Lecture Notes in Computer Science 6409

Commenced Publication in 1973
Founding and Former Series Editors:
Gerhard Goos, Juris Hartmanis, and Jan van Leeuwen

W0227570

Regina Bernhaupt   Peter Forbrig
Jan Gulliksen   Marta Lárusdóttir (Eds.)

Human-Centred Software Engineering

Third International Conference, HCSE 2010
Reykjavik, Iceland, October 14-15, 2010
Proceedings

 Springer

Volume Editors

Regina Bernhaupt
IRIT-ICS, 118, Route de Narbonne, 31062, Toulouse Cedex 9, France
E-mail: Regina.Bernhaupt@irit.fr

Peter Forbrig
Universität Rostock, Institut für Informatik
Albert-Einstein-Straße 21, 18059 Rostock, Germany
E-mail: peter.forbrig@uni-rostock.de

Jan Gulliksen
HCI Group, CSC, KTH, 100 44 Stockholm, Sweden
E-mail: gulliksen@kth.se

Marta Lárusdóttir
Reykjavik University, Menntavegur 1, 101 Reykjavik, Iceland
E-mail: Marta@hr.is

Library of Congress Control Number: 2010936363

CR Subject Classification (1998): D.2, H.5.2, H.5, I.2, H.4, C.2

LNCS Sublibrary: SL 2 – Programming and Software Engineering

ISSN   0302-9743
ISBN-10   3-642-16487-0 Springer Berlin Heidelberg New York
ISBN-13   978-3-642-16487-3 Springer Berlin Heidelberg New York

springer.com

© IFIP International Federation for Information Processing 2010
Printed in Germany

Typesetting: Camera-ready by author, data conversion by Scientific Publishing Services, Chennai, India
Printed on acid-free paper   06/3180

Preface

The conference series HCSE (Human-Centred Software Engineering) was established four years ago in Salamanca. HCSE 2010 is the third working conference of IFIP Working Group 13.2, Methodologies for User-Centered Systems Design.

The goal of HCSE is to bring together researchers and practitioners interested in strengthening the scientific foundations of user interface design, examining the relationship between software engineering and human-computer interaction and focusing on how to strengthen user-centered design as an essential part of software engineering processes. As a working conference, substantial time was devoted to the open and lively discussion of papers.

The interest in the conference was positive in terms of submissions and participation. We received 42 contributions that resulted in 10 long papers, 5 short papers and 3 poster papers. The selection was carried out carefully by the International Program Committee. The result is a set of interesting and stimulating papers that address such important issues as contextual design, user-aware systems, ubiquitous environments and usability evaluation.

The final program of the conference included a keynote by Liam Bannon with the title "Approaches to Software Engineering: A Human-Centred Perspective." This talk raised a lot of interesting questions for IFIP WG 13.2 and might have had some impact for participants to become a member of the working group.

We hope that participants considered HCSE 2010 as successful as its two predesessors in terms of interesting discussions and new ideas for scientific co-operation.

August 2010

Regina Bernhaupt
Peter Forbrig
Jan Gulliksen
Marta Kristín Lárusdóttir

Third Conference on Human-Centred Software Engineering (HCSE 2010)

was organized
in Reykjavik, Iceland

General Chairs

Regina Bernhaupt	IRIT-ICS, Université Paul Sabatier, France
Peter Forbrig	University of Rostock, Germany
Jan Gulliksen	KTH - Royal Institute of Technology, Sweden
Marta Kristín Lárusdóttir	Reykjavík University, Iceland

HCSE 2010 Program Committee

Simone D.J. Barbosa	Informatics Department, PUC-Rio, Brazil
Birgit Bomsdorf	University of Applied Sciences Fulda, Germany
Ann Blandford	University College London, UK
José C. Campos	DI/CCTC, Universidade do Minho, Portugal
Pedro Campos	INESC-ID, Technical University of Lisbon, Portugal
Anke Dittmar	University of Rostock, Germany
Bertrand David	Ecole Centrale de Lyon, France
Xavier Ferre	Universidad Politecnica de Madrid, Spain
Michael Harrison	University of Newcastle upon Tyne, UK
Effi Law	ETH Zürích, Switzerland
Kris Luyten	Hasselt University, Expertise Centre for Digital Media, Belgium
Eduard Metzker	Vector Informatik GmbH, Germany
Tom Moher	University of Illinos, USA
Philippe Palanque	IRIT-ICS, Université Paul Sabatier, France
Oscar Pastor	Valencia University of Technology, Spain
Fabio Paternò	ISTI-CNR, Italy
Costin Pribeanu	ICI Bucuresti, Romania
Matthias Rauterberg	University of Technology Eindhoven, The Netherlands
Corina Sas	Computing Department, Lancaster University
Dominique Scapin	INRIA, France
Ahmed Seffah	University of Lousanne, Switzerland
Daniel Sinnig	Concordia University Montreal, Canada
Christian Stary	University of Linz, Austria
Alistair Sutcliffe	University of Manchester, UK
Gerrit van der Veer	University of Amsteradam, The Netherlands

Jean Vanderdonckt	Université catholique de Louvain, Belgium
Janet Wesson	Nelson Mandela Metropolitan University, South Africa
Marco Winckler	IRIT-ICS, Université Paul Sabatier, France
Thomas Ziegert	SAP Research CEC Darmstadt, Germany
Jürgen Ziegler	University of Duisburg-Essen, Germany

Table of Contents

Model-Based Development

HCI Activities

Posters

Approaches to Software Engineering: A Human-Centred Perspective

Liam J. Bannon

Interaction Design Centre
Dept. of Computer Science & Information Systems
University of Limerick
Limerick, Ireland
Liam.bannon@ul.ie

Abstract. The field of software engineering has been evolving since its inception in 1968. Arguments as to the exact nature of the field, whether it should be conceived as a real engineering profession, the role of formal methods, whether it is as much an art as a science, etc., continue to divide both practitioners and academics. My purpose here is not to debate these particular topics, but rather to approach the field from the outside, coming as I do from a long period of involvement in the human and social side of the computing discipline, namely, from the fields of Human-Computer Interaction, Computer Supported Cooperative Work, Participative Design, Interaction Design, and Social Informatics, more generally. I wish to examine how this "human-centred" perspective might shed a new light on some issues within the SE field, perhaps opening up topics for further discussion and examination.

Keywords: CSCW, human-centred computing, requirements, sociology, software engineering.

Extended Abstract of the Keynote

It is difficult to talk about issues in the Software Engineering (SE) field without first noting the larger landscape of computing and information systems in which it is embedded. Computing traditionally has focused on answering the question : What can be automated? (e.g. Arden, 1980). While the term computer was originally used to describe real people performing numerical calculations, the human side of computing has tended to be ignored within the emerging discipline of computer science, which has focused on hardware and software issues. Emphasizing this, one of the first professional organizations for people involved in computing was titled The Association for Computing Machinery (ACM). As focus has shifted from mainframe computing to personal and now ubiquitous computing, there has been a slowly increasing awareness of the need to pay greater attention to the human aspects of computing. This implies much more than simply noting the social implications of computing technology, but rather seeks to view the activities of people involved in various aspects of

R. Bernhaupt et al. (Eds.): HCSE 2010, LNCS 6409, pp. 1–5, 2010.

computing, especially systems development and programming, as a legitimate, and necessary part of a computing curriculum.

Many people have been involved in the attempt to shift the focus of computing - and informatics more generally – away from a purely technical approach concerned with hardware and software only, to one that considers the human activities of design and use of information systems as being of central concern. Interestingly, many of these people have come from the Nordic countries. My own selection of pioneers in this space would include people such as Kristen Nygaard, who argued for a perspective on systems development that included the social and political, as well as the technical. People like Peter Naur, whose compilation of papers was published by ACM under the title Computing: A Human Activity, which emphasized the human side of programming and systems development. People like Christiane Floyd, from Germany, who presciently wrote of different paradigms in software engineering and the need to allow for multiple perspectives in the field. In the US, perhaps one of the earliest popular publications that promoted a human-centred approach to software was the 1971 book by Gerry Weinberg, a practitioner and consultant, entitled The Psychology of Computer Programming. Rob Kling spent many years as an advocate of a more open computer science discipline that he labelled "Social Informatics". In recent years, a number of senior figures in the field have also put their hats in the ring: Peter Denning, former President of ACM, arguing for a new and more expansive computing profession; Denis Tsichritzis, head of GMD, the former German national research centre for IT, critiquing much old-fashioned computer science as being akin to "electric motor" science; Peter Wegner, in theoretical computer science, arguing that the concept of interaction in computing is fundamentally more powerful than algorithms; and Terry Winograd, one of a number of people involved in bringing the larger field of Design into computing, and developing the Interaction Design field. All of these authors, despite significant differences in their messages, to my mind share a critique of how the field of computing and the academic discipline of computer science has been defined, circumscribed, and taught to students, and all advocate a more "human-centred" approach, in one form or another. For example, in reflecting on our educational system, Denning (1992) notes: "A curriculum capable of preparing students for the shifting world must incorporate new elements emphasing design, demonstrated proficiency, effective interaction with others, and a greater sensitivity toward the historical and cultural spaces in which we all live and work". The issue here is not simply providing computer science students with a rounded education, but more fundamentally questions the very nature of the discipline, arguing that human activities and interests are part of the core of the computing discipline, whenever we conceptualize, design, build, and test new technologies. It is this tradition that I wish to discuss in the context of human-centred software engineering.

These alternative views of the computing field have, I believe, contributed to the slow emergence of what is beginning to be termed, in some quarters, "human-centred" computing (HCC). The label may appear somewhat meaningless, as who would subscribe to an alternative "system-centred" computing label? However, just as the label "user-centred design" in the field of human-computer interaction hit a chord in the 1980's, it may be the case that the "human-centred computing" label will have similar re-orienting effect on the field of computing today. Likewise with other new terms that are appearing currently. For example, the emergence of new terms and research areas, such as the "new informatics" to augment traditional information systems research, and "interaction design" augmenting traditional HCI, are, in my opinion, examples of shifts in perspective towards a more wholistic view of human-systems interaction that begins to pay more attention to the inextricable inter-weaving of the human, social and cultural with the technical aspects of computing. Note that these are not simply surface changes, nor should they be viewed simply as ancillary issues in relation to the dominant computational approach, but rather they raise foundational issues for the field of computing per se. While this is not the place to further develop this argument, I wish now to briefly examine how this human-centred perspective, loosely described above, might be of interest within the software engineering field. The primary area I will focus on my keynote is in the requirements engineering phase of software development.

Early textbooks on software engineering provided scant coverage of any "human" issues, with perhaps a brief mention concerning meetings with user representatives in the derivation of requirements, and in designing the user interface. However, we can observe an increasing concern with "user issues" in standard SE textbooks over the years. The increasing prominence of Participative Design approaches to system development, involving close cooperation with users in all phases of an iterative design process, and the prominent role of prototyping and testing, was starting to be felt in the HCI arena in the late 80's. Also, the rise of the CSCW field was occurring at this time. The CSCW area brought in researchers from other human sciences than psychology, such as sociology and anthropology, to better understand the everyday lives of people, with a view to providing insights that might be useful in the design of more habitable systems. In the case of the classic Sommerville (2010) text on SE, this can clearly be linked to the rise of the CSCW field and the establishment of a CSCW Centre at Lancaster where sociologists and software engineers were involved in joint projects. However, as I will detail in the keynote, this marriage of social and computing science has not been without some difficulties, especially in the context of "producing requirements". There is an issue as to whether the developing relations between such unlikely bedfellows as technical systems developers and social scientists, particularly ethnographers, and more narrowly ethnomethodological ethnographers, should be seen as a virtuous coupling or a "deadly embrace". While it should be obvious that I am in favor of any and all approaches to requirements that open-up this phase to a richer appreciation of the work context and work practices of people, I also feel that this recent courtship between developers and sociologists may turn sour due to a misalignment of motives and interests. If we are to have a useful interplay between these two professions then perhaps we also need to be aware of their different agendas, so as to reduce confusions and misunderstandings. I will explore this issue in greater detail in the keynote.

Returning to this issue of "requirements" in SE, one finds a number of perspectives on them, as evidenced by the different language used. So, for some people, systems design begins with the need for "requirements capture" - which to me inspires an image of requirements as well-defined entities just waiting to be plucked from the environment. It goes without saying that this particular viewpoint is less widely held today than heretofore. A less extreme view, yet one which is still quite popular in the engineering community is the notion of requirements "gathering", which again has an implicit, if not explicit, conception of requirements as things that are waiting to be harvested. Continuing on this line, one can hear discussion of requirements "elicitation" which begins to acknowledge that requirements may not be immediately apparent, or accessible, and may require some effort to "bring forth" from the user community. Going one step further, we can argue that requirements are not "out there" awaiting collection, but are themselves constructions, jointly and severally produced by a range of actors, including users and developers in specific contexts of discussion, observation and analysis. This view thus requires that we pay close attention to the ways in which we investigate the use situation and work context, and take into account the social, political and economic factors involved in the requirements process. (In this regard, the edited collection by Jirotka and Goguen (1994) provides an interesting range of positions on social and technical issues in requirements engineering.)

A number of commentators have noted how requirements as fixed "texts" can impede a good design process. The designer Chris Jones (1988) argues: "...[we must] recognize that the 'right' requirements are in principle unknowable by users, customers, or designers at the start." This position calls into question the nature of most formal software development contracts today. Similarly, the consultant Tom Gilb (1990) stresses the need to focus on process, not method or static product. He notes that current development methodologies "...are based on a static product model. They do not adequately consider our work to be a continuous process—derived from the past and being maintained into the future." Yet another voice in support of this shift, coming from academic software engineering, is that of Floyd (1987). She argues for more emphasis on the process of software development than on the efficiency of the resulting code: "The product-oriented perspective regards software as a product standing on its own, consisting of a set of programs and related defining texts... considers the usage context of the product to be fixed and well understood, thus allowing software requirements to be determined in advance," while the process-oriented perspective "views software in connection with human learning, work and communication, taking place in an evolving world with changing needs... the actual product is perceived as emerging from the totality of interleaved processes of analysis, design, implementation, evaluation and feedback, carried out by different groups of people involved in system development in various roles." It is interesting that some of the recent moves to Agile Methods in software development and the rise of the Extreme Programming movement would seem to provide support to aspects of the above viewpoints, and thus show, in some respects, a focus on a more "human-centred" approach.

References

1. Arden, B.W. (ed.): What can be Automated? The Computer Science & Engineering Research Study (COSERS). MIT Press series in Computer Science, vol. 3. MIT Press, Cambridge (1980)
2. Denning, P.: Educating a new engineer. Communications of the ACM 35(12), 83–97 (1992)

3. Floyd, C.: Outline of a paradigm change in software engineering. In: Bjerknes, G., Ehn, P., Kyng, M. (eds.) Computers and Democracy – A Scandinavian Challenge, pp. 191–212. Avebury, Aldershot (1987)
4. Gilb, T.: Project Management for the 1990s. The American Programmer, 16–30 (1990)
5. Jirotka, M., Goguen, J. (eds.): Requirements Engineering: Social & Technical Issues. Academic Press, London (1994)
6. Jones, J.C.: Softecnica. In: Thackara, J. (ed.) Design After Modernism: Beyond the Object, pp. 216–226. Thames & Hudson, London (1988)
7. Naur, P.: Programming: A Human Activity. ACM Press, New York (1992)
8. Sommerville, I.: Software Engineering, 9th edn. Addison-Wesley, Reading (2010)
9. Wegner, P.: Why interaction is more powerful than algorithms. Communications of the ACM 40(5), 80–91 (1997)
10. Weinberg, G.: The Psychology of Computer Programming. Van Nostrand Reinhold, New York (1971)

The APEX Framework:
Prototyping of Ubiquitous Environments Based on Petri Nets

José Luís Silva[1,*], Óscar R. Ribeiro[1], João M. Fernandes[1],
José Creissac Campos[1], and Michael D. Harrison[2]

[1] Dep. Informática / CCTC, Universidade do Minho, Braga, Portugal
{jlsilva,orribeiro,jmf,jose.campos}@di.uminho.pt
[2] Newcastle University, United Kingdom
michael.harrison@ncl.ac.uk

Abstract. The user experience of ubiquitous environments is a determining factor in their success. The characteristics of such systems must be explored as early as possible to anticipate potential user problems, and to reduce the cost of redesign. However, the development of early prototypes to be evaluated in the target environment can be disruptive to the ongoing system and therefore unacceptable. This paper reports on an ongoing effort to explore how model-based rapid prototyping of ubiquitous environments might be used to avoid actual deployment while still enabling users to interact with a representation of the system. The paper describes APEX, a framework that brings together an existing 3D Application Server with CPN Tools. APEX-based prototypes enable users to navigate a virtual world simulation of the envisaged ubiquitous environment. The APEX architecture and the proposed CPN-based modelling approach are described. An example illustrates their use.

1 Introduction

Ubiquitous computing poses new challenges for designers and developers of interactive systems. Because these systems *immerse* their users, the effect they have on the users' experience is an important element contributing to the success of a design. Technology enhancement has the potential to have a profound impact on a built environment transforming a sterile space into a place that is in harmony with its purpose. The experience of checking into an airport can be improved by providing information to travellers when and where they need it. Frustrating delays could thereby be removed through the appropriate use of personalised information. The experience of using a library could be improved by providing personal and clear information about the location of the shelf in a large library where the required book is located. Experience therefore becomes an additional interactive characteristic of ubiquitous systems, to be explored in addition to more traditional notions of usability.

---

* José Luís Silva is supported by *Fundação para a Ciência e Tecnologia* (FCT, Portugal) through PhD Grant SFRH/BD/41179/2007.

R. Bernhaupt et al. (Eds.): HCSE 2010, LNCS 6409, pp. 6–21, 2010.

Experience is difficult to specify as a requirement that can be calculated and demonstrated of a system. It is difficult to measure and to obtain early feedback about whether a design will have the required effect. Currently, there are no techniques that can be used to analyse specifications against different notions of experience (for a discussion, see [9]). An important barrier is the difficulty of developing prototypes that could feasibly be used to explore issues of experience.

This paper limits attention to *ubiquitous environments* envisaged as enhancing physical environments. In the envisaged designs, "spaces" are augmented with sensors, public displays and personal devices. Of particular interest in these systems is the way that the user interacts with the environment, as a result of both explicit interaction with the system, and implicit interactions that arise through changes of *context*. Here context could include location, or the steps that have to be taken by a user to achieve some goal (for example check-in, baggage screening, passport control, boarding card scanning).

The paper describes how prototypes can be built to represent the interaction between users, devices and services, as users move within ubiquitous environments. To avoid unnecessary development cost, early designs are explored in this proposal through model-based prototypes explored within a virtual environment. The paper describes a prototyping framework (APEX) that uses Coloured Petri Net (CPN) [11] models. APEX binds a CPN model to a 3D application server (OpenSimulator[1]).

The Petri nets modelling language, being an expressive and graphically informative notation, allows the description of the envisaged design. OpenSimulator provides support for exploring the design based on the Petri net description. Their integration thus allows rapid prototyping of ubiquitous environments, enabling users to navigate a virtual world simulation of the environment to evaluate usability issues, including user experience.

This paper builds on [18]. There, the early concept of the APEX framework was discussed, and some initial results presented. Since then, the framework has been developed, and the modelling approach fully revised. The new models present a number of benefits, including better scalability and support for heterogeneity. The current paper describes the APEX architecture, the new modelling approach, and provides modelling guidelines for developing prototypes.

The structure of the paper is as follows. Section 2 discusses related literature and the goals of the project. Section 3 describes the architecture of APEX. Use of the framework is illustrated by means of a smart library which senses the presence of users, and guides them to the shelves where their required books are located. Section 4 describes how the example is modelled. Section 5 describes usage of the framework. Section 6 presents conclusions and future work.

2 Related Literature and Goals

Despite considerable advances in the development of ubiquitous systems, there continues to be a tendency (see [5] for a concise overview) for the development

---

[1] `http://opensimulator.org` (last accessed June 14, 2010).

and evaluation of ubiquitous systems to be focussed on experimental systems, usually prototype device designs within partial systems. The issue of how to evaluate whole systems in real contexts continues to be a concern, see [2] for a useful discussion of this contrast. Another important aspect of evaluation is how to explore the user experience that a designed system creates. In this respect there is a substantial literature taken from design disciplines, see for example [4]. In design, for example, a typical approach is to use non-functional (for example, clay) prototypes as objects which potential users are asked to carry around in the contexts where the actual system is to be used in order to obtain information about how the proposed design might be experienced. One particularity of the type of systems of interest is that the system is woven into the context, making it harder to prototype.

APEX is designed to satisfy three requirements. The first is that it should enable the rapid development of both prototypes and target systems. While there are several existing platforms for ubiquitous computing ([3, 8, 10] are examples), a software tool is required that facilitates the development of prototypes, while simultaneously providing the hooks for the target system.

The second requirement is that a 3D environment can be used to construct simulations that can be explored realistically by users. 3D Application Servers, such as SecondLife™2 or OpenSimulator, provide a fast track to developing virtual worlds. OpenSimulator, in particular, has the advantage of being open source, which means that the backend can be programmed allowing configurability and extensibility.

Systems such as Topiary [13] enable users to explore prototypes of context-aware application in real world settings. They resort to Wizard of Oz techniques to avoid the actual deployment of sensors. They are targeted to the prototyping of applications running on user devices, and do not support the *enhancement* of the physical space. A different class of systems, such as 3DSim [17], UbiWorld [6] or the work of O'Neill et al. [16], have similar visions to ours (developing simulations of the actual environments).

The third requirement is an approach to modelling ubiquitous computing. While 3DSim and UbiWord envisage the use of programming languages to build the prototypes, we are interested in creating them from models of envisaged systems. A benefit of this approach is the integration of the modelling approach with analytical approaches, to provide leverage on properties of ubiquitous environments that are relevant to their use.

Petri nets constitute an expressive and graphically informative modelling language that has been used to describe virtual environments. Previous modelling approaches based on Petri nets include the use of: Hybrid high-level Nets (HyNets) [14], Flownets [19], Interactive Cooperative Objects (ICO) [15], and Coloured Petri Nets (CPN) [11].

CPN modelling and analysis is supported by CPN Tools, enabling analysis either by simulation (similar to program execution) or by more formal analysis (state space analysis and invariant analysis). Simulation can be used to animate

---

2 http://secondlife.com (last accessed June 14, 2010).

the models. State space analysis can be used to check standard properties, such as reachability, boundedness, liveness properties and fairness, as well as specific properties defined using the associated programming language (CPN ML language [12]).

In summary then, given the objectives set forth for APEX, CPN was chosen because: (i) it allows rapid development of prototypes, much faster than equivalent conventional approaches using C#; (ii) it allows analysis of properties of the model (via CPN Tools); (iii) the animation capabilities of CPN Tools allow control of the virtual world simulations directly from the models (hence, the behaviour modelled is exactly what is executed — this improves on current approaches in that in these approaches when a simulation needs to be programmed, what is executed does not necessarily reflect the models and specifications produced in an earlier development stage).

While several approaches aiming at ubiquitous computing prototyping were identified above, they are mostly focused on helping ubiquitous system designers to identify unwanted behaviour in their system, and to support informed decision making in an iterative design cycle. APEX is more focused on the *experience* users will have of the design, and in the use of tools to enable analysis.

The above mentioned approach of O'Neill et al. [16] is the most similar to ours, using models and a 3D simulation for the prototyping of ubiquitous environments. In their case a games engine is used. We believe the use of a 3D application server (OpenSimulator) has some advantages compared with a games engine. It supports the creation of virtual environments in real time using world building tools, and it is easily extendable by the loading of modules. In the case of the games' engine, the environment must be previously fully created using a map editor. Using a 3D application server means the approach is flexible. A variety of clients, customizable in appearance, can access the virtual world on multiple protocols at the same time, and in world application development using a number of different languages is also possible.

3   The APEX Framework

The overall architectural view of the APEX framework is presented in Figure 1. Three main components are identified:

- a *virtual environment component*, responsible for managing the physical appearance and layout of the prototype, including managing the 3D simulation and the construction of the virtual environment;
- a *behavioural component*, responsible for managing the behaviour of the prototype, including the description, analysis and validation of the virtual environment's behaviour;
- a *communication/execution component*, responsible for the data exchange among all components and for the execution of the simulation.

OpenSimulator enables the interactive creation of virtual environments. It provides a sufficiently rich *texture* to enable users to visualise the physical

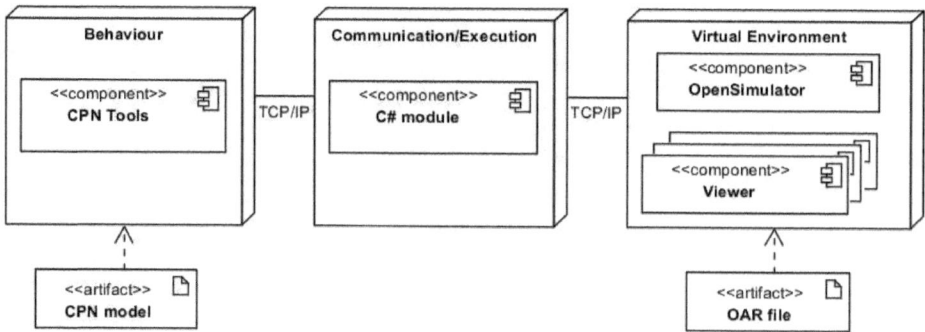

Fig. 1. Logical architecture of the APEX framework

characteristics of the real system. A rich palette of features provides for easy object/environment creation and manipulation. These objects, together with the insertion and manipulation of textures, lighting, animation and sounds also provided, enable a simulation which can create a realistic visualisation of the proposed real system. Pre-defined environments and devices can be used in this creation process.

To create a prototype, besides creating the virtual environment, the developer needs to extend the CPN base model provided. APEX uses CPN Tools to model the behaviour of the virtual environment. Models of each type of dynamic object/device in the environment (e.g., sensors, displays, personal devices) need to be inserted into the global model of the environment. Adequate models must either be available or must be created using CPN Tools. Section 4.2 will provide a more detailed description of how that can be done.

Once the CPN model and the environment are created a component of the framework binds them together. To achieve this, transitions in the CPN link the behaviour described by the models to the respective objects in the environment.

Several users can be connected to the simulation using different viewpoints onto the OpenSimulator server. Users can navigate and interact with the virtual world simulation of the envisaged ubiquitous environment, enabling the evaluation of usability and experience issues with the proposed design.

3.1 Behavioural Component

This component is responsible for driving the simulation using the information from the model, and to send relevant data to the virtual environment. It contains the CPN tools, which use CPN models to describe the behaviour of the virtual environment in response to user actions and context changes.

A generic CPN base model is provided from which virtual environment models can be derived. The aim in developing this base model was to develop a generic style of CPN relevant to the modelling of virtual environments, including models that can be instantiated to the physical space in which the system is to be defined to operate. The model consists of: (a) a module to initialise the simulation, and to establish the connection between the CPN model, as represented by CPN Tools, and OpenSimulator; (b) a module that receives user data (for example user identity and position) from OpenSimulator when a user moves and uses it to update appropriate tokens; (c) modules describing the behaviour of each device in the system. An example is presented in Section 4.

3.2   Virtual Environment Component

This component sends information about the simulation (e.g. user position) to the behavioural component which takes a *decision* and sends indications to reflect these changes in the simulation. It contains the OpenSimulator server and viewers for each client who connect to it.

The OpenSimulator server is responsible for maintaining the virtual environment information available to viewers. The features of the 3D simulation include location, the viewing aspect and the physics of each of the objects in the environment. Pre-defined environments and objects can be saved/loaded in/from Opensim ARchive files (OAR). All the different entities (object, terrain, textures, etc.) are packaged in these files in the format used by Opensimulator to keep data within an archive. The server enables the connection of several users from, possibly, different locations to the same virtual environment via the web through appropriate viewers.

Viewers interact with the server and are used to define features of the 3D simulation presented to users, and to allow users to navigate and interact within the simulated environment. Interaction is achieved both explicitly by a user using (virtual) devices, and implicitly through changes of context. Possible viewers include the Hippo OpenSim Viewer[3] or the Linden Lab's Second Life viewer[4]. However, a number of alternative compatible viewers exist[5]. Note that, currently, some of these alternative viewers only enable the environment exploration without providing any modelling tool.

The behaviour described in the previous section is linked to the objects which are identified by unique names. For instance, to open a gate in the simulation, the CPN model of the gates must indicate in its open transition code the identifier of the gate to open. Objects identifiers are easily accessible through the properties panel provided by the viewer and associated to each object of the environment.

3.3   Communication/Execution Component

This component is a DLL (dynamic-link library) responsible for loading the simulated ubiquitous environment into the OpenSimulator server, and for using the CPN models to drive it. It is positioned between the two other components managing the exchange of information between them.

---

[3] http://mjm-labs.com/viewer/ (last accessed June 14, 2010).

[4] http://secondlife.com/support/downloads (last accessed June 14, 2010).

[5] http://opensimulator.org/wiki/Connecting (last accessed June 14, 2010).

Communication in the CPN models is achieved through Comms/CPN [7], a CPN ML library for connecting between CPN Tools and external processes, provided with the CPN Tools. The BRITNeY Suite [20] also enables the communication between CPN models and a Java-based animation package. Comms/CPN is more adequate and simple to use for our case. Unlike Comms/CPN the BRITNeY Suite has a more general purpose, providing more features besides the communication package, which make it more complex to use.

In order to use Comms/CPN a module must be loaded into the external process. Java and C modules are available with the distribution. However, OpenSimulator modules (DLLs) are developed in C#. No alternatives were found for this communication so a new C#/CPN communication package has been developed. With this development the communication of the CPN models, using the Comms/CPN functions, and C# processes becomes possible.

The developed module sends information to CPN Tools when changes in the environment happen, and is responsible for changing the environment in response to data sent by CPN Tools. Additionally, it handles the loading/saving of OpenSimulator objects/environments and the execution of commands invoked by the user in the viewer. When inserted in the OpenSimulator server location, this DLL is automatically loaded by the OpenSimulator. After the establishment of the communication between the CPN model and the simulator, by the evocation of a function in the CPN model (explained in the next section), the APEX is ready to use.

4   Modelling with CPNs (The Example)

As previously stated, a generic CPN modelling approach was developed to enable the easy creation of new ubiquitous systems prototypes. In this section the modules of this approach are described. Figure 2 presents the setup model. As will be discussed, this model needs small modifications only when being adapted to different applications. The model in figure 3 deals with user position and is generic. The developer then needs to develop a module for each device type present in the ubiquitous system. Figure 4 presents the module for a specific type of object present in the example used (a gate). How these modules are created will be described in section 4.5.

4.1   The Example

The example used to illustrate the system is a smart library. Books are identified by RFID tags and are stored on bookshelves. Screens are used to provide information to library users. A registred library user is allowed entry/exit via gates. When a registered user arrives at the entry gate, a screen displays which books have been requested by the user (e.g., earlier via a web interface) and opens the entry gate. The system guides the user to the required books through the use of sensors that recognise the user's position in real-time. As the user approaches the book's location a light with a specific colour is turned on. Hence several users looking for books in nearby locations can distinguish their own request. When the book is removed, the light on the book is turned off. As the user returns to the exit gate a personalised list of requested and returned books is displayed on a screen by the gate which is opened so that the user can leave.

4.2 Modelling Approach

There are a number of styles of specification that can be achieved using CPN. These styles vary according to the extent to which the semantics of the underlying objects are made explicit in the structure of the CPN specification, or encoded into the tokens. The following two extremes are possible:

- placing all the semantics in the tokens, in other words, minimising the number of places in the net;
- using places to characterize each different relevant situation (user action, context change, etc.), thereby adding transitions that explicitly describe aspects of the semantics of the objects.

A small example is presented to clarify these two approaches. Suppose a device which can be in two different states (*on* and *off*) is to be modelled. Following the two approaches above, two different results will be reached. In the first, the model will consist of only one place, and one transition from and to this place. The place will hold tokens with a semantics which can represent all the different states of the device. The state of the device will be encoded as an attribute (a colour) of the token representing the device. The transition will be responsible for changing the colour of the token, reflecting the new state of the device. In this situation all the meaning is in the value of the tokens.

Following the second approach, the model will be represented by two places each representing a possible state of the device, and by transitions between them (two in this case). No semantics will be carried by the token, all the meaning will be represented by the structure of the model. The state of the device is known by looking to the position of the token, i.e. at the place which holds the token.

In APEX, a mixed approach is used where the states of the dynamic objects (open, closed, etc.) are modelled as places and user actions and context changes modelled as transitions. Each device and user is represented in the CPN model as a token in the respective place. Each of these tokens has an identifier which is used as the identifier of the objects present in the simulation.

The users and object features (e.g. identifier, position) are modelled as attributes in their respective tokens. These values are used by CPN ML functions together with instructions (e.g. *open, close*) to indicate changes that must be reflected in OpenSimulator. Section 4.5 will provide a description of how this is done. The guards on the transitions as well as the functions associated with transitions are responsible for part of the behaviour of the system. Both of these are modelled in the CPN ML language, so this behaviour is modelled functionally.

This combination gives more expressiveness to the ubiquitous systems modelling while avoiding clutter in the CPN specification. In the next sub sections, the approach will be illustrated using the example.

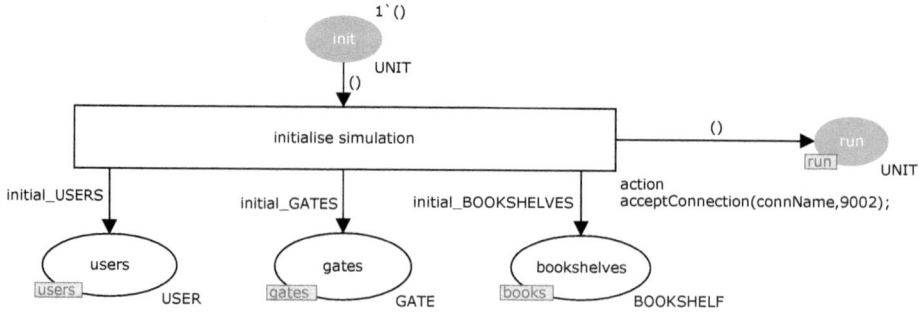

Fig. 2. The CPN module to setup the library simulation

4.3   Setting Up the Simulation

The initial conditions of the simulation are defined in the CPN module shown in
Figure 2. Firing the "`initialise simulation`" transition sets the initial configuration of the simulation, and executes the associated CPN ML code. For example, "`acceptConnection(connName,9002)`" is a function of the Comms/CPN
library used to establish the connection between CPN Tools and OpenSimulator.

In this case the configuration includes three places: "`users`", "`gates`" and
"`bookshelves`". Fusion tags (inset into the lower left corner of the places) enable
instances of these places to appear in other parts of the CPN model. Hence, these
places are called *fusion places*. The utilization of these places will be described
in section 4.5.

Annotations at the bottom right side of the places indicate the type of token
each place can hold. Place "`users`" holds "`USER`" tokens representing information about users in the virtual environments. This particular place is mandatory,
since whatever the model the handling of users must be supported. The remaining places ("`gates`" and "`bookshelves`") hold tokens representing devices. These
places are system dependent and will vary for each prototype. The colour (structure) of the tokens which these places can hold is defined in CPN Tools, and
characterises the information held in the model for each type of device.

Besides establishing the connection between the CPN tools and OpenSimulator, and initializing user and device places, the "`initialise simulation`" uses
two places to control the execution of the CPN model: "`init`" to limit execution
of the transition to one occurrence, and "`run`" to inform other CPN modules
that the simulation is running.

4.4   Reading Users' Positions

Figure 3 presents the CPN module that collects users' data from the Open-
Simulator. Transition "`read user id`" reads a user identifier sent by the Open-
Simulator server (c.f., "`receiveString()`" function on the code block associated

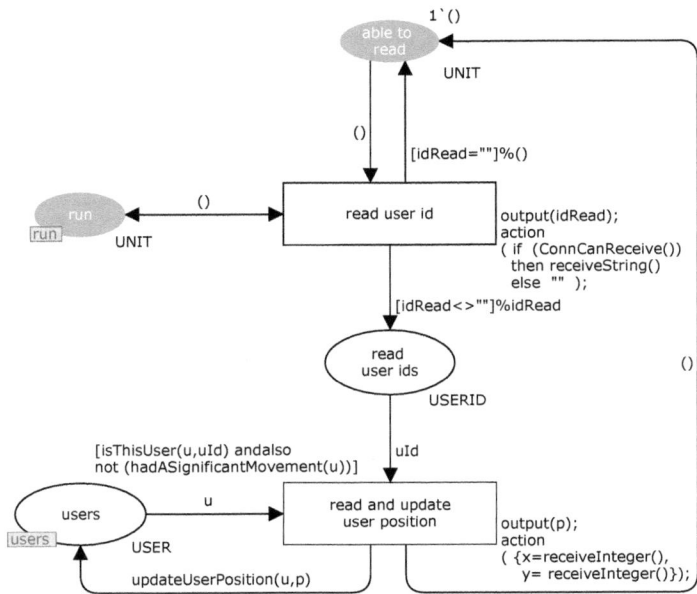

Fig. 3. The CPN module for acquiring users' data

with the transition). A token with the value of the read user identifier is introduced in the "**read user ids**" place (c.f., "**output(idRead)**"). This is used to read the new position by means of the transition "**read and update user position**", which also updates the relevant user token (taken from the user's fusion place). The new coordinates x and y are read in the *action* part of the transition using the function "**receiveInteger()**" and a pair of coordinates (p) is produced. This pair is then used to update the user position through the "**updateUserPosition**" function. The expression "**isThisUser(u,uId)**", in the guard of this transition, guarantees that the user token which is updated corresponds to the previously read identifier. In this model the number of users remains constant during each simulation session. To add more users to the system one must add the corresponding tokens in the place "**users**". The automatic addition and deletion of users at runtime, in accord with the users connected to the simulation, is planned. This will be achieved via the addition of new models to generate user tokens, and by enhancements to the C# module.

CPN modules for reading the user's position, and for managing devices' behaviour execute concurrently. Precedence of devices' transitions over data acquisition transitions is guaranteed through the guard "**not (hadASignificant-Movement(u))**" on the transition "**read and update user position**". Movement of a user is significant (for a device) when the new position is "near" the device. Hence, if a user is near a device, no new data will be acquired until the device has processed the current data.

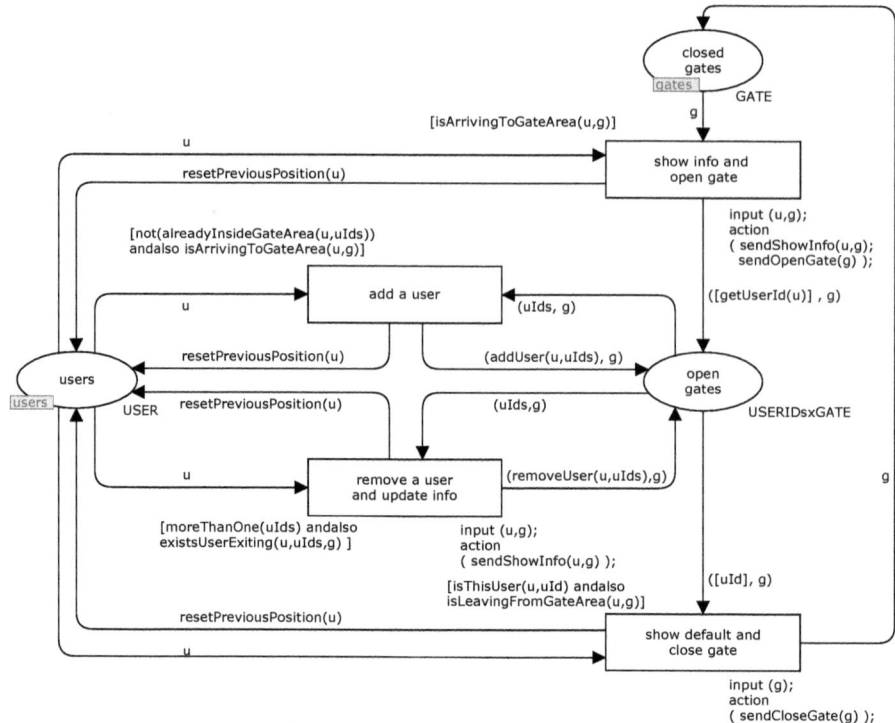

Fig. 4. The CPN module for a entry gate device

4.5 Modelling the Devices of the System

Each device type in the ubiquitous environment simulation needs a corresponding CPN module describing its behaviour. It is envisaged that a library of models will be made available for supported devices. When new (unsupported) devices are to be used, a new model must be developed and added to the library. This section explains the process through the example of the entry gate.

Device behaviour is modelled through a combination of fusion places, normal places, transitions, functions (described in the CPN ML language) and conditions. State transitions play an important role in this process since it is through them that the connection between the model and the simulation is accomplished, via the associated CPN ML functions. These functions are also responsible for describing functional behaviour not structurally expressed by the net.

Fusion places are the basis for the creation of these behavioral modules. They establish the link between the models of the devices and the setup model presented in figure 2. The device model for the entry gate model is presented in Figure 4. In this example the users and gates fusion places hold the (user and gate) tokens needed to model the behaviour.

The entry gate is equipped with a sensor to capture a user approaching it. Transition "show info and open gate" represents the actions of the entry gate. It displays requested books on the screen and opens the entry gate. Functions "sendShowInfo" and "sendOpenGate" are responsible for these actions sending relevant instructions to OpenSimulator. These actions occur when the gate's sensor detects a registered user arriving at the entry gate (modelled by "isArrivingToGateArea(u,g)" evaluating to true). When the gate is open and another registered user enters the gate area the transition "add a user" occurs and this user is included in the set of users that are near the gate. This set of users is represented in the tokens held by the place "open gates". As already stated, each place has an associated token type which it holds. In this case the type of this place is "USERIDsxGATE". It means that each token is a product of a set of user IDs ("USERIDs") and the gate ("GATE") which they are near.

When the transition "show default and close gate" is taken, default information is displayed on the screen and the gate is closed. For this to happen a user must have moved away from the gate, and there should be no more users near it. If other users are near the gate, the transition "remove a user and update info" removes the designated user from the list of users who are near the gate (function "removeUser") and, if that user's information was being displayed, the information currently on the screen is changed to one of the other user's (function "sendShowInfo").

As explained, the different CPN models are connected via *fusion places*, enabling token flow between them (e.g. the models in figures 3 and 4 are connected to the setup model via the "users", "gates" and "run" *fusion places*). Put together they form the model of the envisaged ubiquitous system.

The focus of this paper had been the architecture of the framework, and the CPN-based modelling. Of course, a virtual environment to match the model must also be developed. This is done through the virtual world viewer. Once both models and virtual world simulations for all devices are in place, animation of the envisaged ubiquitous system can start.

5   Support for Design

As stated in Section 1, APEX supports both the design and the analysis of ubiquitous systems. The developer creates the CPN model, as illustrated in Section 4. Depending on the new types of devices that are used the developer is required to modify a small piece of the Communication/Execution C# module responsible for reflecting the changes in the simulation. The code responds to changes in objects of the environment consistent with the state of the CPN model. As an example, Figure 5 is a code snippet that searches for objects where changes are directed to occur by the CPN model and makes the changes. In this snippet an *open* or *close* action is received and the position of the gate is changed accordingly.

A typical runtime configuration of the framework (see figure 6) will involve deploying the OpenSimulator server, CPN tools, and the Communication/Execution

```
foreach (KeyValuePair<Scene, List<SceneObjectGroup>> kvp in HelloWorldModule.scene_prims)
{
        foreach (SceneObjectGroup sog in kvp.Value)
        {

            //Object: gate

            if (sog.Name.Equals("gate"))
            {
                if (action.Equals("open"))           //Open the gate
                    sog.AbsolutePosition = new Vector3(130.7f,130.9f,25.9f)
                else                                 //Close the gate
                    if (action.Equals("close"))
                        sog.AbsolutePosition = new Vector3(128.6f,130.9f,25.9f)

            }

            //Object: screen

            ...

        }
}
```

Fig. 5. OpenSimulator objects behavior code

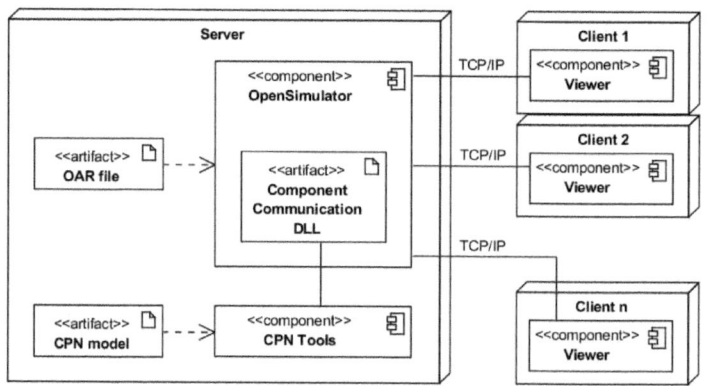

Fig. 6. Physical architecture of the APEX framework

module on a server. Once the CPN model is loaded, the server is ready to allow free exploration and interaction with the virtual environment. At this point, exploration and interaction with the virtual environment is possible. Currently this is achieved by means of viewers deployed on client machines. It is envisaged that higher fidelity prototypes will be possible, for example, using a CAVE system.

Using these prototypes, it becomes possible to test different design alternatives with real users, without the cost of developing the actual system. As an illustration, figure 7 shows a user collecting a book. As the (registered) user approaches the gate (step a) the gate opens and the user is able to enter the library (step b). Once the user is close to the book, the light on the book is turned on so that the user can quickly identify it (step c).

Validating the usefulness of these prototypes in assessing users' experience of the envisaged systems will be the subject of a next phase in the project. However, the literature on virtual reality for purposes such as education, training

a - user near entry gate   b – user inside library   c – user taking wanted book

Fig. 7. Viewer interface - user common path

or medical treatment, contains good indications these systems provide for a rich enough experience to allow relevant results to be reached (e.g., see [1] for some interesting papers on the applicability of virtual reality to behavioural sciences).

In addition to exploring the environment, it is also possible to use the viewer to manipulate it, load objects into the environment and to save and clear the environment. This is achieved in the viewer by an avatar "shouting" commands: *load-oar file*, *save-oar file* and *clear*.

Besides exploration of the prototype, analysis of the models can also be considered. Using the State Space tool, provided with the CPN Tools, properties can be check in the model. For instance, reachability properties (e.g. all the states are reachable, a state is reachable from another one) can be expressed using functions provided by the State Space tool for this effect (e.g. AllReachable(), Reachable(node,node)). In the example, given specific assumptions about user behaviour, captured by adding an automated avatar to replace free user interaction, the model can be used to check properties such as that the required book will always be reached, collected and taken out of the library.

6   Conclusions and Future Work

The user experience of ubiquitous environments is a determining factor in their success. Enabling early exploration of the characteristics of such systems will help anticipate potential user problems and reduce the cost of redesign. However, the deployment of prototypes in the target environment is, in many cases, infeasible. This happens both because of the cost of deploying such prototypes, and because doing it can be disruptive to the ongoing system. Alternatives must be sought that capture the experience of being immersed within the proposed ubiquitous system, without the cost of actually fielding it.

This paper described one such alternative. A simulation-based prototyping framework for ubiquitous computing systems. The framework brings together the expressive and analytic power of Petri nets, with the possibility of exploring a 3D virtual simulation of the modelled system. Petri nets constitute an expressive graphical notation. Development of the models and 3D environments is accelerated by the use of the CPN base model, and pre-defined devices. By enabling potential users to explore the simulation of the system before deployment, it becomes possible to have a low-cost approach to the prototyping problem.

Ongoing work on the development of the framework is addressing a number of technical issues in order to better support developers and users. One immediate aspect is the possibility of adding users to the simulation at runtime. In the current version of APEX, the number of users must be set at the start of the simulation run. This will be fixed in the next version of the framework. Another goal is reducing the amount of information exchanged by CPN Tools and APEX to a minimum. This is relevant both to prevent CPN Tools from running out of resources, and because it is envisaged that simulations will be deployed via the web. Connecting the simulation to user devices via bluetooth is also being addressed. This will encourage a more immersive and realist usage experience by allowing mixed reality. It also allows the possibility of moving progressively as part of the design and implementation process from a simulated system to a real system. Exploring the formal analysis of the models is also being considered. This requires the development of simulated users (capturing assumptions about user behaviour) to allow for a complete analysis. Hence, combining this feature with the the previous one, progress will be made towards a mixed economy of simulated and actual components of a proposed design. This will also support exploring how different levels of abstraction can be accomplished and supported. For example, supporting and enabling the migration of devices at the physical level via Bluetooth, at the virtual level as virtual devices in OpenSimulator, at the model level as CPN models.

Further development of the framework will involve its evaluation with users and developers. User evaluation concerns the fidelity of the results. Whether prototype environments can be used effectively to enable users to experience the design. Developer evaluation is concerned with the approach's agility. It is concerned with the ease with which accurate prototypes can be developed for ubiquitous environments.

References

[1] CyberPsychology & Behavior 6(3/4) (2003)
[2] Abowd, G., Hayes, G., Iachello, G., Kientz, J., Patel, S., Stevens, M., Truong, K.: Prototypes and paratypes: designing mobile and ubiquitous computing applications. IEEE Pervasive Computing 4(4), 67–73 (2005)
[3] Braubach, L., Pokahr, A., Moldt, D., Bartelt, A., Lamersdorf, W.: Tool-supported interpreter-based user interface architecture for ubiquitous computing. In: Forbrig, P., Limbourg, Q., Urban, B., Vanderdonckt, J. (eds.) DSV-IS 2002. LNCS, vol. 2545, pp. 89–103. Springer, Heidelberg (2002)
[4] Buchenau, M., Suri, J.: Experience prototyping. In: Proceedings Designing Interactive Systems (DIS 2000), pp. 424–433. ACM Press, New York (2000)
[5] Davies, N., Landay, J., Hudson, S., Schmidt, A.: Rapid prototyping for ubiquitous computing — guest editors' introduction. IEEE Pervasive Computing 4(4), 15–17 (2005)

[6] Disz, T., Papka, M., Stevens, R.: UbiWorld: an environment integrating virtual reality, supercomputing, and design. In: Proceedings of the Heterogeneous Computing Workshop, pp. 46–59 (April 1997)

[7] Gallasch, G., Kristensen, L.: Comms/CPN: A communication infrastructure for external communication with design/CPN. In: Jensen, K. (ed.) 3rd Workshop and Tutorial on Practical Use of Coloured Petri Nets and the CPN Tools (CPN 2001), DAIMI PB-554, Aarhus University, pp. 75–90 (2001)

[8] Garlan, D., Siewiorek, D., Smailagic, A., Steenkiste, P.: Project Aura: toward distraction-free pervasive computing. IEEE Pervasive Computing, 22–31 (April - June 2002)

[9] Harrison, M., Campos, J., Doherty, G., Loer, K.: Connecting rigorous system analysis to experience centred design. In: Law, E., Hvannberg, E., Cockton, G. (eds.) Maturing Usability: Quality in Software, Interaction and Value. Human Computer Interaction Series, pp. 56–74. Springer, Heidelberg (2008)

[10] Harter, A., Hopper, A., Steggles, P., Ward, A., Webster, P.: The anatomy of a context-aware application. Wireless Networks 1, 1–16 (2001)

[11] Jensen, K., Kristensen, L., Wells, L.: Coloured petri nets and CPN tools for modelling and validation of concurrent systems. International Journal on Software Tools for Technology Transfer (STTT) 9(3-4), 213–254 (2007)

[12] Jensen, K., Kristensen, L.M.: Coloured Petri Nets – Modelling and Validation of Concurrent Systems. Springer, Heidelberg (2009)

[13] Li, Y., Hong, J., Landay, J.: Topiary: a tool for prototyping location-enhanced applications. In: UIST 2004: Proceedings of the 17th Annual ACM Symposium on User Interface Software and Technology, pp. 217–226. ACM, New York (2004)

[14] Massink, M., Duke, D., Smith, S.: Towards hybrid interface specification for virtual environments. In: Duke, D., Puerta, A. (eds.) Design, Specification and Verification of Interactive Systems 1999, pp. 30–51. Springer, Heidelberg (1999)

[15] Navarre, D., Palanque, P., Bastide, R., Schyn, A., Winckler, M., Nedel, L., Freitas, C.: A formal description of multimodal interaction techniques for immersive virtual reality applications. In: Costabile, M.F., Paternó, F. (eds.) INTERACT 2005. LNCS, vol. 3585, pp. 170–183. Springer, Heidelberg (2005)

[16] O'Neill, E., Lewis, D., Conlan, O.: A simulation-based approach to highly iterative prototyping of ubiquitous computing systems. In: 2nd International Conference on Simulation Tools and Techniques, ICST, pp. 1–10 (2009)

[17] Shirehjini, A.A.N., Klar, F.: 3DSim: rapid prototyping ambient intelligence. In: Proceedings of the 2005 Joint Conference on Smart Objects and Abient Intelligence: Innovative Context-Aware Services: Usages and Technologies (2005)

[18] Silva, J., Campos, J., Harrison, M.: An infrastructure for experience centred agile prototyping of ambient intelligence. In: Calvary, G., Graham, T., Gray, P. (eds.) Proceedings of the ACM SIGCHI Symposium on Engineering Interactive Computing Systems, pp. 79–84. ACM Press, New York (2009)

[19] Smith, S., Duke, D., Massink, M.: The hybrid world of virtual environments. Computer Graphics Forum 18(3), C287–C307 (1999)

[20] Westergaard, M., Lassen, K.B.: The britney suite animation tool. In: Donatelli, S., Thiagarajan, P.S. (eds.) ICATPN 2006. LNCS, vol. 4024, pp. 431–440. Springer, Heidelberg (2006)

Model-Based Design and Implementation of Interactive Spaces for Information Interaction

Hans-Christian Jetter, Jens Gerken, Michael Zöllner, and Harald Reiterer

AG Mensch-Computer-Interaktion, Universität Konstanz,
Universitätsstraße 10, 78457 Konstanz, Germany
{hans-christian.jetter,michael.zoellner,
jens.gerken,harald.reiterer}@uni-konstanz.de
http://hci.uni-konstanz.de

Abstract. Interactive spaces with multiple networked devices and interactive surfaces are an effective means to support multi-user collocated collaboration. In these spaces, surfaces like tablet PCs, tabletops, or display walls can be combined to allow users to interact naturally with their personal or shared information, e.g. during presentation, discussion, or annotation. However, designing and implementing such interactive spaces is a challenging task due to the lack of appropriate interaction abstractions and the shortcomings of current user interface toolkits. We believe that these challenges can be addressed by revisiting model-based design techniques for object-oriented user interfaces (OOUI). We discuss the potential of OOUIs for the design of interactive spaces and introduce our own object-oriented design and implementation approach. Furthermore we introduce the ZOIL (Zoomable Object-Oriented Information Landscape) paradigm that we have used as an experimental testbed. While our approach does not provide automated model-driven procedures to create user interfaces without human intervention, we illustrate how it provides efficient support throughout design and implementation. We conclude with the results from a case study in which we collected empirical data on the utility and ease of use of our approach.

Keywords: Interactive Spaces, Information Interaction, Zoomable User Interfaces, Model-based Design.

1 Introduction

Recent work in Human-Computer Interaction (HCI) suggests the use of physical work environments with multiple interactive surfaces (e.g. multi-touch tabletops or walls) for the collocated collaboration of multiple users. These "interactive spaces" are often used to support groups during the collaborative management, presentation, and discussion of information items, e.g. in science, design, and engineering [23,7,17]. Following the Weiserian vision of ubiquitous computing, a fundamental requirement for such interactive spaces is a "natural" style of human-computer interaction where computing interfaces ideally become invisible and unobtrusive. They vanish into the background of our familiar non-digital

R. Bernhaupt et al. (Eds.): HCSE 2010, LNCS 6409, pp. 22–37, 2010.

reality. Therefore the essential operations of our information interaction such as viewing, editing, (re)locating, sharing, and annotating information items should be provided by natural or "reality-based" interfaces. Following Jacob et al.'s notion of reality-based interaction, such interfaces "draw strength by building on users pre-existing knowledge of the everyday, non-digital world to a much greater extent than before." They attempt to make computer interaction more like interacting with the real, non-digital world by employing themes of reality such as users understanding of physical objects or their body and social skills. Fig. 1 shows an example of an interactive space and different reality-based interaction techniques that can provide a more natural and fluid user experience that is ideally not impaired by obtrusive computer user interfaces and technology-induced barriers between them.

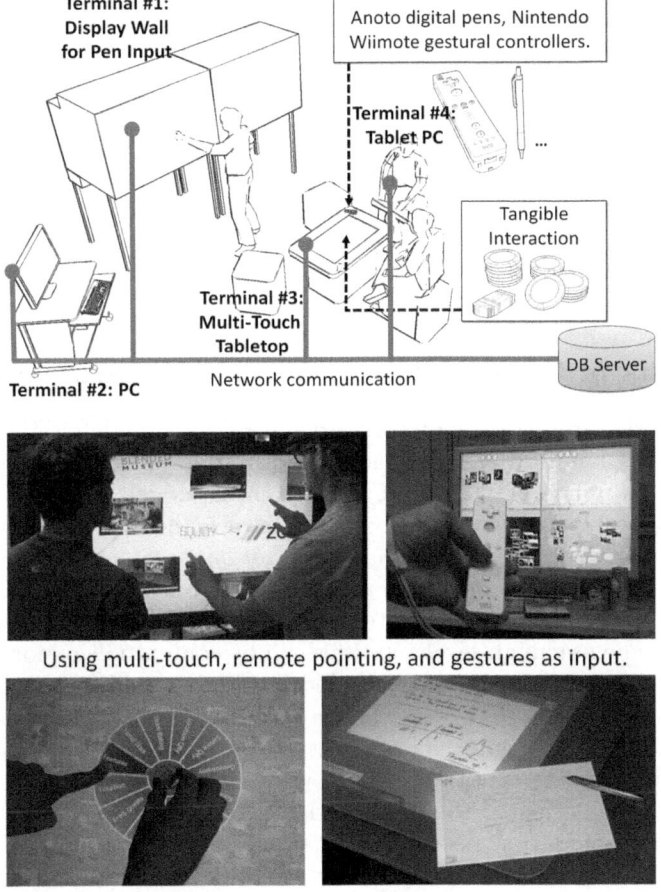

Using multi-touch, remote pointing, and gestures as input.

Using physical tangibles and paper for search and annotation.

Fig. 1. A ZOIL-based interactive space as realized in our lab (top). Natural interaction styles used in our ZOIL case studies, e.g. tangibles and digital pens (bottom).

To this day, designing and implementing reality-based and tangible user interfaces (UI) for interactive spaces is a challenging task. As discussed by Shaer and Jacob, typical challenges are the lack of appropriate interaction abstractions, the shortcomings of current user interface software tools to address continuous and parallel interactions, as well as the excessive effort required to integrate novel input and output technologies [22]. We believe that these challenges can be addressed by viewing interaction through the lens of object-orientation. We suggest to revisit the user interface modeling and design techniques for object-oriented user interfaces (OOUI) from the 1990's that have widely fallen into oblivion and to apply them on today's novel post-WIMP (post-*"windows icons menus pointer"*) technologies and user interface toolkits. In this paper, we make three contributions to this field of research: In chapter 2, we discuss why we believe that this step into the past era of OOUIs has great potential for the design of future computing environments and why this is especially true when considering collaborative interactive spaces for reality-based information interaction. In chapter 3, we introduce the ZOIL (Zoomable Object-Oriented Information Landscape) paradigm that we have used as an experimental testbed for our model-based design and implementation approach. In chapter 4, we illustrate and discuss our approach for modeling OOUIs in detail. While our approach does not provide automated model-driven procedures to create user interfaces without human intervention, we illustrate how it can provide efficient model-based support throughout the design and implementation and we present results from a case study in which we collected empirical data on the utility and ease of use of our OOUI approach from designers and developers.

2   Objects in Collaborative Information Interaction

There is a variety of high-level frameworks in HCI for modeling information interaction, e.g. Blandford and Attfield's "information journey" [4] or the GEMS model from Salminen et al. [15]. Typically these models consider information interaction as a task-oriented series of phases of higher level activities that are separated in time, e.g. *recognizing an information need, acquiring information, interpreting information*, and *using interpretation*. Such generic frameworks can be used as a starting point for interaction design: During a *top-down* design process, these generic high-level activities can be contextualized for the targeted application domain and can be hierarchically decomposed into domain-specific lower level task models (e.g. essential use cases or scenarios). These are used to define the abstract user interface architecture (e.g. the navigation map) and to later flesh out the details of the concrete visual design of individual pages or dialogs. Such a task-oriented top-down design process (e.g. usage-centered design [6]) creates interfaces that resemble virtual pathways to guide users through all the stages, information resources, and interaction contexts that are necessary for completing the tasks from the application domain. These page flows or series of dialogs define the virtual routes that users can take when working with the system. Under the influence of the page-oriented World Wide Web, interaction designers have become very experienced in designing interfaces as such task-oriented stepwise conversations between a single user and a system that move along predefined paths. They achieve great usability for domains with a finite number of clearly defined tasks or business processes (e.g. in e-commerce). However, we believe that in the post-WIMP era such purely task-oriented thinking during design and implementation cannot leverage the true power of today's novel ways of natural and collaborative interaction.

2.1 Task-Orientation vs. Object-Orientation

In the case of collaborative information interaction in post-WIMP environments like in Fig. 1, designers have to consider interaction not only as a task-oriented sequential process supported by a single interface and its hard-coded functionality. In such settings, information interaction becomes a distributed, concurrent, and sometimes seemingly chaotic activity that does not follow simple task models. Instead, the users' actions are situated in a constantly changing social and technological setting, in which multiple users at multiple points of action simultaneously pick up, use, manipulate, recombine, create, and destroy virtual information objects without following clearly defined processes that terminate at clearly defined goals. Furthermore, such post-WIMP environments with multitouch or tangible user interfaces) also afford more natural interaction styles. Instead of clicking hyperlinks or widgets as an intermediary language to sequentially converse with a system about intended actions, users want to continuously touch, grab, and manipulate physical or virtual objects from the application domain. Ideally the application domain itself becomes directly user-accessible and user tasks are carried out by directly manipulating the objects representing it. Thus the user interface changes its nature from being a task-oriented intermediary language medium based on widgets into a computer-mediated world of cooperating visual and tangible objects that provide users with more means for flexibility, improvisation, and establishing individual working styles.

The challenge of designing and programming interfaces that are entirely based on the direct manipulation of cooperating objects instead of sequential conversations is not new. It is similar to the challenge that designers were facing during the advent of graphical user interfaces and direct manipulation in the 1980s [22]. At that time, Hutchins et al. referred to this new kind of direct manipulation interfaces as "model-world interfaces" as opposed to traditional interfaces which have been designed with a conversation metaphor of human-computer interaction in mind [10]. Model-world interfaces provide a coherent and consistent overall representation of the application domain in which the user can freely navigate and directly act on domain objects using a series of low-level direct manipulations that in sum constitute the intended high-level tasks and activities. Essentially, the design challenges we face now in the design of interactive spaces are the same: How can we break down an application domain and its higher level tasks into cooperating visual and tangible objects inside an interactive space, in which higher level tasks can be carried out in natural ways by lower level direct manipulations of objects?

2.2   Revisiting Object-Oriented User Interfaces (OOUI)

In the 1990s, IBM introduced the term *Object-Oriented User Interfaces* (OOUI) to describe a new kind of direct manipulation model-world interfaces: "An object-oriented user interface focuses the user on objects - the "things" people use to accomplish their work. Users see and manipulate object representations of their information. Each different kind of object supports actions appropriate for the information it represents" [21]. At that time, OOUIs were considered as more usable due to the closer match between the application domain and its virtual counterpart on the screen. Furthermore, unlike application-oriented user interfaces, OOUIs provided greater flexibility and consistency following a "flexible structure-by object" instead of a "rigid structure-by function" [16]. Today, this makes OOUIs particularly interesting for post-WIMP designs that are intended to better support the unpredictable and ill-defined needs and actions of situated users which cannot be anticipated by the task models of the design phase.

During OOUI design it is important to avoid unnecessary realism in interface metaphors or an unintelligible plethora of different object types and behaviors. To achieve this, OOUI designers employ rigid object-oriented mechanisms such as *inheritance, generalization*, and *polymorphism* to analyze and model the essential characteristics of the application domain. Thereby they view the domain through the lens of object-orientation from a user's perspective. Using these mechanisms, the user-perceived similarities and differences between domain object types are modeled in common base classes or subclasses. "Interactions should be consistent across objects of the same class; where possible, operations should be polymorphic - applicable to different object types. This reduces the number of interaction behaviors and simplifies the interface" [5]. This way the modeled class hierarchy can integrate very different types of domain objects into a single model while preserving a maximum degree of consistency in interaction. This model is then used to design and implement an interface with consistent behavior, functionality, and appearance. If properly applied users experience a "logical" behavior throughout the entire OOUI. Thus they can more easily apply their previous experiences to infer their strategies for handling novel tasks.

Although OOUIs strongly influenced the design of the "desktop metaphor" in today's operating systems, OOUI design approaches have not been subject of intense scientific research. Most efforts only lasted until the late 1990s (e.g. [1,2,16,5,21]) and after that there has only been some OOUI-related work in the context of Pawson's radical *Naked Objects Pattern* which tries to eliminate the need for specific user interface design by making all code objects and data models directly user accessible [18]. In conclusion, we are aware of only two publications that have proposed entire OOUI design methodologies: IBM's comprehensive description of the OVID methodology in [21] and the brief description of Beck et al.'s TASK methodology in [2].

The OVID methodology *(Object, View, and Interaction Design)* for OOUI design was intended to bridge user interface and software engineering by using the UML notation and modeling techniques of successful code design and combine these with user interface design and usability engineering. At the heart of OVID is the *designer's model*, a conceptual model that includes "descriptions of the objects users will employ to perform their tasks, the properties of those objects, and the interrelationships between them" [21]. To identify the objects that users have to act on and that should be provided to them on the user interface, textual and formal notations of tasks (e.g. use case diagrams) can be used, so that "task analysis will reveal information about what the users do and which objects they work with". Despite OVID's comprehensive treatment in [21], only high level descriptions of iterative design and prototyping are provided and many of the necessary steps, rules, or tools remain unclear.

Before OVID, Beck et al. introduced the TASK methodology for integrating OO analysis into graphical user interface design for desktop systems [2]. During TASK's analysis activity, a task model and an initial object-oriented *object model* is built, which is then refined to an object-oriented *application specification*. This specification is used as a *conceptual user interface model* during user interface design and the views, dialogs, and the actual screen representations of conceptual objects are derived from it. The successful application of TASK and its supporting tools is mentioned for the design of insurance and production planning systems. However, the detailed tools, rules, and the amount of human intervention for translating the *conceptual user interface model* into concrete user interface design and its implementation are not revealed in detail.

3   Exploring OOUI Approaches Using the ZOIL Paradigm

To explore OOUI methodologies for the design and implementation of post-WIMP collaborative information interaction, we have developed our own model-based approach. Thereby, we have taken the promising parts from the TASK and OVID methodologies and adapted them to the design of present-day multi-user and multi-surface environments (see chapter 4). Three questions have been guiding our work: Can we adapt OOUI analysis and design techniques and notations to efficiently inform the domain-specific design of present-day interactive spaces? Can we define concise translation rules for creating the initial visual and interaction design for the user interface directly from our model in a simple step-by-step process? How well can designers and programmers apply our OOUI approaches and how do they assess their practical value?

As a testbed for our experimental approach, we have chosen our Zoomable Object-Oriented Information Landscape (ZOIL) paradigm. ZOIL provides a reference interface design for interactive spaces, a reference client-server architecture for distributed information interaction, and a software framework facilitating their implementation. Thus ZOIL provided us with the necessary infrastructure to efficiently explore our model-based approach. The ZOIL reference design, architecture, and framework have been used before in different projects to realize domain-specific prototypes for information interaction. For example Jetter et al. have designed a ZOIL-based user interface for basic personal information management for interactive television devices [12] and two interactive spaces for discussion and presentation, e.g. for students of media science or for scientists in the field of nano photonics. Heilig et al. have designed

an interactive wall for a public library [9]. In future, Geyer at al. will be using
ZOIL to create collaborative design rooms for interaction design [8].[1]

A ZOIL-based interactive space consists of several interactive surfaces (e.g.
tabletop, tablet PC, wall-sized display) that serve as user terminals to access
the shared information space (Fig. 1 top). Each of the terminals thereby provides a window into a much larger planar visual workspace that contains all
the shared information and functionality of the application domain. This visual
workspace resembles a zoomable whiteboard of infinite size and resolution and
is called the "information landscape". ZOIL's zoomable information landscape
facilitates the navigation in the application domain and its information spaces
by "tapping into our natural spatial and geographic ways of thinking" [19]. All
domain objects and their relations are organized and visualized in space and
scale to foster natural visual-spatial approaches to accessing, sharing, and manipulating information. Regions of the landscape with items, piles, or clusters
can represent certain user activities, domain processes, or personal vs. shared
information repositories. The landscape is used as a flexible multi-scale medium
for visually accessing the application domain and its information spaces and objects. Content and functionality of an individual object can be accessed spatially
using panning and "semantic zooming" [19] without the need for opening folders
or dedicated applications and the then-necessary management of overlaying or
occluding windows (Fig. 2). This zoom navigation is also in line with reality-
based interaction: It draws strength from the users' environment awareness and
skills, e.g. their familiarity with approaching, touching, moving, and organizing
objects in physical space and the simple fact that "all objects in the real world
have spatial relationships between them" [11]. Therefore visual objects at different locations and scales (e.g. virtual Post-It notes, project logos) can further
augment the landscape with global or relative landmarks that support orientation. Furthermore, all regions of ZOIL's landscape can be visually annotated
with ink strokes using stylus, touch, or digital Anoto pens on physical paper.
Annotations can also be made directly on objects, e.g. slides (Fig. 2).

Multi-user collaboration becomes possible by using ensembles of personal and
shared user terminals. All terminals inside the interactive space share the same
information landscape. All user-initiated changes to the content of the landscape
such as moving, resizing, rotating, or annotating information items are immediately sent to a central server and synchronized with the other terminals in real
time (typically within 50-250 ms). However, what region of the landscape is currently visible on each terminal can be individually controlled by the users. For
example, users can use a tabletop to interactively zoom into the tiniest details
of the landscape at many orders of magnification. At the same time they can
display the entire landscape on a peripheral wall-sized screen to provide them
with an overview for orientation when needed. The boundaries of the currently
visible regions can also be transmitted between terminals. For example, users
can instruct the remote wall-sized display to zoom and pan to the region of the

---

[1] Videos of these prototypes are available at http://www.vimeo.com/12737554 and
http://hci.uni-konstanz.de/jetter/hcse2010.mp4

landscape that is currently visible on the tabletop or vice versa. Thus, by using terminals as "cameras", the roles of stationary or mobile terminals can be flexibly adjusted by the users depending on the group's task and preference.

In large information landscapes, users also need efficient ways to find, filter, and analyze single objects or specific clusters. For this reason, ZOIL also integrates physical and virtual "magic lenses" [3] that float above the landscape and through which the underlying content of the landscape can be viewed (Fig. 2). These lenses provide movable filters and visualization tools such as lists, bar charts, scatter plots, or tables to provide an analytical view on the landscape and to facilitate the search and filtering of items using spatial metaphors.

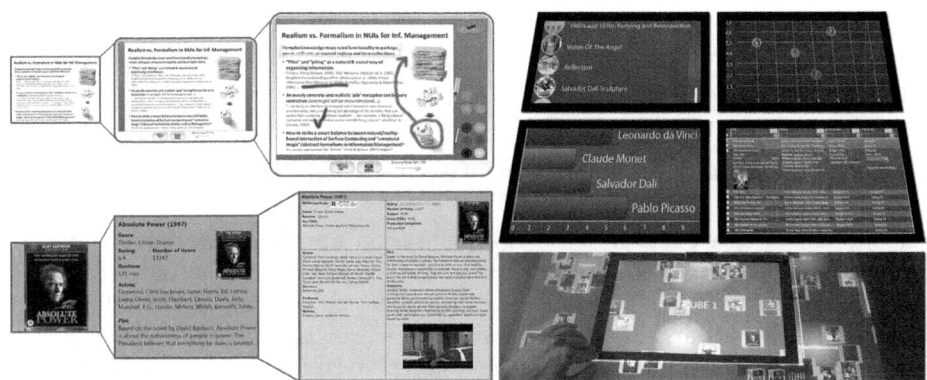

Fig. 2. *Left*: Semantic zooming into objects in ZOIL uses the available screen estate for smooth changes between iconic representations, metadata display, and full content and functionality, e.g. for viewing, editing, or annotating the content. The example shows a slide object (top) and a movie object (bottom) at different zoom levels. *Right*: Physical or virtual magic lenses allow users to view the underlying landscape using different information visualization tools.

To realize ZOIL's distributed multi-user and multi-device ZUI, the reference architecture is based on a client-server architecture that provides and synchronizes the data model of the information landscape for all user terminals or clients within an interactive space (Fig. 1). Inspired by Prante et al.'s i-Land with its COAST framework for object distribution [20], we have implemented a dedicated ZOIL server and a client-side data backend as part of our ZOIL software framework for C#/.NET that is based on the db4o object database and its mechanism of *transparent persistence*[2]. For peer-to-peer communication between clients and for input device connectivity, we have chosen the simple but robust stateless *Open Sound Control (OSC)* protocol that can be used for UDP broadcasting within the subnet of an interactive space and enables developers to easily integrate novel input devices (e.g. Nintendo Wiimote Controllers or Anoto

---

[2] http://www.db4o.com/

digital pens) by connecting to input device middleware such as OpenInterface [14] or Squidy [13]. Equally important for ZOIL's realization is the framework's support for fast client-side rendering of complex rich-media zoomable user interfaces. For ZOIL, we have chosen Microsoft's Windows Presentation Foundation (WPF) technology because of following reasons: First, the technology must support high-performance hardware-accelerated renderings of vector-based user interface components, so that smooth zooming animations over many orders of magnification become possible without pixelation. Second, an initial set of fundamental user interface widgets such as buttons or sliders, but also more complex widgets such as video players, document viewers of web browsers should be available from the start to accelerate implementation. Third, a declarative language for user interface definition should be available that supports a clear separation between business logic and visual presentation. In the following we discuss the central role of WPF's declarative XAML language in our model-based design and implementation approach.

4   Model-Based Design and Implementation with ZOIL

For our model-based design and implementation approach, we have employed an object model similar to the *designer's model* in OVID or the *conceptual user interface model* in TASK as a core artifact. The model uses a UML-like notation to define what kind of information objects are visually exposed to the user and become user manipulatable on the different terminals inside the interactive space. Furthermore it reveals what attributes or metadata these objects carry for the user, and what operations or behaviors these objects share and provide. Fig. 3 shows an example conceptual model for an interactive space in which users can collaboratively explore hotel objects that are contained in ZOIL's zoomable information landscape using semantic zooming. Hotels carry (meta)data such as

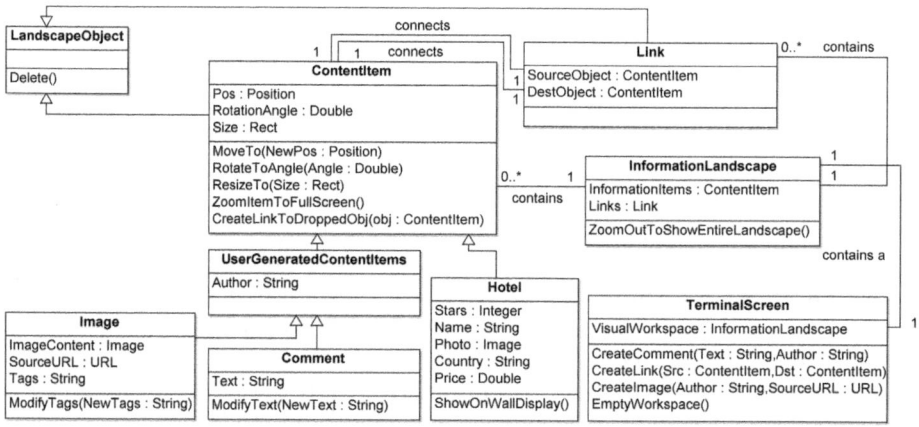

Fig. 3. An object-oriented conceptual model of a ZOIL user interface

the name of the hotel, a photo of the hotel, the country of the hotel, etc. Users can add images from the Web or textual comments as user generated content. Users can explicitly connect all hotels, images, and comments with visual links to structure, annotate, or discuss. It is important to notice that Fig. 3 is not representing the programmer's model of the user interface or its code objects and methods, but that it describes the classes, attributes, and operations of the domain objects and conceptual objects that the user will perceive and act on when interacting with the system's OOUI. "The primary distinction that designers and programmers must keep in mind is that OOUI design concentrates on objects *that are perceived by users*. OO programming focuses on implementation details that often need to be hidden from the user" [21]. Since the conceptual model is used to inform design and implementation based on human intervention, it is not necessary that the notation completely complies with the UML standard and covers all details. It only has to cover the essentials of the UI from a user's perspective using a notation that has been agreed on and is intelligible for all designers and programmers. In our exploration, we have experienced that our UML-like notation used in Fig. 3 has met these requirements.

We have based our example of a conceptual model on typical user tasks during collaborative holiday planning and an OO analysis of the surrounding information space. Task analysis and OO analysis of the information space revealed the objects and their relations, e.g. whether an object of a certain class should contain or refer to one or many objects of a different class. These relations are specific to the application domain and information space, e.g. the landscape in our example contains 0-n objects of the class *ContentItem*, i.e. hotels, comments, or images. Furthermore, all *ContentItem* objects can be linked to other *ContentItem* object via a *Link* object. The OO analysis of the information space also helps to identify the task-relevant metadata or attributes of an class that should be provided to the users, e.g. alphanumeric fields such as *Name* and *Country* of a hotel, or visual images such as the *Photo* of an hotel. In a ZOIL user interface, objects also carry implicit visual properties such as position, size, and rotation angle that are not provided to the user as numeric values but are used to place and render objects. In Fig. 3 all these different attributes are listed in the middle section of each UML class definition.

After having identified the task-relevant classes, relations and attributes of objects, the bottom section of the UML class definition is used to specify the functions or *operations* that objects of this class should expose to the user. Based on the task analysis, basic operations such as creating, editing or deleting an object have to be identified and have to be attached to the object itself or to other user interface objects. For example a virtual Post-It note as *Comment* object should become editable after zooming in to modify its content. Furthermore users should be able to delete outdated comments. Therefore a *Delete()* function should be provided to the user that is attached to the object, e.g. a delete button similar to the close button of a GUI window. However, the functionality to create a new comment *CreateComment(...)* must be attached to the enclosing visual workspace or screen as the create-functionality must be accessible before the *Comment* object itself exists. Other operations can be modeled for facilitating the zooming navigation, e.g. an object can be assigned a *ZoomItemToFullScreen()* functionality to offer an automated zooming that reveals all attributes, metadata, and operations by a simple tap or click on the object. While modeling the operations of objects, further design decisions have to be made, e.g. whether an object is movable, resizable, or rotatable. Also the functionality that should be executed when using drag-and-drop manipulations can be modeled. For example, the behaviors section of a class can define what should happen as soon as an object of a certain class has been dropped onto it, e.g. creating a link to the dropped object in *CreateLinkToDroppedObj(...)*.

The design of the conceptual model should be accompanied by two continuous activities to ensure its quality: First, choosing appropriate class hierarchies is essential for the OOUI's coherence and consistency. Therefore the model should be continuously checked if all new commonalities in attributes and operations have been modeled in common base classes. Second, during OOUI design the higher level task models have to be decomposed into sequences of lower level direct manipulations of objects and other invocations of their operations. In many cases it is not immediately visible if a model covers all required tasks and therefore this should be frequently verified. This can be achieved by manually simulating a user task and using the conceptual model for a sequential walkthrough that checks if all necessary objects, attributes, and operations for all tasks are available.

4.1   Model-Based Design and Implementation of UI Objects

ZOIL's reference design and architecture provide a generic design and implementation framework in which only the application-specific details of the user interface and interaction design have to be fleshed out. Our model-based approach provides the necessary translation rules in a simple step-by-step process, thereby allowing designers to create initial sketches of visual and interaction design from the conceptual model of the user interface. It furthermore enables designers and programmers to easily turn the resulting sketches into an implementation model for the user interface object based on XAML. This XAML code can then be used to test the design as an interactive prototype. Our model-based translation process can be described as a four phase process and is visually illustrated in Fig. 4 for the example of a *Hotel* object.

The first step of the translation process is to decide which attributes and operations of an object should appear on which level of semantic zooming. Attributes or operation can either appear globally at all zoom levels or they can be assigned to different zoom levels, so that they only appear or become active after the user has zoomed in. In Fig. 4, the *Delete()* function is global and appears at all levels of detail. This is also true for the manipulation of the object's position, rotation angle, or size (*Move()*, *Rotate()*, *Resize()*) and its functionality to react to objects that have been dropped onto it such as *CreateLinkToDroppedObj()*. The most important attributes that a user frequently needs to recognize or recall an object (e.g. *Photo* or *Name* of an hotel) already appear at small zoom levels in the early stages of zooming. The attributes only necessary for more

in-depth exploration (e.g. *Stars, Country, Price*) appear after enough screen estate is available, e.g. on zoom level 3. This is also true for advanced functions
like *ShowOnWallScreen()* that shows a hotel on a shared wall-sized display.

In the second step, this assignment is used to sketch the global appearance
and behavior of the object (Fig. 4 top right). The different operations and their
triggering manipulations or widgets are modeled using simple sketches: In our
example, the typical multi-touch gestures known from tabletops or smart phones
are used for *Move()*, *Rotate()*, and *Resize()*. A zoom-to-full-screen animation is
issued by a single tap with the finger on an object (*ZoomItemToFullScreen()*).
Another item can be dragged on the object with the finger, activating the *Cre-
ateLinkToDroppedObj()* functionality if the item is of the type *ContentItem*.

In the third step, the individual zoom levels are sketched based on the assign-
ments of attributes and operations from step one (Fig. 4 right). These sketch
models are created for each zoom level to move from conceptual design to the
concrete design of the visual appearance of objects. Since the necessary attributes
and operations for each zoom level are known, the complexity of the design task
is minimized and can be carried out with standard techniques.

In the final step, the sketch models of the different zoom levels are translated into the implementation model of the user interface object (Fig. 4 bottom). This translation is supported by ZOIL's software framework that extends
the declarative XAML user interface description language of WPF with ZOIL-
specific elements. By introducing ZOIL's *ZComponent* user interface control, an
object's appearance at different semantic zoom levels can be defined entirely using declarative approaches (similar to HTML) without the need for procedural
programming. The different zoom levels are managed by ZOIL's *ZComponent-
Frames* container that selects the appearance of an object depending on the
available render size. To avoid harsh visual changes, zoom levels smoothly blend
between two appearances using an opacity animation. Furthermore designers
and programmers can easily assign predefined ZOIL behaviors to an object using the *attached behavior* software pattern[3]. This pattern helps to encapsulate
frequently used ZOIL-specific behaviors (e.g. "object can be manipulated with
multi-touch", "object zooms to full-screen after tap", "object is a target for drop-
ping another object") in a central behavior library. Behaviors from the library
can be easily attached to classes or individual instances of objects using declarative XAML code without the need to know procedural programming or to fully
understand the underlying class hierarchies. We believe that this combination of
the *ZComponent* object and the attached behavior pattern introduces a great
expressive power to the declarative XAML language and a very natural view of
interactive behavior into user interface programming. It greatly facilitates the
translation of sketch models with their visual appearance and behavioral properties into implementation models. As illustrated in the implementation model in
Fig. 4, the process of translating a sketch model in XAML is thereby a straightforward task that does not rely on advanced programming skills.

---

[3] http://blogs.msdn.com/b/johngossman/archive/2008/05/07/
the-attached-behavior-pattern.aspx

4.2   Case Study

In order to investigate the utility and applicability of our OOUI approach in practice, we conducted a case study with 11 participants (9 graduate-level and 2 undergraduate students of computer science). The question guiding our study was how well participants can apply our approach and how they assess its practical value during a small-scale project. We divided the participants into five teams (4 teams with 2 members, 1 team with 3 members). In a first one-hour session we presented our modeling approach to all teams: We created and explained a conceptual model of a ZOIL user interface for accessing a fictitious image database. The teams were then given the assignment to create an own conceptual model for a different ZOIL user interface until the next session in two weeks. The user interface to model should allow users to explore and discuss hotels as described in the example in the previous sections. We provided the teams with the same input for their modeling and design activity that we used ourselves to create the example model in Fig. 3, i.e. all teams were handed 8 informal functional requirements (e.g. "user must be able to add a textual comment to the workspace") and a list of 22 required object properties (e.g. "each *Comment* has an *Author*", "each *Image* carries *Tags*").

Two weeks later, we carried out individual one-hour team sessions during which each team completed three tasks. First, each team presented and explained their prepared conceptual model. Then we asked the team to check if their model really supports the 8 functional requirements by carrying out a walkthrough. We then presented the team our alternative model (Fig. 3) and asked them to validate this unknown model by another walkthrough. After this, each team member filled out a questionnaire to rate the difficulty of the three tasks. At the end of the sessions, the teams were instructed to design and implement a user interface with the ZOIL framework based on Fig. 3 until the next sessions in the following week. In these last sessions, each team individually presented the resulting interactive prototype and each team member filled out a further questionnaire to rate the overall usefulness of the modeling approach and the difficulty to apply it on user interface design and implementation.

During the case study, all teams presented conceptual models that were formally correct and supported the 8 functional requirements. All teams were able to carry out a walkthrough to validate their own and unknown models. Furthermore, the presented interactive prototypes covered the requested functionality. However, during the first and second session participants reported initial problems regarding the unfamiliar use of UML class diagrams to model user interfaces. Repeatedly participants mentioned that they sometimes had fallen back into the familiar modeling of code objects and lost track of their original intention to model the user interface from a user's perspective. However, the participants reported that they got increasingly used to the approach and found it useful to support the design and implementation. Fig. 5 shows the results from the questionnaires: the creation of a model (mean=3.45, sd=0.93) and checking the own or someone else's model with a walkthrough (mean=3.1, sd=2.9 and mean=2.9, sd=1.14) was not considered as particularly difficult nor very easy.

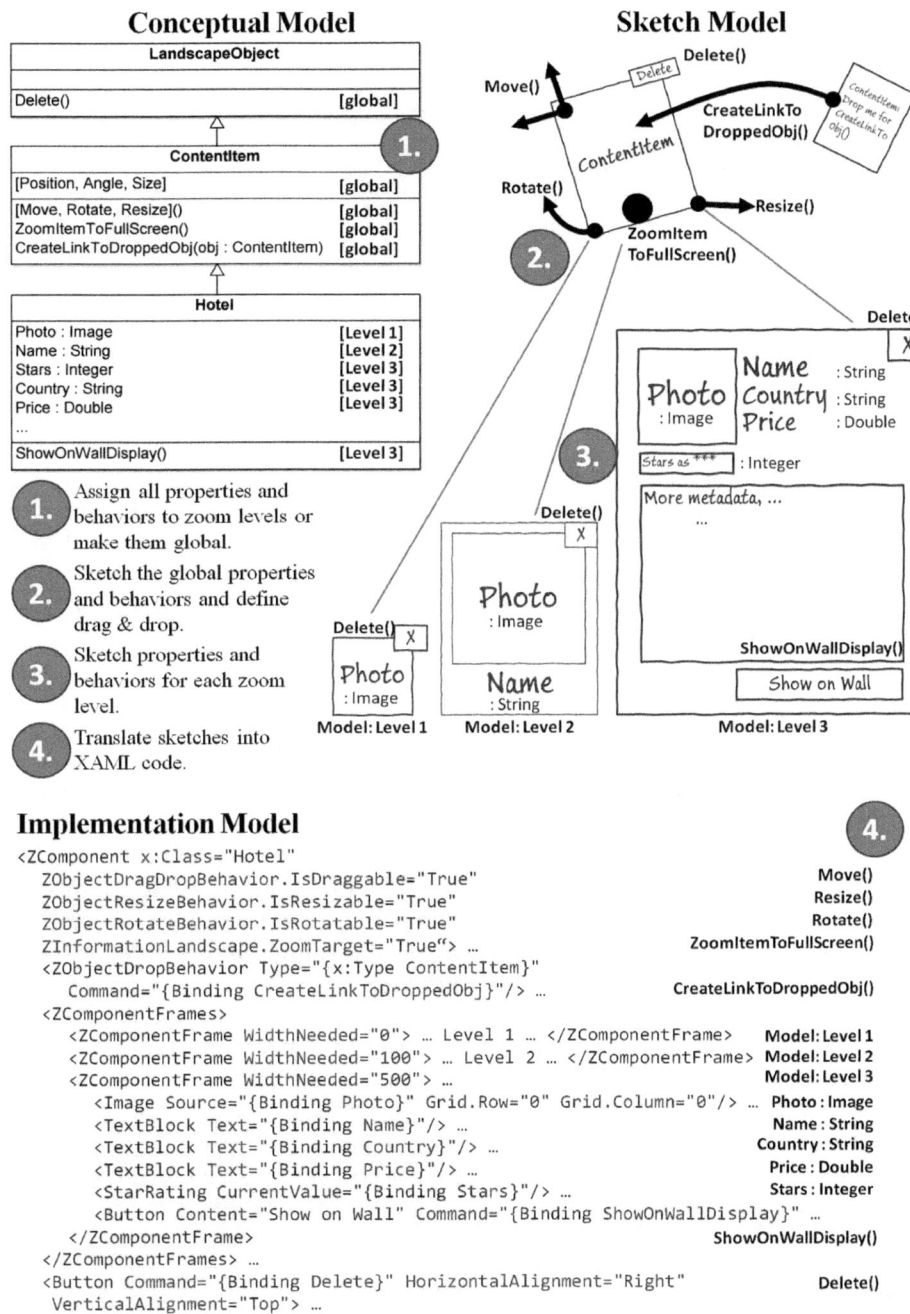

Fig. 4. ZOIL's translation process and rules to translate the object model to user interface design and implementation

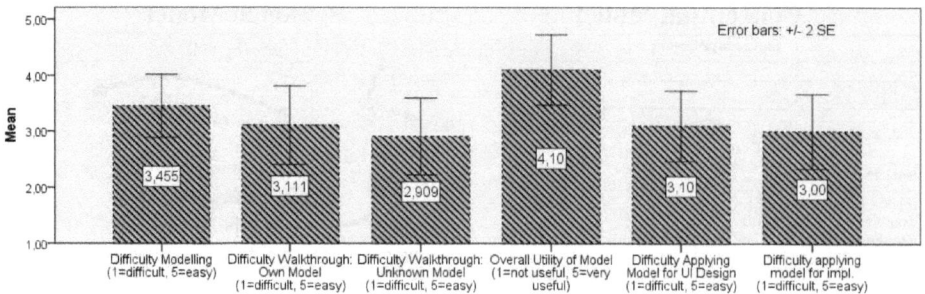

Fig. 5. Collected feedback from the questionnaires of the case study

This is rather encouraging, as the students were given only a very brief introduction to the approach without any proper training phase. Furthermore, the overall utility of the modeling technique was considered as useful (mean=4.1, sd=0.99) by the participants. Regarding the early stage of our approach and the unfamiliar use of object-oriented modeling and design for user interfaces, we consider these results as a promising first evidence that OOUI approaches can be indeed useful for designing interactive spaces.

5   Conclusion and Future Work

We have discussed why we believe that revisiting OOUIs has a great potential for the design of future post-WIMP environments, particularly for collaborative information interaction. We have introduced our ZOIL paradigm that we have used as an experimental testbed for creating and evaluating our OOUI approach. We have illustrated and discussed our approach in detail and have shown how it can efficiently inform the design and implementation of user interface objects following simple translation rules. Furthermore, we have presented promising results from a first case study on the practical utility of our approach. At the current stage, we consider our approach as a successful first step. However, ZOIL-based interactive spaces offer a great design space and currently only small parts of it have been covered by our approach. For example, the design of ZOIL's magic lenses, visualization tools, or the integration of physical objects or paper is not covered yet. Therefore we will investigate how new and extended modeling notations and translation rules can be used to cover these aspects in future.

References

1. Common User Access Guide to User Interface Design. IBM Corporation (1991)
2. Beck, A., Janssen, C., Weisbecker, A., Ziegler, J.: Integrating object-oriented analysis and graphical user interface design. In: Taylor, R.N., Coutaz, J. (eds.) ICSE-WS 1994 and SE-HCI 1994. LNCS, vol. 896, pp. 127–140. Springer, Heidelberg (1995)

3. Bier, E.A., Stone, M.C., Pier, K., et al.: Toolglass and magic lenses: the see-through interface. In: Proc. SIGGRAPH 1993, pp. 73–80. ACM, New York (1993)
4. Blandford, A., Attfield, S.: Interacting with information. In: Carroll, J.M. (ed.) Synthesis Lectures on Human-Centered Informatics. Morgan & Claypool (2010)
5. Collins, D.: Designing object-oriented user interfaces. Benjamin Cummings, Redwood City (1995)
6. Constantine, L.L., Lockwood, L.A.D.: Software for use. ACM Press/Addison-Wesley Publishing Co., New York (1999)
7. Fitzmaurice, G.W., Khan, A., Buxton, W., Kurtenbach, G., Balakrishnan, R.: Sentient data access via a diverse society of devices. Queue 1(8), 52–62 (2003)
8. Geyer, F., Reiterer, H.: A cross-device spatial workspace supporting artifact-mediated collaboration in interaction design. In: Proc. CHI EA 2010, pp. 3787–3792. ACM, New York (2010)
9. Heilig, M., Demarmels, M., Rexhausen, S., Huber, S., Runge, O.: Search, explore and navigate - designing a next generation knowledge media workbench. In: Proc. SIDeR 2009, pp. 40–43. Eindhoven University of Technology, Eindhoven (2009)
10. Hutchins, E.L., Hollan, J.D., Norman, D.A.: Direct manipulation interfaces. Hum. Comput. Interact. 1(4), 311–338 (1985)
11. Jacob, R.J., Girouard, A., Hirshfield, L.M., Horn, M.S., Shaer, O., Solovey, E.T., Zigelbaum, J.: Reality-based interaction: a framework for post-wimp interfaces. In: Proc. CHI 2008, pp. 201–210. ACM, New York (2008)
12. Jetter, H.C., Engl, A., Schubert, S., Reiterer, H.: Zooming not zapping: Demonstrating the zoil user interface paradigm for itv applications. In: Adjunct Proceedings of EuroITV 2008. Springer, Heidelberg (2008)
13. König, W.A., Rädle, R., Reiterer, H.: Interactive design of multimodal user interfaces. Journal on Multimodal User Interfaces 3(3), 197–213 (2010)
14. Lawson, J.Y.L., Al-Akkad, A.A., Vanderdonckt, J., Macq, B.: An open source workbench for prototyping multimodal interactions based on off-the-shelf heterogeneous components. In: Proc. EICS 2009. ACM, New York (2009)
15. Lehikoinen, J., Aaltonen, A., Huuskonen, P., Salminen, I.: Personal Content Experience: Managing Digital Life in the Mobile Age. Wiley, Chichester (2007)
16. Mandel, T.: The GUI-OOUI War, Windows vs. OS/2: the designer's guide to human-computer interfaces. Van Nostrand Reinhold, New York (1994)
17. Memmel, T., Reiterer, H.: Model-based and prototyping-driven user interface specification to support collaboration and creativity. J.UCS 14(19), 3217–3235 (2009)
18. Pawson, R., Matthews, R.: Naked objects: a technique for designing more expressive systems. SIGPLAN Not. 36(12), 61–67 (2001)
19. Perlin, K., Fox, D.: Pad: an alternative approach to the computer interface. In: Proc. SIGGRAPH 1993, pp. 57–64. ACM, New York (1993)
20. Prante, T., Streitz, N., Tandler, P.: Roomware: Computers disappear and interaction evolves. Computer 37(12), 47–54 (2004)
21. Roberts, D., Berry, D., Isensee, S., Mullaly, J.: Designing for the User with OVID. Macmillan Technical Publishing, Basingstoke (1998)
22. Shaer, O., Jacob, R.J.: A specification paradigm for the design and implementation of tangible user interfaces. ACM Trans. Comput. Hum. Interact. 16(4), 1–39 (2009)
23. Wigdor, D., Jiang, H., Forlines, C., et al.: Wespace: the design development and deployment of a walk-up and share multi-surface visual collaboration system. In: Proc. CHI 2009, pp. 1237–1246. ACM, New York (2009)

ViSE – A Virtual Smart Environment for Usability Evaluation

Stefan Propp and Peter Forbrig

University of Rostock, Institute of Computer Science,
Albert Einstein Str. 21, 18059 Rostock, Germany
{stefan.propp,peter.forbrig}@uni-rostock.de

Abstract. Within the research field of HCI task models are widely used for model-based development of interactive systems. Recently introduced approaches applied task models further to model cooperative behaviour of people interacting in smart environments. However there is a lack of usability methods to support the needs of evaluations during a model-based development process for smart environments. Particularly during early stages of development building a prototypical environment for user evaluations is resource consuming. To overcome the challenges we present a process model and according tool support. We provide the virtual smart environment ViSE to conduct expert evaluations and user studies during a user-centred design process, supporting iterative evaluations.

Keywords: Model-based Usability Evaluation, Task Models, Smart Environment.

1 Introduction

According to Weiser's vision [9] of ubiquitous computing, devices are weaving themselves into everyday life, allowing people to fully concentrate on performing their tasks, while hiding complexity of necessary devices. A smart environment (SE) recognizes user behavior and provides assistance to achieve the users' objectives. For instance within a meeting scenario the presenter should concentrate on the talk, while the SE assists by adjusting the projector and capturing audiovisual data for meeting documentation if needed.

While offering a higher degree of comfort, also new challenges are introduced. In contrast to desktop computing, where a user focuses the attention on a single device, in a SE multiple devices influence user behavior. Reflected from a task-oriented point of view, a certain task can be started at one device, while being finished at another device. For instance during a discussion some comments are quickly typed into a PDA, being revised later back in the office at a notebook. Different user interactions lead to a wide variety of options [7] for the design of the SE, comprising modalities (like speech or gestures), device selection (like direct access by a user or dynamic selection by the SE) and the initiative (explicit or implicit). An example for explicit

R. Bernhaupt et al. (Eds.): HCSE 2010, LNCS 6409, pp. 38–45, 2010.

initiative is a user manually turning the light on via switch, whereas an example for implicit initiative describes a scenario where the SE senses that it is too dark and decides autonomously to turn the light on. As we can see, an interaction needs to be interpreted within a certain context. Contextual conditions like available devices, currently present users, light or temperature, may influence task performance for each user. Furthermore cooperation is an important aspect. Within SEs a certain task may be performed cooperatively by several users, who reflect certain roles.

These characteristics of SEs impose challenges for usability evaluation. An evaluation is particularly resource consuming. To conduct a user study within a real SE a completely functional prototype has to be set up, while evaluating a simulated environment needs effort for instance to prepare a "Wizard of Oz"-experiment.

For model-based development of SEs some approaches apply task models [1, 2, 3, 8, 10]. We suggest reusing these task models also for usability evaluation to integrate evaluation into development. Advantages are (a) the reduced effort to prepare evaluations rapidly at all stages of development, (b) an easier interpretation of task-based log files than of low level events and (c) the direct link back to the development models facilitates their improvement.

2 Related Work

Several recently published approaches apply task models for model-based development of SEs. Trapp et al. [8] define each device's capabilities with a task model chunk. When a new device connects to the room infrastructure, the corresponding model chunk is added to the room task model. As a result combined functionalities may be offered. For instance a scanner and a printer may offer an additional copying functionality. Wurdel et al. [10] model behaviour of persons with task models and describe their collaboration. For instance, that person "A" has to finish the talk first to give person "B" the floor. Each task is described by a set of preconditions and effects on the environment. Feuerstack et al. [1] enhance the task modelling notation CTT to serve as model for runtime interpretation. Domain concepts are annotated and the object flow is modeled. Different users' task models are synchronized with domain objects. Luyten et al. [3] focus on modelling distributed user interfaces for dynamic environments. Task and environment models are visualized to reduce complexity.

While several approaches for the development of SEs are available, there are only a few appropriate usability methods. Scholtz et al. [6] suggest a general framework with evaluation metrics to give a starting point for structuring the evolving evaluation techniques. Maly et al. [4] describe an approach of visualizing the user's behaviour as 3D representation and allow experts to create artificial scenarios when sensor data is not available yet. However, task models are not used. In [5] we suggest a task model-based process for evaluating smart envionments. Performed tasks are visualized within animated task models and serve for analysis. In this paper we extend the approach to build a virtual smart environment, which visualizes user interactions as a 2D representation of a physical SE.

3   Usability Evaluation Method

Software development is structured into several stages, comprising requirements analysis, design and implementation of the final product. Accordingly we describe a structured process of development and evaluation of SEs. This section presents the process model (section 3.1) and subsequently discusses the usage of ViSE to conduct expert evaluations (section 3.2) and user studies (section 3.3).

3.1   Process Model

The process model (fig.1) describes an approach for the iterative development and evaluation of SEs. During each development cycle three stages are considered.

(1) During planning stage the development methods and evaluation techniques are chosen. If any developed artifacts of a previous cycle exist, their evaluation results are taken into account.

(2) During development stage existing artifacts are refined and new artifacts are developed. Examples are requirements documents, models and source code.

(3) Iterative evaluations comprise direct feedback for the developed artifacts based on feedback of user studies and expert evaluations.

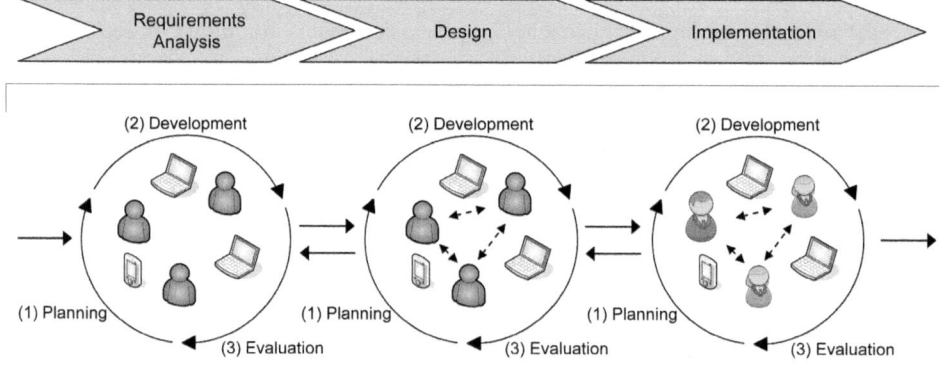

Fig. 1. Process model for design and evaluation of Smart Environments

Depending on progress within development different activities are carried out during each cycle, which should be subsequently outlined.

Requirements analysis. To elicit requirements a dialog with customers and prospective users is conducted. We identify user roles and create a task model for each role. A task model captures task hierarchies and their temporal relations. To provide additional insights (e.g. context dependencies) textual scenarios are captured, which may serve as test cases during evaluations.

During evaluation the consistency of the designed task models has to be analyzed. A task model animation tool allows interactively walking through the models.

Another challenge is to evaluate the users' stated assistance functionalities, which the smart environment should provide, like automatically switching lights on or showing presentation slides of a presenters' laptop. We provide a virtual smart environment (ViSE), which allows conducting "Wizard of Oz"-Experiments for SEs: An expert hides in another room, observing user interactions via video camera. The expert operates the devices within the physical environment remotely to mimic the envisioned assistance. Changing devices' states in ViSE allows changing the devices' states in the physical SE accordingly. Involved users get a feeling of the envisioned assistance and reflect their requirements

Design. Within the design stage task models have to be enriched with further details to more accurately reflect user behavior and to serve as initial models for implementation. Textual scenarios elicited during requirements stage contain additional details about cooperative dependencies between different users, like a chairman is required to give a presenter the floor. Further details comprise contextual dependencies for performing tasks, like having a laptop containing slides to give a presentation. These aspects are modeled in CTML ("collaborative task modeling language") [10]. Each task is annotated with preconditions and effects. A precondition formalizes the environments' state before a particular task can be performed. An effect describes the environments' state after a task is performed.

To ensure the consistency of the designed models, the virtual SE visualizes the modeled SE and allows an interactive walk-through as collaborative animation. Scenarios from requirements stage are animated by a usability expert and identified inconsistencies can be corrected.

Implementation. Based on the designed task models the SE's software has to be implemented. The envisioned SE assists users while performing their tasks and proceeds in three steps: firstly it senses user movements and further context information (e.g. location sensors to separate presenter and audience), secondly it infers the task currently performed (e.g. a person is beginning to present) and finally it triggers devices accordingly (e.g. a projector performs a system task "show agenda"). Within our physical SE this recognition of performed tasks is accomplished by a probabilistic behavior model, which is derived from previously specified task models as discussed in [2]. Finally the software is deployed at the devices within the environment.

To ensure an adequate integration of all software and hardware components, user studies have to be conducted. During evaluation a vast amount of sensor data within the SE is captured, leading to the challenge of a suitable interpretation of user behavior to discover usability issues. Our virtual SE allows playing captured data forth and back to interactively explore issues.

After having introduced the process model and provided tool support we take a closer look at expert evaluations during design stage and user evaluations during implementation stage.

3.2 Expert Evaluation of Cooperative Task Models

After having specified a CTML design model its consistency according to the elicited requirements has to be evaluated. Fig. 2 depicts ViSE within an expert evaluation.

The left part of ViSE contains a birds' view of the environment, comprising users, devices (e.g. laptops and projectors) and other objects (e.g. pens and whiteboard erasers). Interactions with these entities allow changing the SEs' state and performing tasks. The following interactions are supported:

- Changing the persons' location
  (e.g. moving to a an empty seat)
- Changing the persons' corpus orientation
  (e.g. to look to the front, where the presenter is speaking)
- Attaching items to persons
  (e.g. a presenter is taking up a laptop)
- Changing devices' states
  (e.g. switching a laptop on)
- Establishing connections between devices
  (e.g. connecting a laptop to a VGA port to connect it to the room infrastructure)

The upper right part contains the persons within the current scenario with their associated roles. For each role a task model is animated. A task can be performed if both the temporal relations and the preconditions are fulfilled.

The lower right part contains the preconditions for the current task and indicates which conditions are currently "true" and "false". For the task "present with projector" three preconditions are specified (see fig.2, lower right part):

- The person with the role "presenter" has to be located at the "PresentationZone".
- The person has to carry a device of type laptop or PDA.
- The persons' device has to be connected to a VGA port.

In the scenario in fig.2 requirements engineer Stefan fulfills all three preconditions and the temporal relation that he has already performed task "enters room". Hence he is allowed to perform the task "presents with projector".

If any preconditions are differing from the requirements, they can be edited textually to directly improve the evaluated artifacts. As an alternative preconditions can be edited graphically. A designer may move persons to a certain location and equip them with devices. A subsequent option "generate preconditions" allows updating the preconditions accordingly.

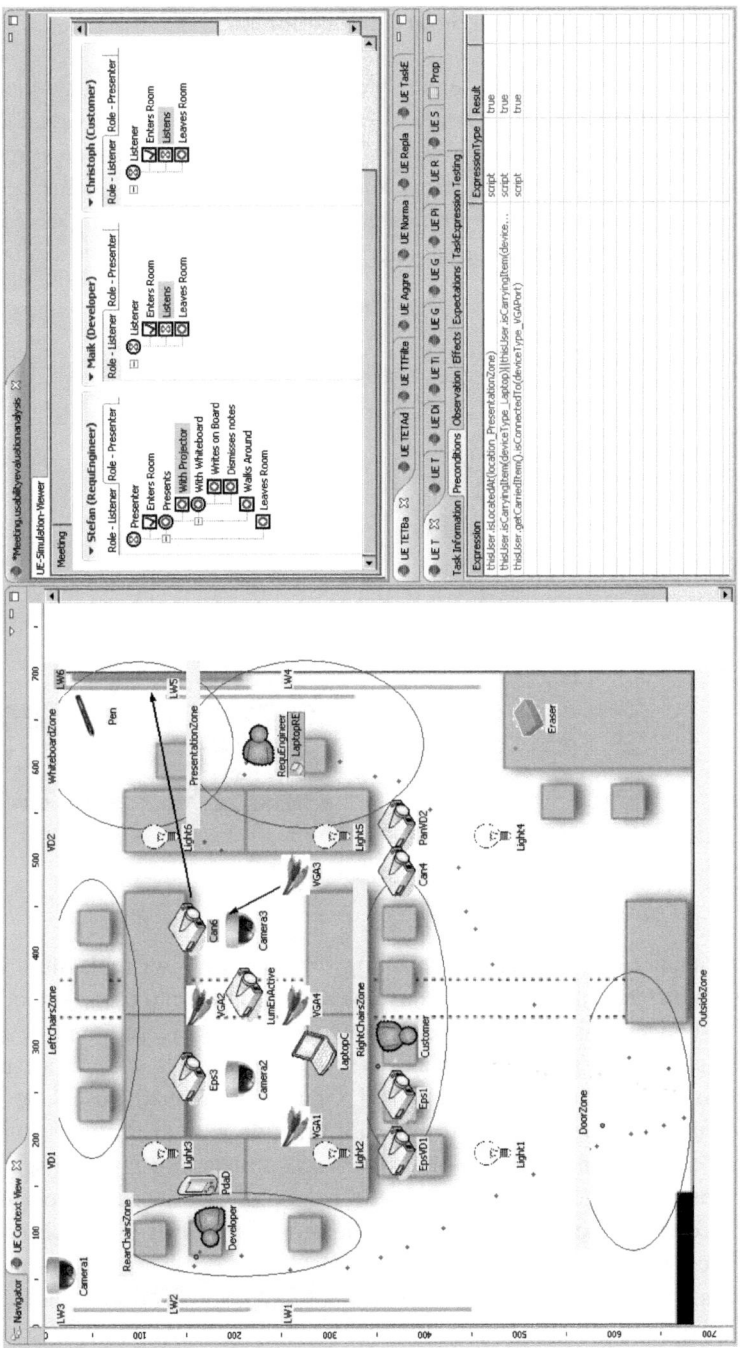

Fig. 2. Interactive walk-through of a design model with ViSE

3.3 User Evaluation of a Physical Smart Environment

After all components are set up, a user study can be conducted to evaluate the physical SE. Users are invited to perform tasks specified in a test plan as individual tasks or within a cooperative scenario. At the same time user interactions are captured: user movements via UbiSense location sensors, handled devices or other items via RFID tags, performed tasks via task recognition algorithms and video streams via cameras. Most data is already captured for normal operation of the SE. Hence it is available for evaluation.

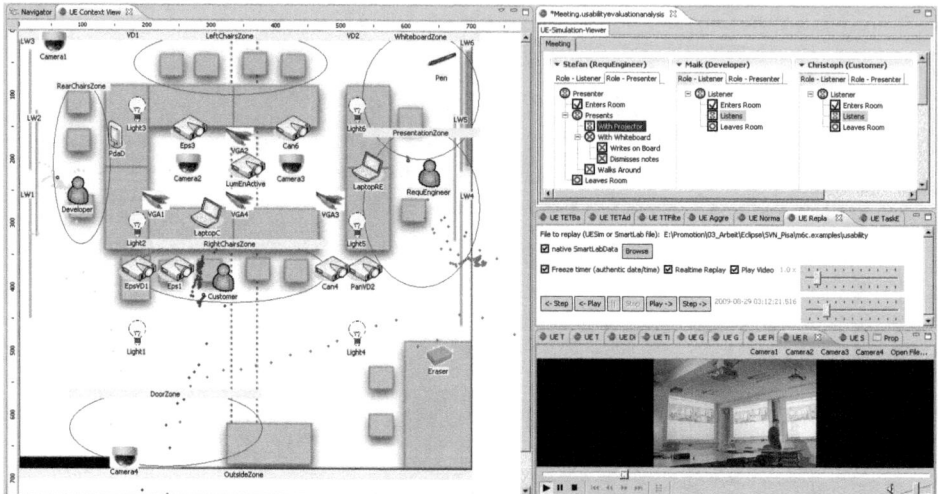

Fig. 3. Replay of sensor data with ViSE

ViSE was enhanced with a replay mode (fig. 3), which allows replaying captured sensor data with different animation speeds to provide insights into user interactions. A birds' view visualizes user movements, depicting locations of users and devices as according icons and way points reflecting past location sensor data with a particular focus on locations where tasks were performed. Graphically selecting users, devices or way points of user movements gives further information as tool tip (e.g. which task was performed at a certain way point) and filters sensor data. For instance spanning a selection rectangle over the presentation zone in front of the audience delivers an overview of all performed tasks within that area. During replay further expert observations can be annotated. For instance currently our physical SE recognizes only a limited set of tasks automatically. Additional tasks can be identified manually during video replay. According replay controls are depicted within a view at the right of fig. 3. Further views provide several logs and visualizations of sensor data on demand, for instance the progress of task performance as animated task model or gantt chart.

4 Conclusion

In this paper we have given an overview of model-based development of SEs and shown how to exploit designed task models for usability evaluation. A process model describes a process of iterative development and evaluation. The virtual smart environment ViSE provides tool support at requirements, design and implementation stage. In early development stages, when a physical SE for user studies is not available, ViSE allows conducting expert evaluations for SEs. After a physical SE is set up ViSE helps to cope with the vast amount of captured sensor data. We emphasize on providing an integrated view on task performance, a graphical presentation of user and device movements and video streams, for both presenting and interactively exploring usability data.

Future research avenues comprise gathering further real life experiences to improve the presented method and tools.

Acknowledgments. The work of the first author was supported by a grant of the German National Research Foundation (DFG), Graduate School 1424.

References

1. Feuerstack, S., Blumendorf, M., Albayrak, S.: Prototyping of Multimodal Interactions for Smart Environments based on Task Models. In: AMI 2007 Workshop on Model-Driven Software Engineering, Darmstadt, Germany (2007)
2. Giersich, M., Forbrig, P., Fuchs, G., Kirste, T., Reichart, D., Schuhmann, H.: Towards an Integrated Approach for Task Modeling and Human Behavior Recognition. In: Jacko, J.A. (ed.) HCI 2007. LNCS, vol. 4550, pp. 1109–1118. Springer, Heidelberg (2007)
3. Luyten, K., Vandervelpen, C., Coninx, K.: Task modeling for ambient intelligent environments - design support for situated task. In: TAMODIA 2005, Gdansk, Poland (2005)
4. Maly, I., Curin, J., Kleindienst, J., Slavik, P.: Creation and Visualization of User Behavior in Ambient Intelligent Environment. In: Information Visualisation, London, Great Britain (2008)
5. Propp, S., Buchholz, G., Forbrig, P.: Task Model-based Usability Evaluation for Smart Environments. In: Forbrig, P., Paternò, F. (eds.) HCSE/TAMODIA 2008. LNCS, vol. 5247, pp. 29–40. Springer, Heidelberg (2008)
6. Scholtz, J., Consolvo, S.: Towards a Discipline for Evaluating Ubiquitous Computing Applications, Technical Report of Intel Research (2004)
7. Shirehjini, A.: A Multidimensional Classification Model for the Interaction in Reactive Media Rooms. In: Jacko, J.A. (ed.) HCI 2007. LNCS, vol. 4552, pp. 431–439. Springer, Heidelberg (2007)
8. Trapp, M., Schmettow, M.: Consistency in use through Model based User Interface Development. In: Workshop at CHI 2006, Montreal, Canada (2006)
9. Weiser, M.: The Computer for the 21st Century. Scientific American 265, 94–104 (1991)
10. Wurdel, M., Propp, S., Forbrig, P.: HCI-Task Models and Smart Environments. In: HCIS 2008, Mailand, Italy (2008)

A Domain Specific Language for Contextual Design

Balbir S. Barn and Tony Clark

Middlesex University, Hendon, London, UK, NW4 4BT

Abstract. This paper examines the role of user-centered design (UCD) approaches to design and implementation of a mobile social software application to support student social workers in their work place. The experience of using a variant of UCD is outlined. The principles and expected norms of UCD raised a number of key lessons. It is proposed that these problems and lessons are a result of the inadequacy of precision of modeling the outcomes of UCD, which prevents model driven approaches to method integration between UCD approaches. Given this, it is proposed that the Contextual Design method is a good candidate for enhancing with model driven principles. A subset of the Work model focussing on Cultural and Flow models are described using a domain specific language and supporting tool built using the MetaEdit+ platform.

1 Introduction

This paper examines the role of user-centered design (UCD) to the design and implementation of a mobile social software application for supporting student social workers in their work place. The principles and expected norms of UCD raise a number of issues which lead us to propose that these problems are a result of the inadequacy of precision of modeling the outcomes of UCD, which prevents model driven approaches to method integration between UCD and established software engineering practice. A particular UCD approach - Contextual Design [3] is explored in detail from a model/language design perspective by first critiquing the key issues of ambiguity and lack of precision of diagrams normally produced as a result of Contextual Design activities. Following on from this, a subset of Contextual Design, namely, the Cultural Model is developed in terms of abstract and concrete syntax together with its accompanying semantics diagram using an approach to language design described by Clark et al [7]. An implementation using the MetaEdit+ tool [17] is also briefly described. The issues of a lack of precision of UCD methods represents an ongoing research challenge in the field of requirements engineering and a key outcome of this paper is to encourage discussion of these problems and lessons to enable method re-engineering of UCD practice.

The paper contributes to current research in human centred software engineering by providing a formal syntax and semantics for aspects of the Contextual Design methodology and in doing so provides a route whereby the exploration of how UCD and software engineering can be integrated.

R. Bernhaupt et al. (Eds.): HCSE 2010, LNCS 6409, pp. 46–61, 2010.

The remainder of the paper is structured as follows: section 2 introduces key aspects of UCD and model driven development; section 3 presents the key motivation of this work, our experience of using UCD and the lessons learnt, and provides a short introduction to Contextual Design, the UCD approach we have selected to be subject to a formal treatment; section 4 puts the case for using a *model driven* approach to UCD; section 5 presents the approach we have taken to develop a modelling language with more precise syntax and semantics; section 6 presents the domain specific language version for Contextual Design along with an illustrative example of its use; section 7 presents concluding remarks and notes for further research.

2   Background to UCD and MDD

2.1   From User-Centered Design to Participatory Design

A detailed review of the literature concerning user-centered design is not possible within the constraints of this paper but it is useful to present an overview of key phases in development of user engagement in systems design processes. User-Centered Design (UCD) or the variant, User-Centered Systems Design [22] emerged in the 1980s as an important development recognizing the move from batch computing to interactive computing applications where there was a need to involve users in the design process. At that time, however, as Marti and Bannon [20] indicate: UCD did not imply that "users were ... active participants in the design process", rather they were studied, observed, measured as a way of gathering requirements for the system development [8]. An implication of UCD is thus one of where the designer (hopefully) reacts to feedback from the user. A more radical school of user involvement is that attributed to the so-called Scandinavian Model of UCD, namely, Participatory Design (PD) that emerged from the research activity of people such as Bjerknes et al [5]. In PD, users are seen as equal partners in the design and development of systems. This involvement of users implies users as "active agents" and later became known as Cooperative Design [11] or more latterly as "Co-Design". In PD, interestingly, there is a focus on primary work processes and identification of technology to enhance and better support work activities. (The basis of business process modeling). As UCD concepts became established they were further elaborated as ISO Standard 13407, Human-centred design processes for interactive systems [23]. These concepts were developed and extended into 12 key principles for UCD by Gulliksen [15].

While the mantra of involving users in the design process is now well ingrained [26] it has been contested and more recently Marti and Bannon [20] outline caveats where they argue that involving users can present problems. The characterization of problems they have identified forms part of the evaluation of our experience of co-design when applied to our development of a mobile application for e-learning, and which led us to consider how such issues may be addressed by model driven practice for UCD.

2.2   Model Driven Development

Orthogonal but related to UCD is the need to recognize that software engineering development methods have also evolved and more recently model driven development is increasingly seen as critical to good design: see [10] for an overview of MDD where it is argued that modelling is a key technology that is necessary to address the representation gap between human understanding of complex modern systems and their implementations and where precision at all levels of development is key to the increased scope of computer-based support for systems development. We argue that precision is key to increasing all aspects of system quality including reliability, usability, efficiency, and that MDD offers an approach that provides precision from a range of appropriate perspectives. MDD is increasingly being used for user-centred aspects of systems such as HCI [27,25,24] and safety [1].

Modeling in general is viewed as a capstone of many software engineering approaches where it is used to as an approach to user requirements definition and as a basis for developing information systems to meet those requirements. Models provide a vehicle for explaining and sharing understanding of complex problems and provide capabilities for different views of the underlying problem at different levels of abstraction. Model driven architecture takes this premise further by providing an overarching conceptual structure for using and applying transformations to models in a structured and controlled manner in all stages of the software engineering development process.

The Object Management Group (OMG) provides a set of standards to express models and model-model transformation and has been leading industry initiatives in the promotion of technologies, methods and standards under the banner of model driven architecture (MDA) [13]. Our position is: MDA has key role to play in systems development and are in agreement with Constantine and Lockwood [8], who assert that UCD can be ambiguous and vague. In contrast, Gulliksen et al assert that "model driven approaches represent a move away from user-centered design reducing their involvement to that of the users being informants rather than co-designers". This assertion needs re-visiting in the light of MDA approaches to user interface design and recent advances in domain specific languages. Certainly Fisher [9] has identified that Collaborative Design and meta-design (using MDA principles) are key themes facing software engineering research and practice.

3   Experience of User Centered Design

This section describes some of our experiences from a recent research project that utilised UCD and software engineering approaches to developing a mobile application for Social Work education. We discuss some of the key issues and lessons arising from that experience and present an argument for model driven UCD.

3.1   Case Study

The motivation for exploring how model driven principles could be applied to user centred design arose from a recent research project where we applied a variant of user centred design to design and implement a mobile device application to support Social Work Education in the UK.

In common with many other professions, the training of social workers requires students to be placed in social work settings and to undergo assessment in the workplace. Trainee social workers in England (those on an accredited social work degree (UG or PG) must successfully complete 200 days in a practice setting. Such placement can occur in different size blocks according to structures and requirements of individual degree programmes. These requirements are maintained and regulated by the Social Work professional body – the General Social Care Council (http://www.gscc.org.uk/Home/).

During the practice learning process, there are several key stakeholders involved, including: the student; the practice mentor and assessor; the University academic tutor; the work based supervisor. The key outcome of the placement is a report that outlines the skills and competencies raised along with supporting evidence collected from the placement.

Given these background concepts the research project aimed to develop a set of applications both mobile and web-based that supported student social workers in the planning and design of practice learning assessments and in the collation of research and practice evidence towards a final report.

3.2   Experience Using UCD

The project team assigned to the project was multidisciplinary. There were academic experts from Computer Science, Sociology, Social Work, along with practitioners from the Social Work field. Further, the project development teams were located in multiple locations across the UK South. As well as the multiple disciplines located within the team, the Computer Science team further represented alternative approaches to systems design, with representation from both MDA and UCD. These different approaches led to some creative tension manifested in early debates similar to that discussed between Gulliksen and Constantine. Given the make-up of the project team, it was essential to agree to a methodology that could accommodate disparate views. The team had previous experience of using a co-design process for developing mobile applications for the Nursing domain [21]. Hence this approach was adapted to suit the needs of this project and the software engineering principles influencing members of the team. Thus the project deployed a variety of methodological techniques that draw upon software engineering, social sciences research and usability.

3.3   Problems Encountered

While the system was successfully developed, its deployment and use was very limited, and is consequently still ongoing (past the project completion date).

This is partially attributed to the implementation of the co-design approach and it is here that it is considered that there are many lessons to be learnt. Using the putative framework of problems identified by Marti and Bannon [20] as a starting point the following lessons are presented:

user types. The intended software applications were designed for several types of users.

users as designers. While it is accepted that all users can design at some level – that is have ideas, think creatively about different uses of tools and convey those thoughts in some form explicit knowledge transfer – it is clearly not the case that users have the necessary design skills to engage in all stages of the design process.

new technologies. Mobile technology is evolving at a rapid pace. Increasing power, capability and software applications possible makes it very difficult for non-technologists to remain abreast with such change. In order for users to make a significant contribution to the design process they need to have a logical understanding of technological solutions in order to be able to conceptualize new scenarios of use. This problem manifested itself very early in the co-design process: many of our participants had their first direct contact with current mobile devices in our show and tell workshops.

work environments. Project champions tend to be located at management level where there is often limited understanding of operational requirements. This can have a detrimental effect on active user involvement throughout the design process. The Social Work environment in a public sector setting meant there were work pressures that often prevented users from securing sufficient time to effect a meaningful engagement in the co-design activities.

deployment risk. The need for sufficient training, guidance, support and impact assessment in the work environment also need to be sufficiently defined. Issues of risk and technology in the workplace, although correctly identified at the beginning of the project manifested themselves resulting low usages in the work place context. There has been considerable interest within the social sciences in developing ideas related to risk. Beck in his seminal text Risk Society [2] argued that the "technisisation" of risk derives form the omnipresence of technology. The experience here could be seen as reflecting fear on a number of dimensions. Reluctance to engage with the project could be seen as a fear of technology itself and the ability of some individuals to cope with technological demands. The social work task is in itself high risk and high profile and the use of technological devices for training purposes could be seen as representing a 'reflexive' form of risk. The findings could also reflect the so-called 'precautionary principle'. Practitioners and students were anticipating possible difficulties in areas such as confidentiality and data protection which prevented them from considering the possible full benefit of the opportunity offered by the project.

user confusion. Confusing what users want with what they truly need. Numerous user studies and approaches can create a wide and detailed user understanding however such studies can create confusion with what users say they want with what they really need.

multi-faceted design team. The make-up of the design team can influence the nature of user involvement. For example, a team that is equipped with skills in UI, prototyping, and software design will likely involve users at stages in the design process. A team with predominantly HCI researchers will likely involve more users and at more stages. In this case, there was a relatively balanced team in terms of skills and knowledge – our problems were arriving at shared common vocabularies, and attempting to involve all users and all design team members all the time.

4   The Case for Modelling in User Centered Design

These lessons or observations from the co-design approach have the potential to be mitigated by taking a model-driven integrated approach to the artifact development from the co-design activities. This paper argues that artifacts from user-centred design should be model based so that transformations between viewpoints can be integrated. This requires a user-centered design approach that is both rich, for capturing key user requirements and is also model driven such that it can be subject to model driven transformations during the design and implementation process.

Currently, UCD approaches are strong on user engagement and communication but tend not to be model-based in the software engineering sense. Thus it is difficult to derive a single viewpoint to meet both the needs of stakeholders and software engineers. Such design-slicing could be a powerful feature in presenting key features of an overall design without information overload.

Multiple viewpoints are a recognized approach to such a challenge but tend to driven by software engineering needs. For example, Rational Unified Process [18] has attempted to integrate user centered design activities. Such models serve software engineering well but present notational and technique challenges to the stakeholder in the usability domain. Here, it is proposed that multiple viewpoints that are driven from UCD method approaches have the potential to reduce or mitigate the problems/issues raised earlier. Hence it is proposed that taking steps to move UCD to a more model driven software engineering approach has the potential to be more effective than taking steps to make Software Engineering more UCD focussed.

4.1   Contextual Design

The Contextual Design approach described by Beyer and Holtzblatt [3] is a good candidate for enhancing using model driven principles as it already exhibits language that one might see comfortably in the software design arena but is still a rich user-centered design approach. The method supports the production of a number of artifacts such as: key customer data as the basis for decision making; processes where work is done; interactions using "flow models"; cultural models for capturing intuitive elements of environment; consolidation using affinity diagrams.

These elements are present in a number of models enumerated here and we also indicate if there is an existing language and notation feature available from the Unified Modeling Language (UML) [14] available:

Artifact Model: produces the key customer data relevant to the system. These data are referred to in other models and also inform the technical architecture element that is part of the User Environment Design stage. The Conceptual Design method does not advocate data modeling approaches explicitly but the strong similarity suggests that UML Class Models would be a strong technique for capturing such data.

Flow Model: is an analysis tool that is used to capture communication and coordination between roles. It will typically describe what interactions take place such as request for information, supply of information or an action. In Contextual Design such a model is informal – but it can easily be modeled in UML in a variety of ways. For example flow models have been described by Activity Diagrams with additional features in [28].

Cultural Model: is an analysis tool that shows the cultural or political forces in the organization. Issues addressed are forces that may impinge on roles to prevent or modify how work is done. For the purposes of this paper, we view cultural forces having an effect on belief values held by individuals who are participating in a given task.

Sequence Model: shows the detailed steps that are performed to accomplish a task. The terminology used in Contextual Design shows strong correspondence to process modeling and can be represented by UML Activity Diagrams. This correlation provides a useful language tool for sharing of information between usability designers and systems designers. For the purposes of this paper we view sequence models as capturing the many alternative workflows that individuals can undertake when directed to perform a given task. The choice between different workflows is partially determined by the belief values held by a given individual. It follows that cultural models have a part to play in influencing workflow choices.

Contextual Design provides a stage that aims to consolidate findings from the analysis. In this stage tools such as Affinity Diagrams for mapping issues across the organization, and Consolidated work models for identifying common strategies are available. These tools help in addressing the problems of multiple types of users, users as designers, confusing what users want and what they truly need because an overall view is possible. Such models could be captured using stereotypes and UML class diagrams.

Similarly, process models described from different user perspectives may be organized in models so that commonality and variability may be explicitly specified. However, no formal language for expressing such variation is described. Interestingly, the method also has elements that are focused on software architecture These elements produce artifacts that include object models and the functions and structures needed by the re-designed systems expressed as a detailed architectural model.

4.2   The Semantics of Cultural Models

We now look at the Cultural model in detail and in particular examine the concepts represented in Cultural models from the perspectives of key components of language design - abstract and concrete syntax and the accompanying semantics. Inspection of examples of cultural models [4]) raises key questions. At first the diagrams appear to convey a significant amount of information. A closer examination requires a full answer to many questions. Many of the diagrams represent Influencers as overlapping circles of different sizes. Consider the following: Is there a significance in the size of circles? Is there significance to the overlaps? What does an overlap mean? Are the length of the arrows important and do they signify anything? Is there a particular style to annotating the circles and arrows? Even if the questions can be answered - and it make take many pages of explanatory text there are still issues of interpretation between users and stakeholders. Generally, these are the same class of problems that modelling design methods have addressed and which led to the standardisation of the Unified Modelling Language (UML) [14] and solutions to these problems boil down to the creation (and agreement) of an abstract syntax (a set of concepts, relationships and well-formed rules), a concrete syntax (typically a graphical notation that supports the concrete syntax), and semantic model for the domain which will allow unambiguous interpretation of instances of concepts from abstract syntax. A model-enhanced version of this diagram would therefore need to be based on a language that is specifically designed to represent cultural forces in an organization - the domain. Such a class of language is often termed a domain specific language (DSL) [6].

5   Approach

Our approach to the problem of formalising Cultural model aspects of Contextual Design (CD) is based on the principles of model driven language engineering [7]and through a process of analysis of the problem space, a domain specific language (DSL) is created. The second step is to implement the language using a meta modeling tool or by hand-coding.

5.1   Model Driven Language Engineering

A language definition must be provided using a suitable meta-language that can represent the key features of a language (shown in figure 1):

concrete syntax is the human-friendly representation of a language. The concrete syntax defines how the language is to be presented on the screen or the page.

abstract syntax is a machine friendly representation of language. The abstract syntax defines the information structures that are used to represent the essential features of the language so that they can be processed as data values by a machine without worrying about how they are displayed on the screen or the page.

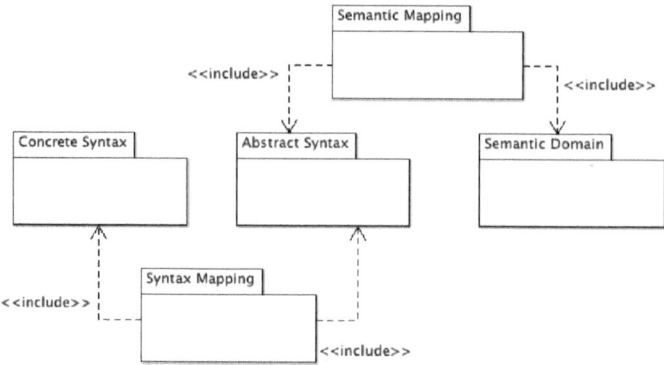

Fig. 1. Model Driven Language Engineering

syntax mapping relates the abstract syntax structures to their valid concrete representation. A syntax mapping is used by a tool to link what the user sees to how the language is stored internally.

semantic domain is a definition of the things we mean when constructing models in our language. The relationship between syntax and semantics is the same as that between relational database schemas and the tables that conform to them: there are conformance rules and there may be many databases that conform the same schema.

semantic mapping are the conformance rules between the syntax and the semantics. For example, the semantic mapping defines the rules by which a database table is considered to be correct with respect to a given schema.

In addition to the elements defined above, a language definition must contain well-formedness rules that define when concrete syntax, abstract syntax and semantic domain elements are valid. These correspond to database rules that, for example, require all column names to be unique.

Simple UML-style class models and associated constraints can be used as a suitable meta-language for representing the language components listed above. The syntax and semantics are represented as independent class diagrams and the mappings are class diagrams that include elements from the appropriate models and define relationships (associations) between the elements. There are other meta-languages available e.g. MOF [12]. Also, Halpin and Morgan's work [16] was used as the meta-modelling language for Archimate - the enterprise architecture modelling language [19].

5.2   Tooling

The next step is to provide an implementation of the language, that is, a tool that provides a binding of the various syntactic and semantic models and thus allows users to construct cultural models of the target (or subject) domain. To develop a proof of concept of this toolset, we utilised the meta modelling toolset

MetaEdit+ [17]. Meta Edit+ is a software toolset that supports the design and implementation of domain specific languages. It uses a meta modelling language GOPRR that is broadly similar to one that we used to specify our abstract syntax and has the following concepts: **Graph** specifies one modelling language such as Cultural Model; **Object** describes the basic concepts of a modeling language. Objects are the main elements of the language; Examples include the concept of Force, Role and so on; **Relationship** describes the properties for the objects' connections such as inheritance, call and transition; within the toolset, the relationship mechanism is used to form bindings with objects and roles; **Role** specifies the lines and endpoints of relationships; **Property** defines the attributes which can be used to characterise any of the previous concepts. Properties are of different data types and can be used to link to external concepts. The abstract syntax for Contextual Design was encoded in the GOPRR modelling language within the MetaEdit+ toolset in order to define the concrete syntax and the production of the accompanying tool.

6 A DSL for Contextual Design

Contextual Design (CD) invoves four different types of model: flow models; sequence models; artifact models; contextual models. It is important that we understand what these models mean in order to use them effectively. This section applies the approach to language design described in section 5.1 to CD.

6.1 Abstract Syntax

The abstract syntax is the cornerstone of a language definition. In principle there may be many different concrete syntax models and many different semantics for the same abstract syntax model. This section defines the abstract syntax for each of the main models in the CD modelling language.

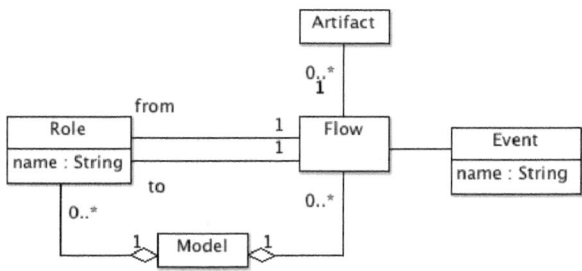

Fig. 2. Flow Models

Flow Models. Figure 2 shows the abstract syntax of flow-models. The element *Model* is used as the top level container for all CD model elements. A model consists of a collection of roles with flows between them. Each flow represents an interaction between roles and is labelled with both an event that it generates and the artifacts that are involved in the interaction. An example of a well-formedness rule associated with the class *Model* is: *every role must have a unique name.*

Artifact Models. Artifact models are equivalent to class models in UML. They describe the elements that are involved in the interactions between roles. In terms of our language definition, we do not need to consider artifacts in any more detail.

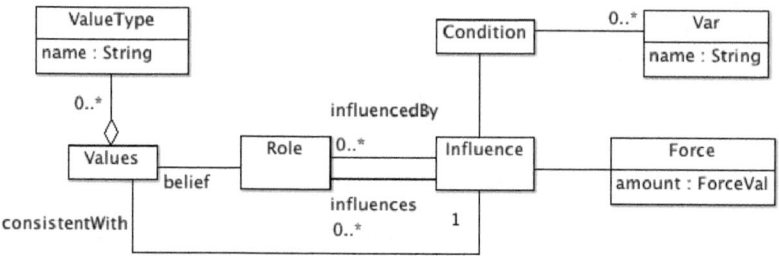

Fig. 3. Cultural Models

Cultural Models. Figure 3 shows the abstract syntax of cultural models that represent influences by one role on another. Each influence has a force associated with it from *weak* to *strong*. Each role manages a collection of values that represent personal beliefs. For example an individual might believe that certain types of technology are effective or that the cost associated with using certain processes is very high. In a CD model, *Values* is an assembly of belief value types in the same way that a class has an assembly of attributes. As we shall see, the specific belief values associated with a person who performs the role is defined in the semantics. An *Influence* together with its *Force* defines a condition which must be met by any valid instance of the belief values associated with an any influenced *Role*. A condition is a boolean expression in terms of variables. The effect of applying an influence to a role is to restrict the set of possible belief values that the role can have. A well-formedness rule that applies is *Influence: the set of variable names in the condition must be a sub-set of the value type names associated with the belief values of all influenced roles.*

Sequence Models. Figure 4 shows the abstract syntax of sequence models. Each role has an interface of activities. Each activity provides a description of what to do when an event is received by the role. Each activity has a number of alternative step assemblies (*Steps*) that reflects the options an individual has when responding to a request to perform a task. For example, if an individual is requested to implement a software component they may choose to implement

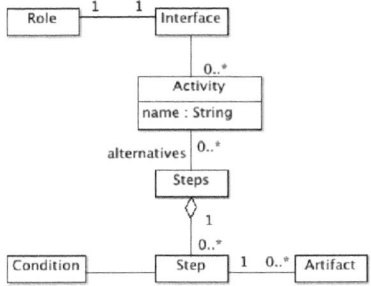

Fig. 4. Sequence Models

the component in one of a number of programming languages and using any one of a number of development methods. Each individual step in a step-assembly processes some artifacts and must satisfy a collection of belief-values. The idea is that a step cannot be performed by a role unless it is consistent with the beliefs of the particular individual.

An example of a well-formeness rule for sequence models is: *the artifacts associated with a step must be a subset of the artifacts associated with the flow that gave rise to the event.*

6.2 Concrete Syntax

The complete abstract syntax for Contextual Design is large. In this paper we have focussed on the Cultural Forces Model as it presents concepts that address areas of the systems design process that are often not captured in software engineering. Consequently we have translated that section of the abstract syntax to the GOPRR meta modelling syntax for Meta-Edit+. The tool capability allows the creation of an concrete syntax - the notations and graphical elements and their binding to the GOPRR representation of the abstract syntax. Diagram 5 shows the abstract syntax for cultural models in MetaEdit+ and figure 6 shows the resulting cultural modelling tool generated from the meta-model and also a partially drawn cultural model of the Social work Domain.

In this diagram example Roles include Student Social Worker. Influencers, those who can assert a force and therefore influence how an activity is performed include: Management, and Academic. Examples of Forces that are brought to bear on a role include the fear of Data security (the loss of data) that was identified during the project deployment. When that force became sufficiently critical, there was a Breakdown (red lightning icon) which resulted in an restriction of the use of the mobile devices. The Toolset for developing and presenting Cultural Models was generated from the set of abstract concepts described in GOPRR, the concrete syntax developed using the graphics tools available in MetaEdit+ and the bindings and rules for how connections work were declaratively specified again in MetaEdit+.

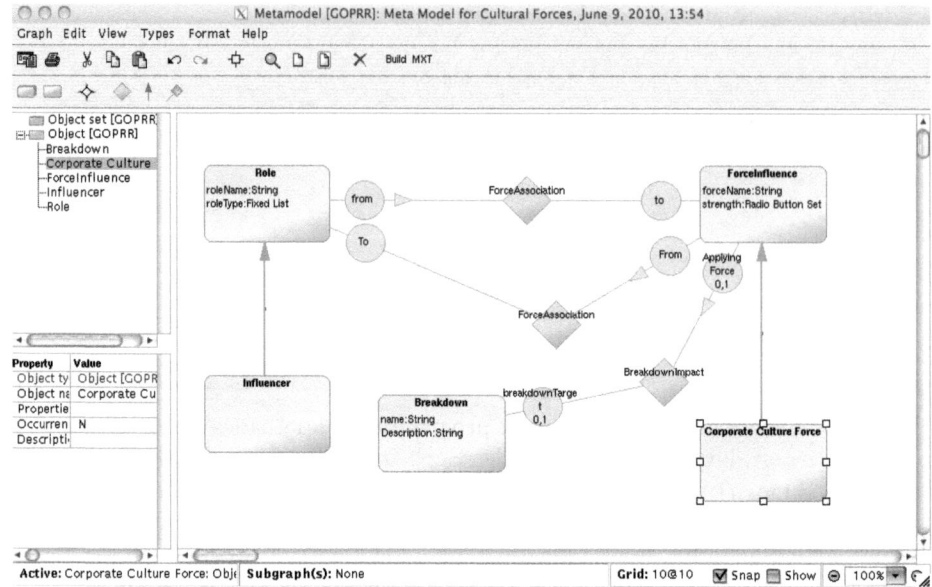

Fig. 5. GOPRR Meta Model

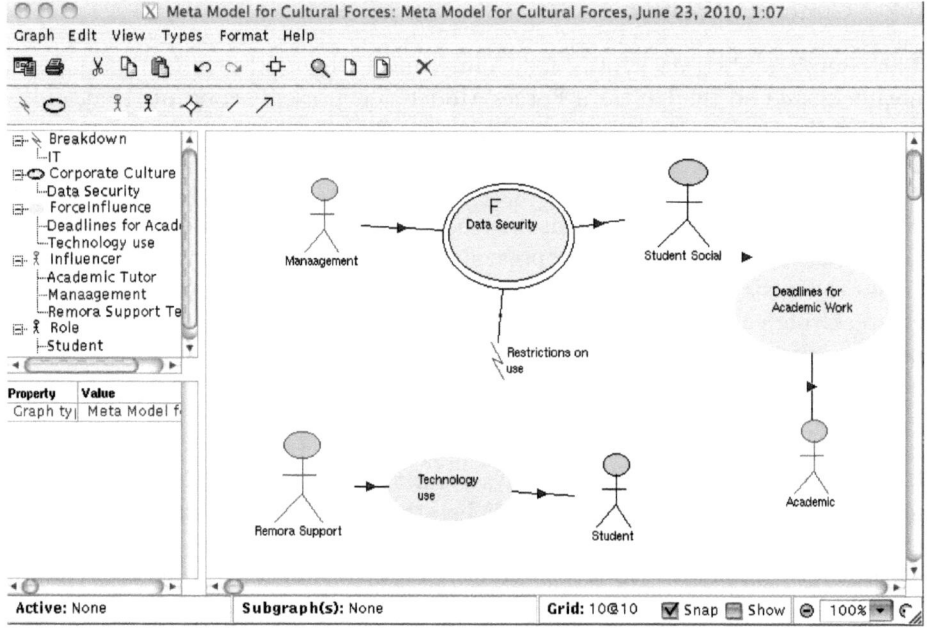

Fig. 6. Toolset for Modelling Cultural Forces

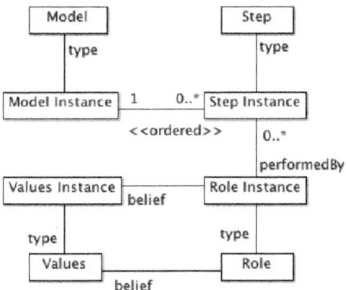

Fig. 7. Semantic Domain

6.3 Semantic Domain and Semantic Mapping

Figure 7 shows both the elements of the semantic domain (classes suffixed with *Instance*) and elements of the syntax domain together with semantic mapping associations between them (labelled *type*). The semantic domain defines the elements that we are denoting using the syntax models. In this case the semantic elements are essentially sequences of step instances that have arisen from the steps associated with activities in the sequence model. However we cannot associate *any* sequence of steps with a model instance because we must satisfy the semantic mapping constraints that are outlined below:

1. *in every role instance the belief values must satisfy the condition on every influencer of the associated role.*
2. *in every step instance, the condition must be satisfied by the belief values associated with the corresponding role instance.*
3. *a step can only be associated with a role instance where the corresponding role has an incoming event with the same name as the activity giving rise to the steps.*

7 Concluding Remarks

The motivating work - the development of a mobile application for a complex domain (Social Work) highlighted that there are potential problems that arise with using co-design and while the core principles of UCD are clearly desirable, the nature of the artifacts that are produced do not transfer to the software engineering community in a straight forward manner. Thus our experience also confirms that there is still mileage on the need to converge "on a science of design through the synthesis of design methodologies" [9]. In particular there is interest are in how design theories, user centred design approaches in general and their outputs can be modeled such that method integration with established software engineering approaches can be more formalized . Hence there a role for model driven engineering in user centered design and this paper has outlined how one established UCD approach may be adapted to make it more model driven (and so artifacts captured using UML modeling tools).

CD models, as defined in the literature, have an informally defined semantics. This limits what can be achieved, especially in terms of tooling to support CD. This paper has taken a precise meta-modelling approach to the definition of a language for CD modelling. In doing so, we have defined both the syntax and (a) semantics for CD. Our semantics defines CD models to denote chains of steps that arise from interactions between roles in a business context and which process business artifacts. The semantics reflects the choices that occur in a business environment that are resolved in terms of belief-systems of the individuals involved; it does this by allowing a single model to denote multiple possible sequences of steps for each single business activity. The semantics attributes influencing factors to the ability of individuals in a business to affect belief systems and thereby influence the way that influenced individuals implement given tasks.

As a result of taking a semantics driven approach to our CD modelling language we can now perform analysis of models. For example, it is possible to determine whether, given a set of influencers on individuals, there are any sequences of steps for a given business interaction. Suppose that this is used in a business that encourages new employees to get advice from established employees when performing tasks. Our semantics allows us to determine whether there are particular sets of 'old-hands' whose collective advice would be unhelpful. Furthermore, we can measure the amount of positive influence that mentoring is likely to have in terms of the reduction in confusion when staff take on a new role. For researchers, future projects will likely consider and evaluate further how such approaches may be used to allow more alignment with the software engineering model driven architecture paradigm.

References

1. Basnyat, R., Chozos, N., Johnson, C.: Incident and accident investigation techniques to inform model based design of safety critical interactive systems. In: Gilroy, S.W., Harrison, M.D. (eds.) DSV-IS 2005. LNCS, vol. 3941, pp. 51–66. Springer, Heidelberg (2006)
2. Beck, U.: Risk society: towards a new modernity. Sage Publications Ltd., Thousand Oaks (1992)
3. Beyer, H., Holtzblatt, K.: Contextual design: defining customer-centered systems. Morgan Kaufmann Pub., San Francisco (1998)
4. Beyer, H., Holtzblatt, K.: Contextual design. Interactions 6(1), 32–42 (1999)
5. Bjerknes, G., Ehn, P., Kyng, M., Nygaard, K.: Computers and democracy: A Scandinavian challenge. Gower Pub. Co., England (1987)
6. Clark, T., Evans, A., Kent, S.: Engineering modelling languages: A precise meta-modelling approach. In: Kutsche, R.-D., Weber, H. (eds.) FASE 2002. LNCS, vol. 2306, pp. 242–260. Springer, Heidelberg (2002)
7. Clark, T., Sammut, P., Willans, J.S.: Applied metamodelling: a foundation for language driven development (2008)
8. Constantine, L.L., Lockwood, L.A.D.: Usage-centered engineering for Web applications. IEEE Software, 42–50 (2002)

 9. Fischer, G.: Software engineering themes for the future. In: Proceedings of the 28th International Conference on Software Engineering, p. 1044. ACM, New York (2006)
10. France, R., Rumpe, B.: Model-driven development of complex software: A research roadmap. In: FOSE 2007: 2007 Future of Software Engineering, Washington, DC, USA, pp. 37–54. IEEE Computer Society Press, Los Alamitos (2007)
11. Greenbaum, J.M., Kyng, M.: Design at work: Cooperative design of computer systems. L. Erlbaum Associates Inc., Hillsdale (1991)
12. Object Management Group. OMG Meta Object Facility (2010), http://www.omg.org/mof/
13. Object Management Group. OMG model driven architecture (2010), http://www.omg.org/mda/
14. Object Management Group. Unified Modeling Language (2010), http://www.uml.org/
15. Gulliksen, J., Goransson, B., Boivie, I., Blomkvist, S., Persson, J., Cajander, Å.: Key principles for user-centred systems design. Behaviour & Information Technology 22(6), 397–409 (2003)
16. Halpin, T., Morgan, T.: Information modeling and relational databases: from conceptual analysis to logical design. Morgan Kaufmann, San Francisco (2008)
17. MetaCase Inc. Metaedit+ workbench - build your own domain-specific modeling language (2009), http://www.metacase.com/mwb/
18. Kruchten, P.: The rational unified process: an introduction. Addison-Wesley Longman Publishing Co., Inc., Boston (2000)
19. Lankhorst, M.M., Proper, H.A., Jonkers, J.: The Anatomy of the ArchiMate Language
20. Marti, P., Bannon, L.J.: Exploring User-Centred Design in Practice: Some Caveats. Knowledge, Technology & Policy 22(1), 7–15 (2009)
21. Millard, D., Howard, Y., Gilbert, L., Wills, G.: Co-design and Co-deployment Methodologies for Innovative m-Learning Systems. In: Multiplatform E-Learning Systems and Technologies: Mobile Devices for Ubiquitous ICT-Based Education (2009)
22. Norman, D.A.: Cognitive engineering. User Centered System Design, 31–61 (1986)
23. International Standards Organization. Human-Centered Design Pocesses for Interactive Systems. ISO (1999)
24. Radeke, F.: Pattern-driven Model-based User-Interface Development (2007)
25. Sottet, J.S., Calvary, G., Favre, J.M.: Towards mapping and model transformation for consistency of plastic user interfaces. In: The Many Faces of Consistency in Cross-Platform Design Workshop at CHI 2006 (2006)
26. Scaife, M., Rogers, Y., Aldrich, F., Davies, M.: Designing for or designing with? Informant design for interactive learning environments. In: Proceedings of the SIGCHI Conference on Human Factors in Computing Systems, p. 350. ACM, New York (1997)
27. Vanderdonckt, J.: A mda-compliant environment for developing user interfaces of information systems. In: Pastor, Ó., Falcão e Cunha, J. (eds.) CAiSE 2005. LNCS, vol. 3520, pp. 13–17. Springer, Heidelberg (2005)
28. Van Welie, M., Van Der Veer, G., Koster, A.: Integrated representations for task modeling. In: Tenth European Conference on Cognitive Ergonomics, pp. 129–138 (2000)

An MDE Approach for User Interface Adaptation to the Context of Use

Wided Bouchelligua[1,2], Adel Mahfoudhi[2], Lassaad Benammar[2],
Sirine Rebai[2], and Mourad Abed[1]

[1] University of Valenciennes
LAMIH, UMR CNRS 8530, BP: 311–59304, Valenciennes cedex 9, France
{wided.bouchelligua,mourad.abed}@univ-valenciennes.fr
[2] University of Sfax
ENIS, CES, Soukra Road km 3.5, B.P: w 3038 Sfax, Tunisia
adel.mahfoudhi@fss.rnu.tn,
{lassaad.benammar,sirine_rebai}@hotmail.com

Abstract. With the advent of new media and the delivery of recent means of communication, associated with the progress of networks, the circumstances of software use, as well as the skills and the preferences of the users who exploit them, are constantly varying. The adaptation of the User Interface (UI) has become a necessity due to the variety of the contexts of use. In this paper, we propose an approach based on models for the generation of adaptive UI. To reach this objective, we have made use of parameterized transformation principle in the framework of the Model Driven Engineering (MDE) for the transformation of the abstract interface into a concrete interface. The parameter of this transformation plays the role of the context of use. The paper develops two parts: meta-models for every constituent of the context of use and the adaptation rules.

Keywords: User Interface, Adaptation, Context of use, Model Driven Engineering, adaptation rules.

1 Introduction

The technological innovations and the evolution of the means of communication have opened new perspectives to guide the use of the usual applications. Besides, the circumstances of software use have constantly varied following the example of the skills and the preferences of the users who exploit them. This is due to the appearance of new media and the delivery of recent means of communication, associated with the progress of networks. It is not only resources of interaction that can appear and disappear, but also the objectives of the user. The latter is considered as a motive, evolving in a varied environment, according to his needs, to diverse platforms of interaction. That is why, in 1999 Thevenin brought a new concept: the plasticity of interfaces [21]. The plasticity is defined as the capacity of a user interface to adapt itself to the context of use which is denoted by the triplet <user, platform, environment>, while preserving usability.

R. Bernhaupt et al. (Eds.): HCSE 2010, LNCS 6409, pp. 62–78, 2010.
© IFIP International Federation for Information Processing 2010

Several approaches are proposed to make User Interfaces (UI) adaptable to the context of use. According to [18], these approaches are classified into four categories: 1) Translation Interface, 2) Reverse-engineering and migration Interfaces 3) approaches based on the markup languages and 4) model-based approach. The latter is adopted in this work because it has the advantage of applying the adaptation to the context of use of the models, leading to a strong abstraction.

The proposed approach in this paper assures the adaptation of the UI to the context of use. It builds on the concept of transformation parameterized by the context as defined within the framework of the Model Driven Engineering (MDE) [1] [8]. MDE goes beyond the framework of Model Driven Architecture (MDA) [15], which can be summarised in the elaboration of the Platform Independent Models (PIM) and in their transformation into Platform Specific Models (PSM) [1], to cover the methodological aspects. We apply the parameter setting at the level of the transformation of an Abstract User Interface (AUI) into a Concrete User Interface (CUI), whose generation is made on three phases. The first transformation parameterized by the model of adaptation describing the user, gives rise to a first CUI, which in turn is going to feed the second module of transformation. But, the latter will be parameterized by the characteristics of the platform to generate a Concrete User Interface in agreement with the preferences of the user and the properties of the interaction platform. In the last phase, the process of adaptation connected with the environmental context is launched to finish with a plastic Concrete User interface to conform to three dimensions of the context of use.

The remainder of this paper is structured as follows. Section 2 presents a state of the art on the model-based approaches for the adaptation of the UI. Next, section 3 clarifies the concept of the parameterized transformation in the MDE approach. Then section 4 describes the proposed approach in terms of context meta-models and adaptation rules. Section 5 provides a case study illustrating the approach. Finally, section 6 draws the conclusion and provides perspectives to future research.

2   State of the Art

This section is limited to the presentation of model-based approaches for UI adaptation. In fact, the Cameleon reference framework [5] represents an excellent framework of UI adaptation as it defines four essential stages for the development of the user interfaces in a pervasive environment (Fig. 1): tasks and concepts, abstract interface, concrete interface, and final interface.

In this area of research, we can quote the TERESA method [17] that supplies the tasks as a single model, and allows the generation of several interfaces for various platforms. We also cite the Comets (COntext sensitive Multi-target widgETS) [4], which proposes essentially a model for the plastic interactors that can be adapted to the variation of the screen size. Likewise, the UsiXML (User Interface eXtensible Markup Language) [23] [14] approach represents a UI approach of engineering defined according to the Cameleon reference framework. Such an approach describes a context model consisted of three constituents: user, environment and platform. But practically only the variant platform is considered during the UI generation.

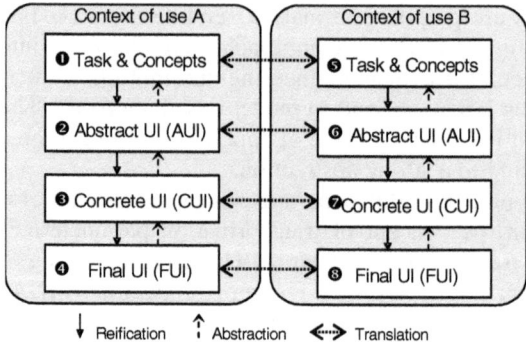

Fig. 1. Cameleon Reference Framework [23]

Sottet [19] [20] is considered as one of the pioneers to have joined his work to the Model Driven Engineering and the domain of Human Computer Interaction (HCI). His approach makes it possible to show that the concepts of the MDE could be successfully applied to the UI engineering. Sottet [19] proposes meta-models and models transformations to generate adaptable UI, and defines a general context meta-model. Based on the same approach (MDE), Hachani [11] suggests the introduction of the context of use at the tasks level rather than at the interactors level. This approach is distinguished by the definition of the generic rules appropriate to all the contexts of use. However, both approaches lack a detailed description of each constituent of the context of use. As in [20] and [11], we opt for the proposition of a model-based approach and its transformation according to the characteristics of the context. Yet, we seek to detail the context in accordance with three generic meta-models (user meta-model, platform meta-model and environment meta-model).

3   MDE Parameterized Transformation

Our objective is to handle the adaptation of the UI to the context of use (platform, environment, user). To do so,our work builds on the parameterized transformations defined by [22]. Vale [22] describes a parameterized transformation within the framework of the model driven engineering for a contextual development. The methodology proposed by [22] (left of Fig. 2) consists in defining the correspondences "match" between the model of the context and the PIM to define a CPIM (Contextual PIM). Then, an ordinary MDE transformation is used to define the CPSM (Contextual PSM).

The correspondences are assured by a parameter setting of the transformation, whose basic principle is to take into consideration the properties of the context during the specification of transformation rules (right of Fig. 2). *"A parameter specifies how arguments are passed into or out of an invocation of a behavioural feature like an operation. The type and multiplicity of a parameter restrict what values can be passed, how many, and whether the values are ordered"* [22].

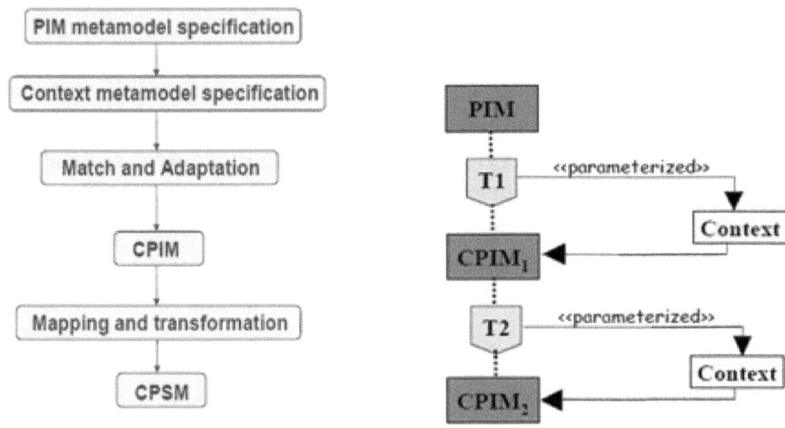

Fig. 2. Parameterized transformation [22]

The use of the parameterized transformations is envisaged with the aim of either improving new features (values, properties, operations) or changing the behaviour of an application. For that purpose, the designer has to specify the parameters which are intended to be inserted during the phase of transformation. In his work, Vale [22] proposes that these parameters are the contextual data, thus and after the transformation, the application will be in harmony with this information passed in parameter.

In the following section, we formulate the principle invoked by Vale, in favour of our approach to implement the notion of plasticity.

4 Proposed Approach

The proposed approach consists in generating the user interface automatically, using the parameterized transformation technique of the Model Driven Engineering domain

4.1 Overview of the Approach

The proposed approach in this paper is shown in Fig. 3. The abstraction levels of the Cameleon framework [5] incorporated in our approach are: abstract user interface and concrete user interface.

In our approach, the Abstract User Interface allows the transition of the specification in the modelling of the abstract components of the interface. In order to describe the Abstract User Interface and the Concrete User interface, we have resorted to the static model of interactions [3]. Aiming at applying a model-to-model transformation, we have refined the static model of the interactions of [3] in the form of two meta-models: the AUI and CUI meta-models. Indeed, AUI meta-model describes the hierarchy of the abstract components corresponding to the logical groups of interactions.

The AUI meta-model and transformations rules to obtain the AUI from the task model are detailed in [2].

The Concrete User Interface is deduced from the Abstract User Interface to describe the interface in terms of graphic containers, interactors and navigation objects. We have extended the CUI meta-model presented in [2] [16] to add the vocal components and to associate with every container of the interface a "PersonnalizationService" component containing properties used to specify the presentation of such an object as well as any object being a part of this container. Quoting for example the service "useoflanguage" which can be active if the user prefers a language other than French. If this service is activated, the attribute language allows the specification of the sought language.

The passage to the concrete level has for objective the generation of a plastic interface adapted to the planned context. Our approach facilitates the adaptation of the UI to the user, because the latter is in the centre of all the problem of the UI and everything revolves around him.

The first transformation (T1 in Fig. 3) allows the generation of the first concrete user interface (CUI1 in Fig. 3) adapted to the preferences of the user having received the information suitable to him and echoing them on this intermediate interface.

On the other side of the coin, we are interested in the injection of the characteristics of the platform used to assure the plasticity towards this context. Indeed, we opted for choosing this injection order of the characteristics for multiple reasons. On the one hand, it is around the user that revolves everything and it is his characteristics that are going to impose the choice of the platform. Besides, it is the user who decides about the device on which he even wishes to post the information. Indeed, this variation is going to require the appearance and the disappearance of the other devices of interaction. Furthermore, it is according to his preferences that the modality: graphic, hearing or even olfactive is going to be chosen. Then, in case of change at the level of one of the contextual dimensions, an adaptation is launched to protect the usability [21]. Certainly, the specific properties and the capacity characteristics of the target device have to satisfy the needs of the user. This second transformation (T2 in Fig. 3) adapts the first CUI1 to the characteristics of the platform which is going to welcome the application, from which the second CUI (CUI2 in Fig. 3) results.

So, having fixed and adapted the characteristics of the target platform to his own motivations and intentions, the user has now nothing but to choose the environment which is going to welcome the application. In fact, this environmental variant has to be in agreement with the characteristics of the user and the target platform. It is the profile of the user, defined as being a first entity for the process of adaptation, as well as these accompanied intentions, naturally, symptomatic of the platform that are going to determine the environmental aspects. The latter are going to be implemented during the process of adaptation to succeed in the generation of a plastic UI while taking into account three speeds of the context. Hence, in the third place, we are going to inject

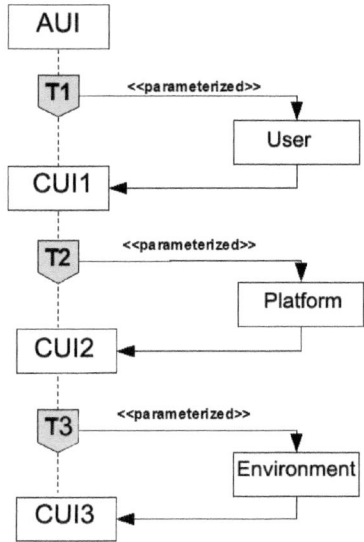

Fig. 3. Parameterized transformation for the UI plasticity

the environmental properties in the third transformation (T3 in Fig. 3) to have the interface (CUI3 in Fig. 3).

Therefore, the generation of the concrete interface (CUI) is made on three phases. To do so, we have to establish three meta-models (the user, platform and environment meta-models), so as to implement the transformation principle to illustrate the process of adaptation.

4.2   Context of Use Meta-models

The context is identified by many teams [5] [18] [23] [20] [12] by the triplet <User Platform, Environment>. Thus, three categories of contextual information can be distinguished [7]:

– So much information pertaining to the platform (processor, memory, peripheral equipments, connection network, the size of the display screen, and the available interaction tools …)
– Those relative to the user (his profile, his current activity, his preferences, his habits, his cultural characteristics…)
– The information corresponding to the environment (light, noise, geographical localization …)

4.2.1   User Meta-model

The user model has to contain information allowing the characterization of the user. Our meta-model (Fig. 4) builds strongly on the work of [10] and [6]. Such information contained is classified in four categories:

- Information staff (the name and the first name of the user, the age, the kind)
- Knowledge (The expertise level of the user in computer science, the expertise level regarding task or manipulated concept)
- Preference (The modality of interaction (graphic, vocal, olfactive, tactile, etc.), police, the character size, colour and the sound volume)
- Capacity (physical (sensory and engine) and cognitive capacities).

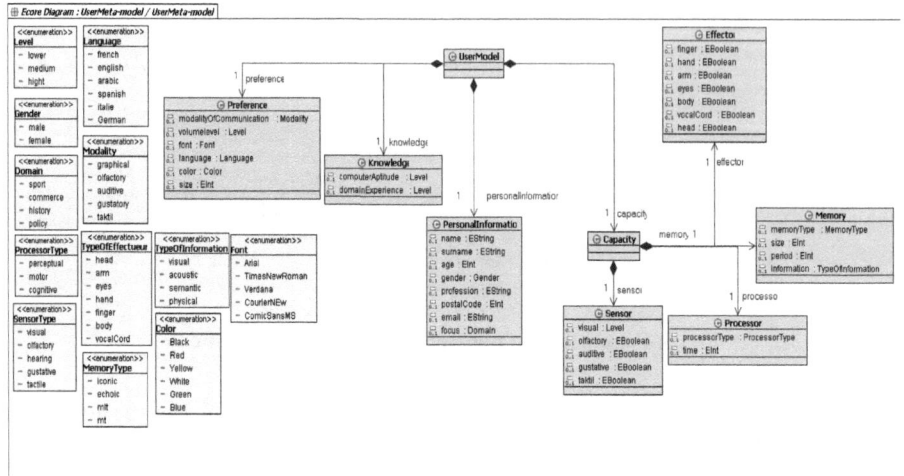

Fig. 4. User Meta-model

4.2.2 Platform Meta-model

Although most of the work done on plastic UI made adaptation to the platform, it does not provide a complete and detailed meta-model. The existing approaches are limited to its description at a high abstraction level or the description of the display surface of the platform which represents the most used interactional resource in the adaptations made so far. However, the adaptation can be prepared in the presence and absence of the other interaction devices. For example, if we do not have a mouse, we can suggest as a form of adaptation using a vocal interactor where the activation of the actions will be made vocally. Fig. 5 presents our platform meta-model [16] [2]. Generally, the platform consists of:

- Calculation resources represented in Fig. 5 by the "ComputationalCapacities" class. These resources does not only include the material aspect, such as the memory or processor but also the software aspect as the supported operating system;
- Interaction resources that are the input-output devices represented in our meta-model by the "InteractionDevices" class. We identify two classes of interaction devices: the input devices (InputDevice class in Fig. 5) and the output devices

(OutputDevice class in Fig. 5). Certain devices inherit both classes and are thus in-put/output devices, such as the touch screen.

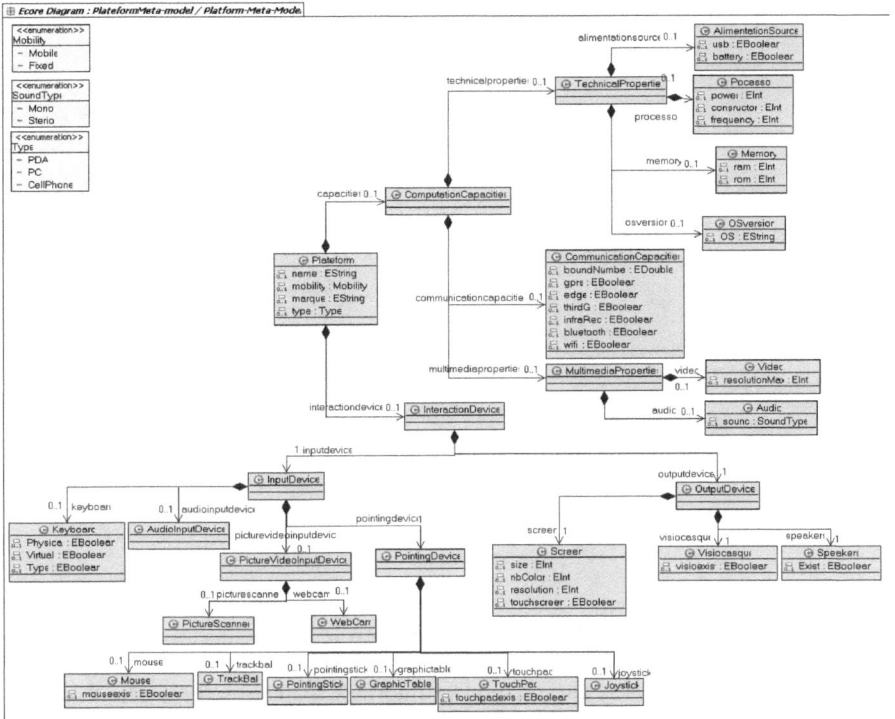

Fig. 5. Platform Meta-model [16]

4.2.3 Environment Meta-model

In this meta-model, illustrated in Fig. 6, we try to cover all the environmental facets of the context susceptible to react directly or indirectly on the interactive system. In fact, we are trying to take into account the maximum of environmental aspects. Therefore, our meta-model consists of four classes that explain the general characteristics.

- The first class characterizes the ambient environment that surrounds the interactive system "AmbientEnvironment". But with the invasion of the ubiquities computer science, the ambient conditions are changeable from one moment to another. This class inherits three under classes: "ClimaticEnvironment", "LuminousEnvironment" and "SonorousEnvironment".
- The second class composing our meta-model is the class "TemporalEnvironment".
- As for the third class, named "SocialEnvironment", it characterizes the social environment receiving the interactive system. This class is decorated with a single attribute: "atmosphere" of type "Atmosphere" enumeration.

- To specify the place receiving the application, we used the fourth class named "SpatialEnvironment". Indeed, this class gives information about the geographical location of the interactive system.

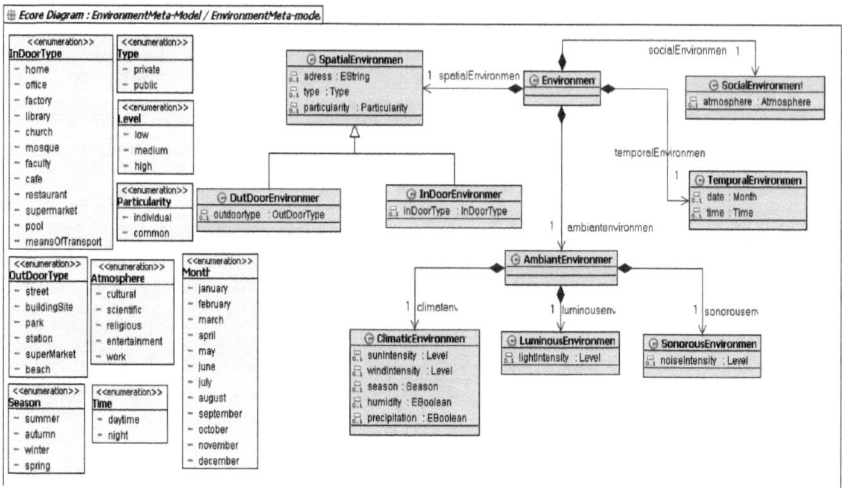

Fig. 6. Environment Meta-model

4.3 Generation Process of CUI and Adaptation Rules

The generation stages of the Concrete User Interface lean strongly on the work of [21] and [14]. The three transformations of the approach are developed with the transformation language Kermeta [13]. The transformation of an *AUI* into a *CUI1* (T1 transformation) is implemented by the following four stages:

- Creation of the application: creation of the application in the "ConcreteUserInterface" target model by the "AbstractUserInterface" of the source model;
- Realization of the abstract containers;
- Choice of the interactors;
- Definition of the navigation.

We have developed a set of rules allowing T1 transformation. As an illustration, in what follows, we clarify the stage of interactor's choice. This stage aims at associating the adequate interactor with the abstract component of *AUI*. Such a choice depends on the properties of the abstract component: its type (Input or Output) its nature (Specify, Select, Turn …) and the user preferences.

The extract of the following code transforms every abstract component of the "CollapsedUIUnit" type into a "UIField" and appeals to the "UIFieldSpecification" method for the choice of the appropriate interactor. In that case, it is a question of executing the interactor's choice for an abstract component of the "Specify" nature.

```
operation createUIField(inputmodel :
AbstractUserInterface,collapseduiunit: CollapsedUIUnit,
uiw : UIWindow)        is do
UIFieldSpecification(inputmodel,collapseduiunit,uiw)
end
//UIFieldSpecification
operation UIFieldSpecification( inputmodel :
AbstractUserInterface,uic : CollapsedUIUnit,uiw :
UIWindow) is do
var lnk : Link
lnk := getAllLinks(inputmodel).detect{c|stdio.writeln
("link" + c.uicomponent.name)c.uicomponent.name ==
uic.name}
//Specify
var nat : Nature init uic.nature
var tp : AnnotationType init lnk.uicomponentannot.type
if (nat == Nature.Specify) then
createStaticField(uiw,uic,lnk)
createFieldIn(uiw,uic,lnk)
end //rest of code
end
```

Several existing characteristics in the model of the user can have an impact during the realization of the *AUI*. Certain characteristics have an impact on the choice of the concrete object of interaction to know the preference of the user in terms of the modality of communication. The impact is thus expressed in terms of the reshaping of the interface. The extract of the Kermeta code below illustrates the impact of the preference modality of communication on the realization.

```
operation      transform      (      inputModel      :
AbstractUserInterface,    paramModel   :   UserModel)   :
ConcreteUserInterface is do
    AUI2CUI := Trace <UIElement, CUIElement>.new
    AUI2CUI.create
    result := ConcreteUserInterface.new
    var      modpref      :      Modality      init
getPreference(paramModel).modalityOfCommunication
    if (modpref == Modality.graphical) then
          stdio.writeln("Graphical Modality")
          //Graphical treatment
    else if modpref == Modality.auditive then
          stdio.writeln("Auditive Modality")
        //Auditive treatment
    end
end
```

Other characteristics in the model of the user influence the properties of the objects of interactions rather than the choice of concrete object. The extract of the following code shows the function allowing the creation of a service (createServicePerso method). It shows the activation of the two services "useoflanguage" and "useof-tooltip" as example. The latter is activated if the user does not have strong computer capacities (computer aptitude).

```
operation  createServicePerso(nameuiw  :String,pref  :
Preference,knl : Knowledge) : PersonnalizationService is
do
     var    srv    :    PersonnalizationService    init
PersonnalizationService.new
        srv.name :=nameuiw
        if pref.language != Language.french then
          srv.useoflanguage := true
          srv.language := pref.language.name
        else
          srv.useoflanguage := false
        end
        if knl.computerAptitude != Level.hight then
          srv.useoftooltip := true
        else
          srv.useoftooltip  := false
        end //rest of code
        result := srv
  end
```

The obtained *CUI1* is the source model of the second transformation that takes as parameters the characteristics of the platform. We have addressed the impact of the property screen size and inputting/outputting devices of the platform. The following code produces the testing for the required devices of graphical or vocal interaction.

```
operation transform ( inputModel :
ConcreteUserInterface, paramModel : Plateform)   :
ConcreteUserInterface is do
CUI2CUI1 := Trace <CUIElement, CUIElement>.new
CUI2CUI1.create
result := inputModel
var width : Integer init
getScreen(getOutputD(getID(paramModel))).width
var height: Integer init
getScreen(getOutputD(getID(paramModel))).height
getCUIWindow(inputModel).each{uiw1|
if (MouseExist(paramModel) and ScreenExist(paramModel)
```

```
and      KeyboardExist(paramModel)) or
(TouchPadExist(paramModel)and ScreenExist(paramModel)
and KeyboardExist(paramModel)) or
TouchscreenExist(paramModel)          then
//rest of code
else
stdio.writeln("Inexistant Device")
end}
getVocalGroup(inputModel).each{vg|
if VisiocasqueExist(paramModel) or
(MicrophoneExist(paramModel)and ScreenExist(paramModel)
and then
getVocalForm(vg).each{vf|
//rest of code
else
stdio.writeln("Inexistant Device")
end}
end
```

The third transformation injects the properties of the environment that will host the application. The impact of environment properties does not affect the objects of inter-action, but affects the existence or nonexistence of services interface. The following code shows the activation of service "useofbackground".

```
getService(inputModel).each{srv|
if(getLuminousEnv(getAmbiantEnv(paramModel)).lightInten
sity == Level.hight) or
(getSocialEnv(paramModel).atmosphere ==
Atmosphere.religious) or
(getSpatialEnv(paramModel).getMetaClass() ==
OutDoorEnvironment and getTemporalEnv(paramModel).time
== Time.daytime) then
srv.useofbackground :=true
srv.background := BackGroundType.light
end
```

5 Illustrating Example

The case study relates to a credit card request by a customer. This application is adapted to the context of use. The following scenario illustrates this adaptation on a precise case. Sarra is connected to the site of the bank to launch her request of credit card. She has to log in first of all by introducing her user name and password. Then she has to choose her type (private individual or company). Then, she is asked to choose the type of card that she seeks to obtain before filling in an information form. In this case study, the following context of use is assumed:

User={Computer aptitude="lower", font="TimesNewRoman", language="english", color="Red" size="14", Modality of communication ="graphical"},

Platform={iPAQ HX2490 Pocket PC},

Environment={Alone, atmosphere="work", light intensity="low"}.

Fig. 7 shows the abstract user interface for the process of the credit card possession. This interface contains a "UIGroup" called "Ask for a credit card". This "UIGroup" gives access to two "UIUnitSuit" ("Login" and "Determine private individual form") and "CollapsedUIUnit" ("Select customer type").

During the detection of a context change, the system is adapted. The *AUI* adapts itself first of all to the preferences of the user. In the following figure, we give the treebased description of the use of our case study. In front of these characteristics, the first module of transformation uses as output the *AUI* model (Fig. 7) and the user model (left of Fig. 8) on which the generic transformations rules are applied, based on their respective meta-models.

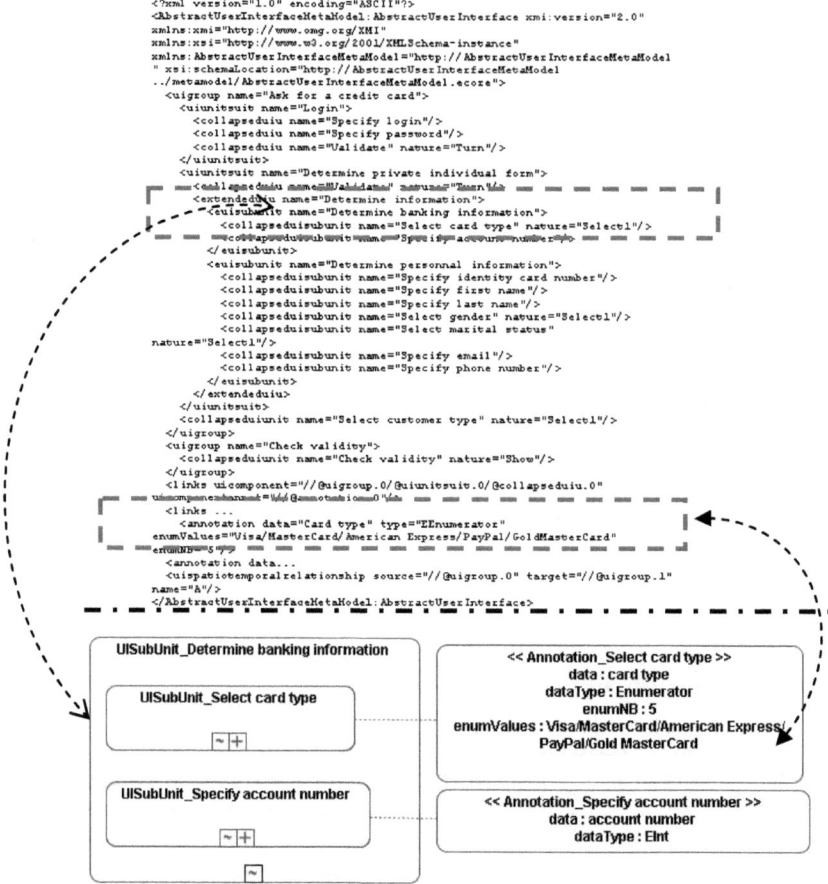

Fig. 7. Abstract User Interface for the process of the credit card possession (case of a private individual customer)

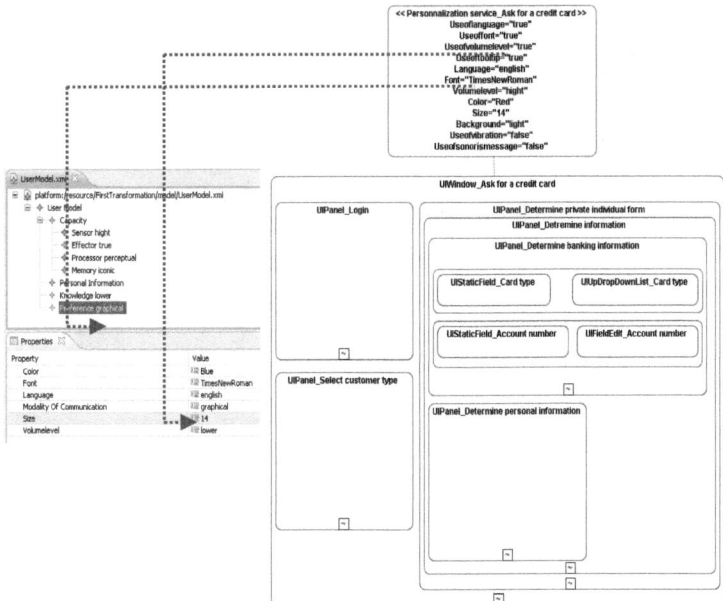

Fig. 8. (Left) The tree-based description of User model. (Right) Concrete User Interface specific to the user model.

The first module of transformation consists in transforming an XML (Extensible Markup Language) file source obtained from an abstract user interface. This file is automatically generated by our AbstractUserInterface editor developed thanks to the Graphical Modeling Framework (GMF) tool [9] of Eclipse. The result of transformation is an XML file that is in harmony with the CUI meta-model. Right of Fig. 8 produces the *CUI1* visualized with our ConcreteUserInterface editor. The realization of the *AUI* is in graphic mode since the user has chosen a modality of graphic communication. A set of personalization services is activated giving as an example the service "Use of tooltip" which results from the fact that the user possesses low computing capacities.

As a concrete example, left of Fig. 9 gives the tree-based description of "iPAQ HX2490 Pocket PC" realized by EMF-based editor. The refinement of the *CUI1* taking into account this platform allows the generation of a concrete interface replying on the properties of this platform, as in the example of the value of the screen size (height="320" width="240"). Moreover, the choice of the appropriate interactor is related to the inputting devices that exist in the platform. In this case, we have a touch screen (TouchScreen) and a text input device (TextInputDevice). That is why the concretisation in the graphic form is possible.

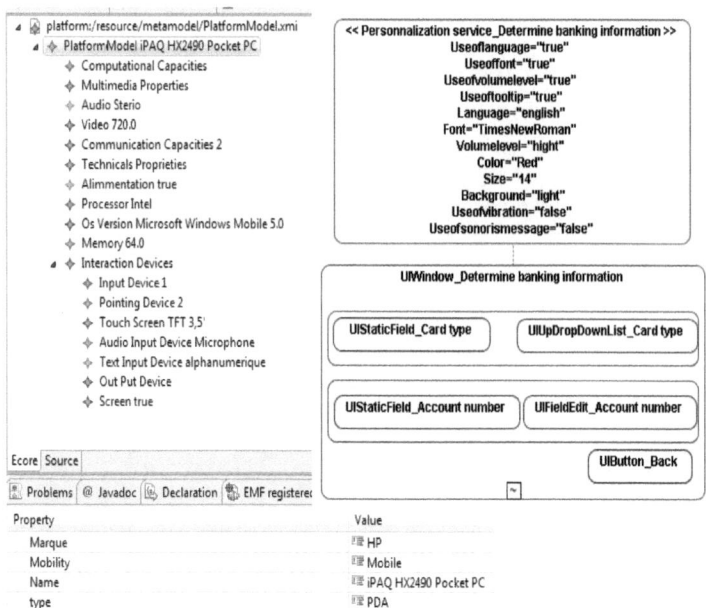

Fig. 9. (Left) The tree-based description of "iPAQ HX2490 Pocket PC". (Right) Concrete User Interface specific to the platform model.

Taking into account the properties of the platform "iPAQ hx2490 Pocket PC" (Left of Fig. 9), the transformation of *CUI1* (Right of Fig. 8) produces a *CUI2* with a re-modelling of containers. Right of Fig. 9 presents the visualization of the *CUI2* with our ConcreteUserInterface editor. For readability we have chosen to present only the window "Determine banking information." For the size of the screen "iPAQ hx2490 Pocket PC" and the number of manipulated concepts (>4), the realization of the abstract component "UISubUnit_Select card type" of *AUI* is a "UIUpDropDownList. A "UIStaticField_Card type" interactor is added, since the user does not have strong computer Capacities (computer aptitude).

Our case study is situated in a closed environment (inDoorType). As regards the ambient characteristics that specify this type of environment, it will be restored to the intensity of light as well as that of the sound level. This model (Left of Fig. 10) is going to feed the third module of transformation which will lead to the generation of a concrete interface adaptable to the context of use passing through the three elements that define it.

Taking into account the properties of environment (Left of Fig. 10), the transformation of *CUI2* (Right of Fig. 9) producing a *CUI3* with new enabled services, such as the background service whose value has become "gloomy" since the light intensity was low. Right of Fig. 10 produces the visualization of the target *CUI3*.

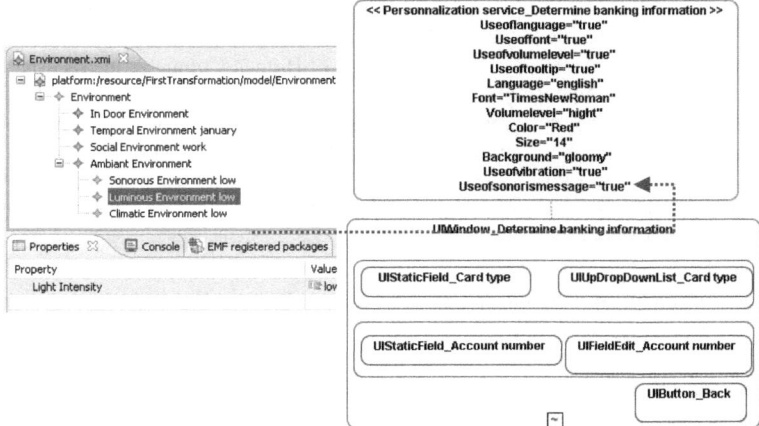

Fig. 10. (Left) The tree-based description of environment model. (Right) Concrete User Interface specific to the environment model.

6   Conclusion

In this paper, we have presented a methodology for the development of the plastic UI of an Information System. To apply "model to model" transformations, we set up two meta-models: Abstract User Interface meta-model and Concrete User Interface meta-model. The characteristic of the interface adaptation to its context of use was our primordial objective. In order to reach this objective, we proposed three meta-models describing the context of use. Encountered by a new context, a definition of a model for this context will be enough. So, our transformations rules are generic.

We foresee multiple perspectives for our work, which concern the integration of the ergonomic properties in our transformations and the determination of causality between the three components of the context of use.

References

1. Bézivin, J., Blay, M., Bouzeghoub, M., et al.: Action spécifique CNRS sur l'Ingénierie Dirigée par les Modèles. Rapport de synthèse (2005)
2. Bouchelligua, W., Mahfoudhi, A., Mezhoudi, N., Daassi, O., Abed, M.: User Interfaces Modelling of Workflow Information Systems. In: Barjis, J. (ed.) Enterprise & Organizational Modeling and Simulation. LNBIP, vol. 63. Springer, Heidelberg (2010)
3. Brossard, A., Abed, M., Kolski, C.: Context Awareness and Model Driven Engineering: A multi-level Approach for the Development of Interactive Applications in Public Transportation. In: Proceedings of 27th European Annual Conference on Human Decision-Making and Manual Control, EAM 2008, Delft, Hollande (2008)
4. Calvary, G., Coutaz, J., Dâassi, O., Balme, L., Demeure, A.: Towards a new generation of widgets for supporting software plasticity: the "comet". In: Bastide, R., Palanque, P., Roth, J. (eds.) DSV-IS 2004 and EHCI 2004. LNCS, vol. 3425, pp. 306–323. Springer, Heidelberg (2005)

5. Calvary, G., Coutaz, J., Thevenin, D., et al.: A Unifying Reference Framework for Multi-Target User Interfaces. Interacting with Computers 15(3), 289–308 (2003)
6. Card, S., Moran, T., Newell, A.: The Psychology of Human-Computer Interaction. Lawrence Erlbaum Associates, Mahwah (1983)
7. Dey, A.: Providing Architectural Support for Building Context-Aware Applications. Thèse de doctorat, Institut Technologique de Géorgie (Georgia Tech), p.170 (2000)
8. Favre, J.-M.: Toward a Basic Theory to Model: Model Driven Engineering. In: Workshop on Software Model Engineering, WISME 2004, Lisbonne, Portugal (2004)
9. GMF, Graphical Modeling Framework, http://www.eclipse.org/gmf
10. Habieb-Mammar, H.: EDPHA: un Environnement de Développement et de Présentation d'Hyperdocuments Adaptatifs. Thèse de doctorat, Institut National des Sciences Appliquées (INSA) de Lyon (2004)
11. Hachani, S., Dupuy-Chessa, S., Front, A.: Une approche générique pour l'adaptation dynamique des IHM au contexte. In: IHM 2009, Grenoble, France (2009)
12. Hariri, M.-A., Lepreux, S., Tabary, D., Kolski, C.: Principes et étude de cas d'adaptation d'IHM dans les SI en fonction du contexte d'interaction de l'utilisateur. Ingénierie des Systèmes d'Information (ISI). Networking and Information Systems 14, 141–162 (2009)
13. Kermeta, Kernel Meta-modeling Framework, http://www.kermeta.org/
14. Limbourg, Q., Vanderdonckt, J.: UsiXML: A User Interface Description Language Supporting Multiple Levels of Independence. In: Matera, M., Comai, S. (eds.) Engineering Advanced Web Applications, pp. 325–338. Rinton Press, Paramus (2004)
15. MDA, Model Driven Architecture, http://www.omg.org/mda
16. Mezhoudi, N.: Méta-modèles et règles pour la plasticité des IHM, Mémoire de mastère, Institut d'Informatique et de Multimédia, Université de Gabès, Tunisie (2010)
17. Mori, G., Paternò, F., Santoro, C.: Tool Support for Designing Nomadic Applications. In: Proceedings of the International Conference on Intelligent User Interfaces, Miami, pp. 141–148 (2003)
18. Samaan, K., Tarpin-Bernard, F.: Task models and Interaction models in a Multiple User Interfaces generation process. In: Proceedings of 3rd International Workshop on TAsk MOdels and DIAgrams for user interface design TAMODIA 2004, Prague, Check Republic, pp. 137–144. ACM, New York (November 2004)
19. Sottet, J., Calvary, G., Favre, J., Coutaz, J., Demeure, A., Balme, L.: Towards Model-Driven Engineering of Plastic User Interfaces. In: Bruel, J.-M. (ed.) MoDELS 2005. LNCS, vol. 3844, pp. 191–200. Springer, Heidelberg (2006)
20. Sottet, J.S., Calvary, G., Favre, J.M.: Mapping Model: A First Step to Ensure Usability for sustaining User Interface Plasticity. In: Proceedings of the Workshop on Model Driven Development of Advanced User Interfaces (2006)
21. Thevenin, D.: Adaptation en Interaction Homme-Machine: Le cas de la Plasticité. Thèse de doctorat, Université Joseph Fourier, Grenoble I, p. 212 (2001)
22. Vale, S., Hammoudi, S.: Context-aware Model Driven Development by Parameterized Transformation. In: Proceedings of MDISIS (2008)
23. Vanderdonckt, J.: A MDA-Compliant Environment for Developing User Interfaces of Information Systems. In: Pastor, Ó., Falcão e Cunha, J. (eds.) CAiSE 2005. LNCS, vol. 3520, pp. 16–31. Springer, Heidelberg (2005)

Desktop-to-Mobile Web Adaptation through Customizable Two-Dimensional Semantic Redesign

Fabio Paternò and Giuseppe Zichittella

CNR-ISTI, HIIS Laboratory, Via Moruzzi 1, 56124 Pisa, Italy
{fabio.paterno,giuseppe.zichittella}@isti.cnr.it

Abstract. In this paper we present a novel method for desktop-to-mobile adaptation. The solution also supports end-users in customizing multi-device ubiquitous user interfaces. In particular, we describe an algorithm and the corresponding tool support to perform desktop-to-mobile adaptation by exploiting logical user interface descriptions able to capture interaction semantic information indicating the purpose of the interface elements. We also compare our solution with existing tools for similar goals.

Keywords: Ubiquitous Applications, Multi-Device Environments, Adaptation.

1 Introduction

One of the main issues in current technological settings is how to design and develop interactive applications that can be accessed through a wide variety of devices (ranging from small watches to very large screens, including various types of smartphones, PDAs and Digital TVs). This is particularly important in Web applications, which are the most common ones.

The vision of ubiquitous computing [16] is that the users operate in intelligent environments, which are aware of users' needs and able to assist, even proactively, the users in performing their activities and reaching their goals. To this end, one important aspect is the possibility for a user surrounded by multiple devices to freely move about and receive user interfaces adapted to the current context of use.

In current mobile devices various solutions are adopted for accessing Web applications originally developed for desktop systems. Some just cut the page to the display area, thus showing only a limited portion. Others, such as those using the Small Screen Rendering Technique in the Opera mini browser, provide the narrow view in which the content is vertically arranged in order to avoid horizontal scrolling. The most sophisticated solutions are those, such as the Safari browser in the IPhone, which automatically resize the Web page to the screen size and allow the user to zoon in and out through gestures in the touch interface. However, their usability is often low in terms of Web navigation, since users have to make various zoom in and out interactions in order to identify the part of content that they are looking for.

The solutions for such issues can benefit from user interface model-based approaches, in which declarative descriptions of the user interface are used in order to avoid dealing with a plethora of low-level implementation details associated with the

R. Bernhaupt et al. (Eds.): HCSE 2010, LNCS 6409, pp. 79–94, 2010.

wide number of available devices and implementation languages. Despite such potential benefits, their adoption has mainly been limited to professional designers, but new solutions have recently been emerging that are able to extend such approaches in order to achieve natural development by enabling end users to develop or modify interactive applications still using conceptual models, but with continuous support that facilitates their development, analysis, and use [1].

Model-based languages are utilized at design time to help the user interface designer cope with the increasing complexity of today's applications and contexts. The underlying user interface models are mostly used to generate a final user interface code, which is then executed at run time. However, approaches utilizing the models at run time are receiving increasing attention. We agree with Sottet et al. [13], who call for keeping the models alive at run time to make the design rationale available.

In the following, we present some research work that exploits model-based approaches for multi-device ubiquitous applications. We show a new tool for desktop-to-mobile adaptation, called customizable two-dimensional semantic redesign. We present its underlying algorithm and compare its results with those of other current tools. The environment also allows end users to customize the adaptation process. Lastly, some conclusions are drawn along with indications for future work.

2 Related Work

Various approaches are possible to support adaptation for mobile devices. Bickmore [2] proposed a classification into five categories: device-specific authoring (one version for each target device type), multiple-device authoring (one version, with subversions for the various targets, e.g. using different stylesheets), client-side navigation (adaptation is performed directly by the client), Web page filtering (adaptation is obtained by content filtering) and automatic re-authoring (one version exists, which is then automatically adapted for the target device). Automatic re-authoring can be further divided into transducing (the original structure is preserved and the elements are adapted, e.g. images resized) and transforming (the structure is adapted as well). Our approach is an example of automatic re-authoring, supporting transforming (since the original pages can even be split into multiple mobile pages if they are too expensive in terms of space consumption).

Various contributions have been put forward in this area and it is not possible to mention all of them. The OPA browser [14] allocates various functions for Web browsing on each numerical key of a cellular phone. Buyukkokten et al. [4] proposed a novel technique for form summarization, which is also able to automatically summarise texts according to various policies. Laakko and Hiltunen [6] proposed a technique for server side adaptation. We too support a solution using an adaptation proxy but we also exploit logical descriptions that allow us to propose a more general solution. The Roam system [5] is another environment for multi-device applications. It also logically partition an application in a set of components but then it requires that developers provide various implementations for different types of devices. Thus there is little support for automatic adaptation. Studies on usability of mobile adaptation [7] by Kaikkonen and Roto indicate that adaptation should not completely destroy the original structure of the desktop pages in order to allow users to still be able to associ-ate the mobile pages with the original ones. One important issue in this adaptation process is how to handle table adaptation. In [10] there is a proposal that allows users to interactively fold and unfold the tables rows and/or columns. However, such man-ual adaptations are lost when users access the tables again.

3   A Model-Based Architecture for User Interface Adaptation

We have designed and developed a model-based architecture for user interface adap-tation, which supports reverse and forward transformations that are able to transform existing desktop Web applications for various interaction platforms. The basic as-sumption is that there exists a huge amount of easily accessible content for desktop Web applications, which can be processed and transformed to support multi-device interfaces, even across non-Web implementation languages. The advantage of this solution with respect to others (e.g. [9]) is that it does not require that the applications be implemented using a particular toolkit in order to make them able to adapt.

When the user accesses the application through an interaction platform other than the desktop, the intermediate adaptation server (which includes a proxy server) trans-forms its user interface by building the corresponding logical description and using it as a starting point for creating the implementation adapted to the accessing device (see Figure 1). Lastly, the user interface implementation for the target device is generated.

The reverse engineering module analyses the content of the HTML and the associ-ated CSS files and builds the logical description of the desktop user interface, which is provided as input to the adaptation module.

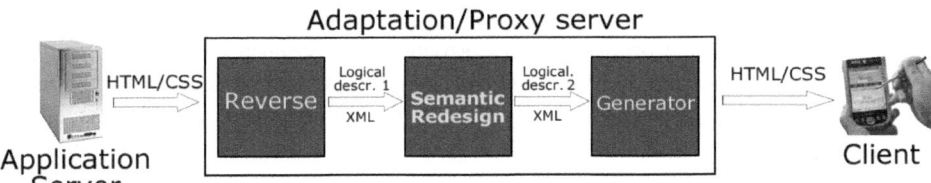

Fig. 1. The Main Phases of the Adaptation Process

In the process of creating an interface version suitable for a platform different from the desktop, we use a semantic redesign module. This part of the environment auto-matically transforms the logical description of the desktop version into the logical description for the new platform. Therefore, the goal of this transformation is to pro-vide a description of the user interface suitable for the new platform. This means that intelligent rules are used for adapting the description of the user interface to the new platform taking into account its capabilities (e.g. using interface elements that are more suitable for the new platform) but ensuring at the same time that the support for the original set of tasks is maintained. This solution allows the environment to exploit the semantic information contained in the logical description. In this case the semantic information is related to the basic tasks that the user interface elements are expected to support.

This software architecture for user interface adaptation currently uses MARIA [12], a recent model-based language, which allows designers to specify abstract and concrete user interface languages according to the CAMELEON Reference framework [3]. This language represents a step forward in this area because it provides abstractions also for describing modern Web 2.0 dynamic user interfaces and Web service access. It provides an abstract language independent of the interaction modalities and concrete languages for a number of platforms. In general, concrete languages are dependent on the typical interaction resources of the target platform but independent of the implementation languages.

In MARIA an abstract user interface is composed of one or multiple presentations, a data model, and a set of external functions. Each presentation contains a number of user interface elements (interactors) and interactor compositions (indicating how to group or relate a set of interactors), a dialogue model describing the dynamic behaviour of such elements, and connections indicating when a change of presentation should occur. The interactors are classified in abstract terms: edit, selection, only_output, control, interactive description, .. Each interactor can be associated with a number of event handlers, which can change properties of other interactors or activate external functions.

4   The Adaptation Transformation

We have designed a new tool for adaptation: *Customizable Two-dimensional Semantic Redesign*. It supports adaptation from desktop-to-mobile devices and overcomes some of the limitations of previous approaches in the area [11] because it allows users to configure the adaptation process and provides more control over costs calculation and the adaptation results. For example, while previous solutions calculated the screen space requested by the user interface elements mainly in terms of vertical extension, the new algorithm calculates both the horizontal and the vertical consumption of screen space.

The new algorithm takes as input the concrete description of a desktop user interface in the MARIA language and goes through a number of steps. First, it performs some basic transformations: if the user provides preferences regarding the minimum and maximum fonts for the target device then the system transforms all the textual content in order to fit it into the given range. Next, it calculates the cost of all the interactors and composition operators in the provided specification. If the resulting total cost is sustainable for the target device, then the corresponding logical description is generated, otherwise it starts the process to reduce the cost in order to make it sustainable. The basic elements are adapted for the target device first: the images are shrunk, while preserving their aspect ratio, some interactors are replaced with others that are semantically equivalent but need less screen space (e.g. a list can be replaced with a drop-down menu), long texts are reduced in such a way that the part exceeding a limit is shown only on request, image and text in tables are reduced in size. After these basic transformations the overall cost is recalculated and if it is not yet sustainable by the target device then the part of the algorithm related to page splitting is activated. The purpose of this phase is to split the original desktop presentation into two or more presentations that are sustainable for the target mobile device. For this purpose the algorithm considers the interactor compositions (groupings of elements or relations that involve two groups) and tables of elements, and associates some of them to newly generated mobile presentations, removing them from the current presentation in order to decrease its overall cost.

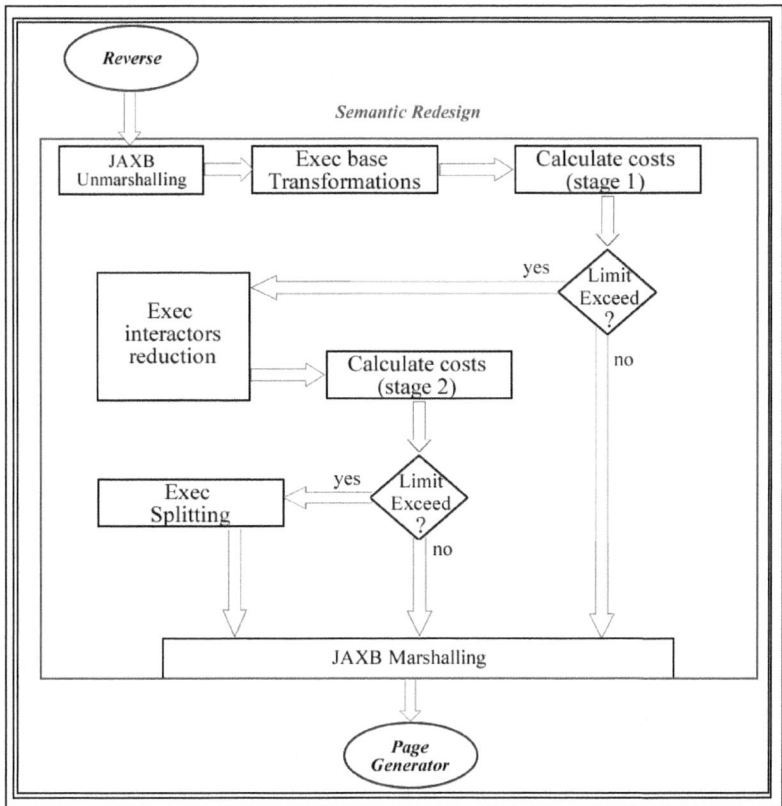

Fig. 2. The adaptation algorithm

The elements that determine the cost of the interactors are: the font attributes (size, style, type), the vertical and horizontal space required by a text, image dimensions, interline value, interactor type, ...

The algorithm has a parameter (Scrolling to Avoid), which allows the specification of which scrolling (vertical or horizontal) to avoid in the case that the presentation cost exceed the limits in both directions.

When the splitting part is activated the algorithm looks for a structured element in the logical description whose cost is sufficiently high that removing it would make the presentation sustainable for the target device. Then, such structured element would be allocated to a newly generated mobile presentation, which would be accessible through a link inserted in the original one. The structured elements considered are groupings, relations, data tables and layout tables. When the element candidate for removal is a data table, the splitting is implemented differently. The table is split into two parts, the part composed of the columns visible without horizontal scrolling remains in the original presentation with an additional link allowing the user to continue to browse it in a separate presentation containing the remaining columns, from which it is possible to return by a similar link.

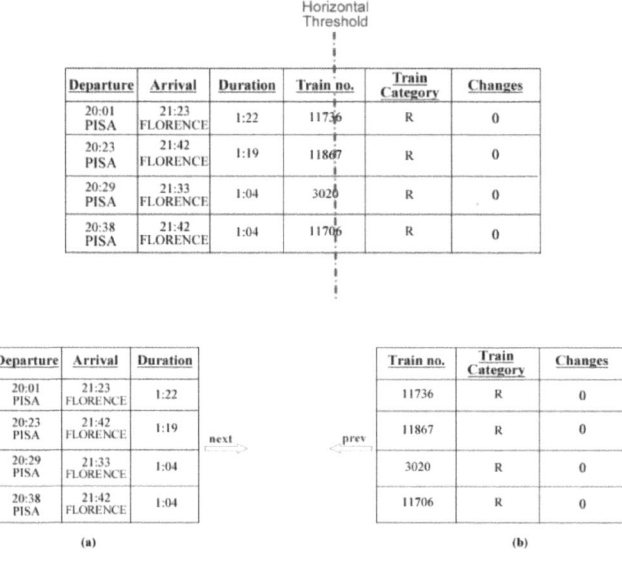

Fig. 3. Example of table splitting

In particular, the tool supports two ways to determine how splitting should be performed. In both cases it analyses the cost of the structured elements, which includes those of the composed interactors, and the cost of the tables (both data and layout tables). Then, the decision of the set of elements to allocate to the newly generated mobile presentation is given in one case by the most expensive element. In the other case the algorithm first calculates the elements whose removal would make the current presentation sustainable by the target device, and then selects the one that has the lowest cost. The rationale for this second option is that it allows obtaining a sustainable presentation but by removing the least amount of information possible, thus preserving the original design as much as possible.

5   End-User Adaptation Customization

In the research on user interface adaptation, one issue that we are considering is how to provide users with more control over the adaptation process in order to improve the usability of its results. In this context more control can mean various things. One important aspect is control over the rules that drive adaptation to the various platforms (the most common case is desktop-to-mobile adaptation). For example, the adaptation engine is able to split the desktop pages when they require considerable amounts of interaction resources but some users may like to have more control over the splitting algorithm. End-User Development [8] (EUD) can be defined as a set of methods, techniques, and tools that allow users of software systems, who are acting as non-professional software developers, at some point to create, modify or extend a software artefact. End-users already have difficulties with single device applications, thus it easy to understand how such difficulties increase when considering applications for multi-device environments. This is one further reason for providing better support for EUD in ubiquitous applications.

Figure 5 and 6 show the user interface that allows end users to configure the adaptation process. The various parameters are grouped according to the related user interface aspect considered. For the fonts, it is possible to specify the minimum and maximum font size in the target device, and the associated measure unit. For the radio buttons it is possible to indicate whether they should be transformed into an interactor that supports the same semantics but using less space screen. In this case, it is possible to specify the threshold, in terms of number of choice options, which should trigger the transformation and the type of interactor to use for its replacement. Similar parameters are available for the list boxes. Other parameters concern the maximum number of characters for texts, maximum and minimum dimensions for images. These parameters determine the cost of rendering a presentation. This cost is compared with the overall sustainable cost in the target device, which is given by the screen resolution multiplied by the horizontal and vertical tolerance. The higher the tolerance coefficient values are, the more scrollable the generated user interface will be. This means that end users have the possibility to specify to what extent the adapted content will be scrollable in the target device. The table tolerance provides an additional factor to consider when calculating the sustainable cost. In practise, this means that when there are tables, more scrolling will be acceptable before deciding to split the presentation.

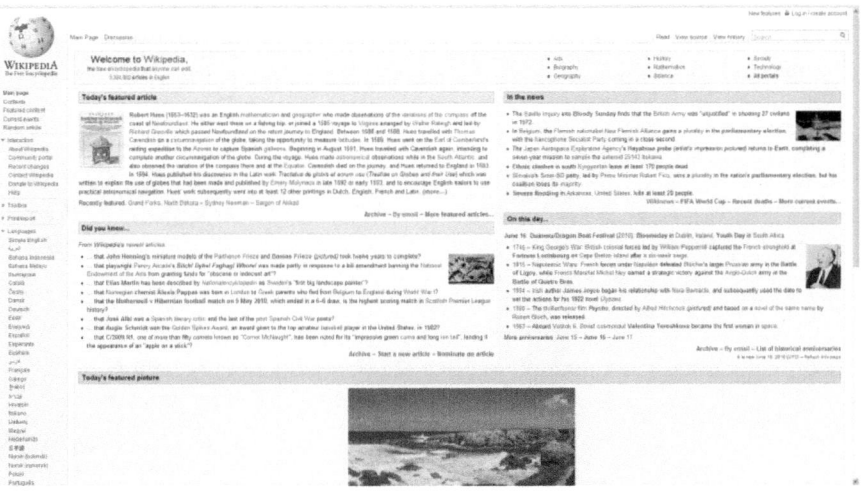

Fig. 4. An example application: Wikipedia

Figure 4 shows the structure of the user interface of a well-known application, Wikipedia, and next we see how the splitting changes depending on the customization parameters specified. In next Figures we show two example configurations, which mainly differ for the scrolling to avoid parameter (in one case is vertical and in the other is horizontal) and the coefficients for display tolerance (in one case they are 20 and 80, in the other one they are 20, 500).

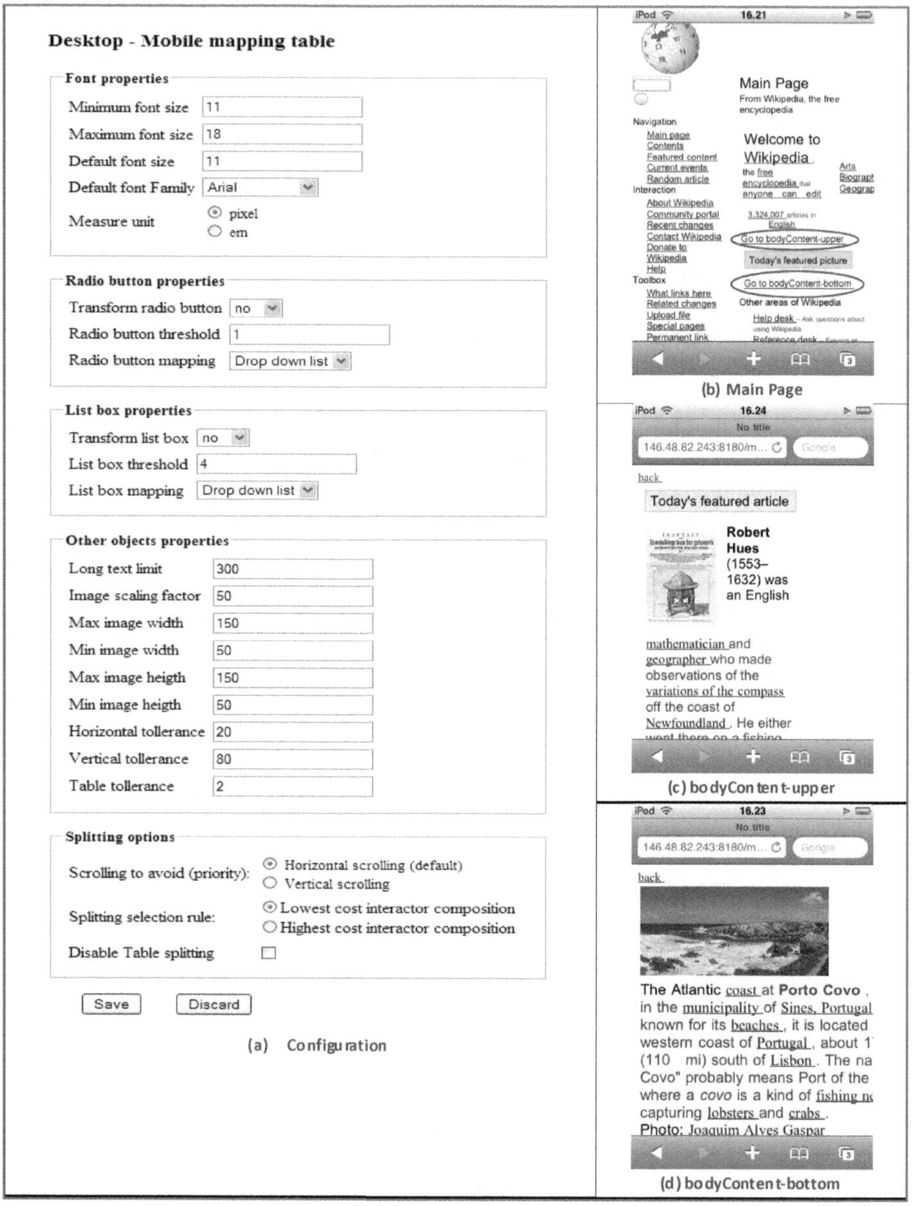

Fig. 5. First Example of Adaptation Configuration and Associated Results

The customization interface also allows the user to set the priority of the type of scrolling (horizontal or vertical) to avoid and the algorithm splitting policy to apply. In this way, we obtain the specification of user preferences regarding adaptation, which can also be reused for other applications more easily than solution such as collapse-to-zoom [15], where the user can express preferences only associated to a given application.

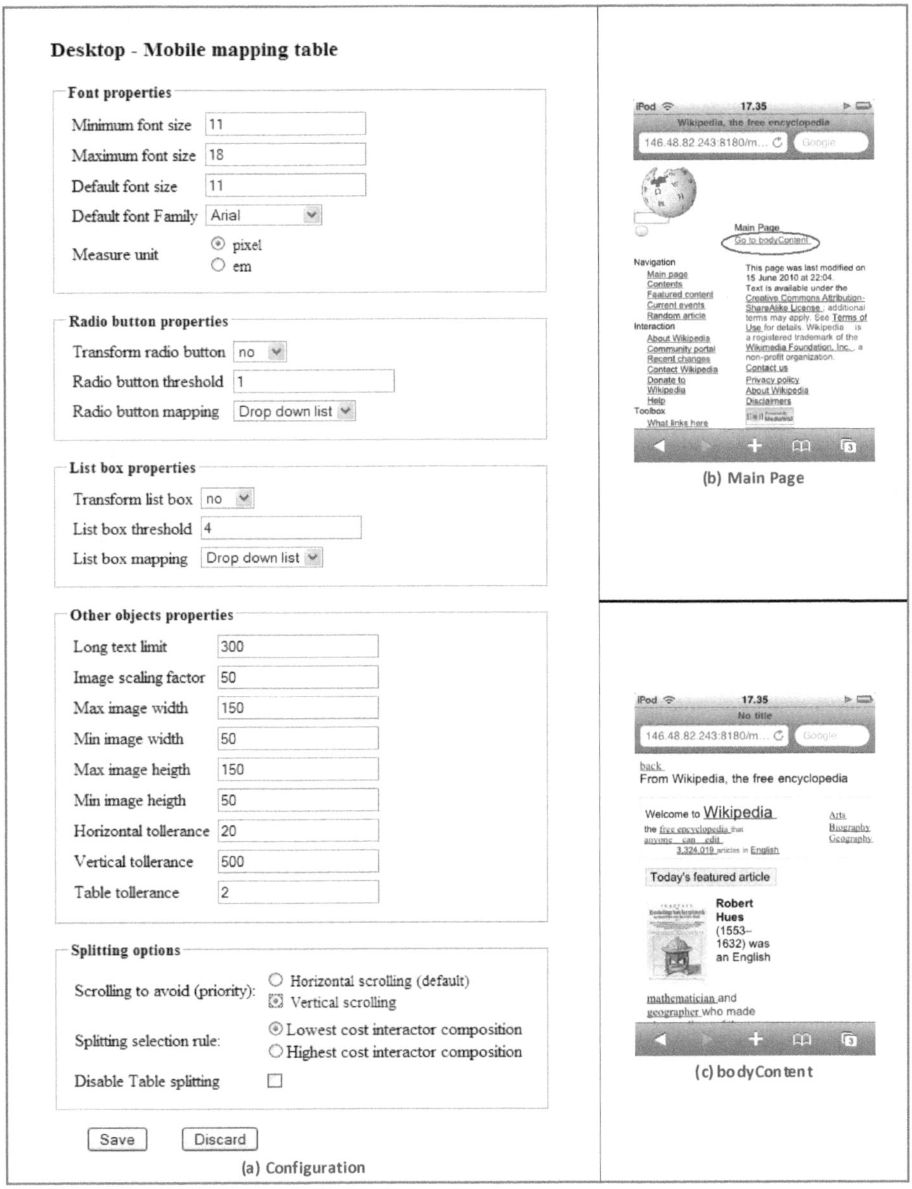

Fig. 6. Second Example of Adaptation Configuration and Associated Results

Then, we can see for each configuration the resulting adapted mobile pages. In the first case the main page is split into three mobile pages (Figure 5). In the first mobile presentation we have highlighted the automatically generated links to the other mobile pages. In the second case (Figure 6), only two pages are generated from the splitting. This is because in order to fit with the vertical scrolling was sufficient to cut only one big element, which referred to the main central content part.

Please note that the results of the adaptation applied to Web sites such as Wikipedia can change depending on the change of the actual content, which continuously varies in such sites.

6 An Example Application

In order to better understand how our approach works we can consider an example desktop Web application (see Figure 7). For the sake of clarity we do not use a particularly complex example.

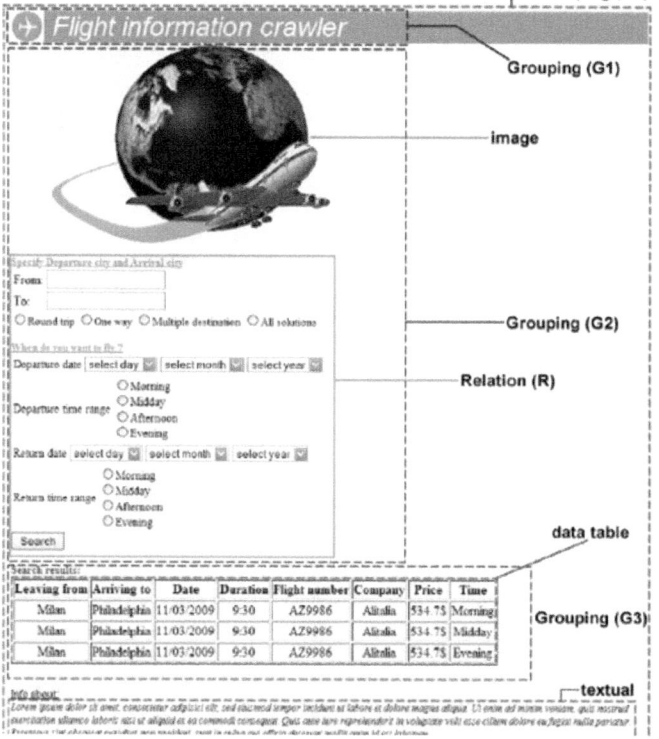

Fig. 7. An example user interface

When the reverse engineering module performs the analysis of this page code, it builds the corresponding logical description (which is highlighted in the Figure).

At the first level it identifies a group (G1) associated with the header, a group (G2) associated with the central part, and one group (G3) mainly associated with the data table. Lastly, a final long text at the bottom is identified. Recursively it identifies the elements included in each group. The top group is composed of an image and some text, the central group is composed of an image and a form, the bottom group is composed of text and a data table. The form is then composed of a number of interactive elements and texts. Now, let us assume that the following parameters have been specified to configure the adaptation process:

Minimum font size = 10px
Maximum font size = 18px
Max image width = 200px
Max image height = 150px
Horizontal tolerance = 10%
Vertical tolerance = 10%
Radio button transformation = yes
Radio button threshold = 3
Radio button mapping = drop down list
Scrolling to Avoid = horizontal
Interactor composition to cut = highest
Long text limit = 300

According to the algorithm previously described, first some basic textual content adaptation is performed. For example, the text "Flight information crawler", contained in Grouping G1, has a size (33px) greater than the value specified in the parameter maximum font size, and consequently is reduced to this limit.

Then, the algorithm calculates the costs in terms of screen consumption of the basic interface elements, and then consequently calculates the costs of the higher elements in the logical structure.

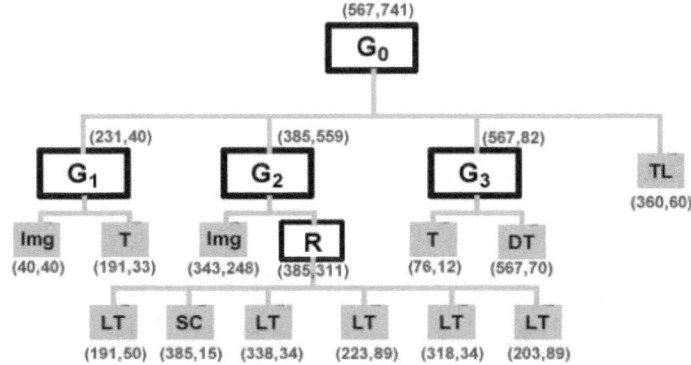

Fig. 8. The costs of the example

Figure 8 shows the resulting costs. For each element a pair of values is provided indicating both the horizontal and the vertical costs. If we consider the specified values for horizontal and vertical tolerance and the resolution of the current device (360x480 pixels), the maximum sustainable horizontal cost would be 396 pixel, and the vertical 528 pixels. If we look at the overall page cost, given by the cost of G0, we can notice that it is higher than the sustainable cost and consequently the adaptation transformation should move on to the next phase, which involves adaptation of the user interface elements. In particular, in this case we have:

- *The transformation of long texts*, since G0 contains a text longer than 300 characters, the text is split into two parts, one reachable only on request through a link;
- *The transformation of images*, the image contained in the G2 grouping is larger than the limits indicated by max image width and max image height, thus it is scaled from 343x248 pixel to a resolution of 198x143 pixels.
- *Conversion into equivalent interactors*, the radio buttons (an example is the interactor SC in the Figure) are transformed according to the adaptation parameters that indicate that radio buttons be converted into drop-down menus when there are more than three options.
- *Reduction of space taken up by data tables*, the data table DT, contained in the Grouping G3, is reduced by decreasing the size of all the texts contained in it.

Figure 9 shows the updated costs in the user interface versions with the elements adapted as described. It is possible to note that even the resulting overall cost is still too large for the target device. Thus, the phase dedicated to page splitting is activated.

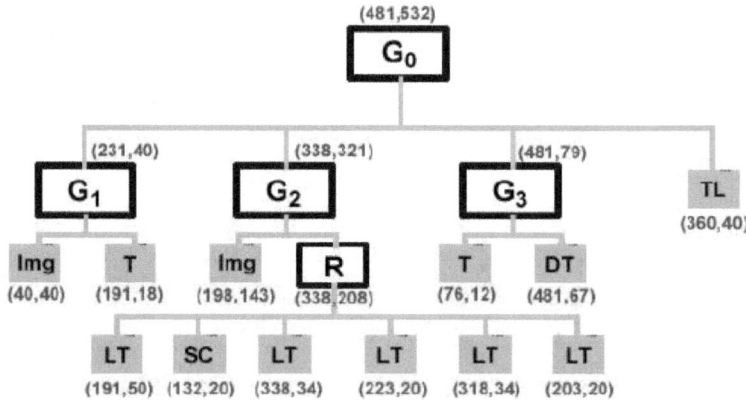

Fig. 9. The updated costs of the example

As described previously the splitting algorithm is driven by two parameters: Scrolling to Avoid and Interactor composition to cut. In our example the first one is set to *horizontal*, and the second one to *highest*. According to these values, the splitting algorithm looks for the element with the highest cost, which is suitable to avoiding horizontal scrolling. In this case it is the data table DT in Figure 9. According to the rules previously introduced the table is split in such a way as to allocate to a newly generated mobile presentation the portion exceeding the horizontal limit. Thus, at the end of the first cycle the algorithm produces two newly generated additional mobile presentations: one for the excessive table portion and one for the excessive text (see Figure 10).

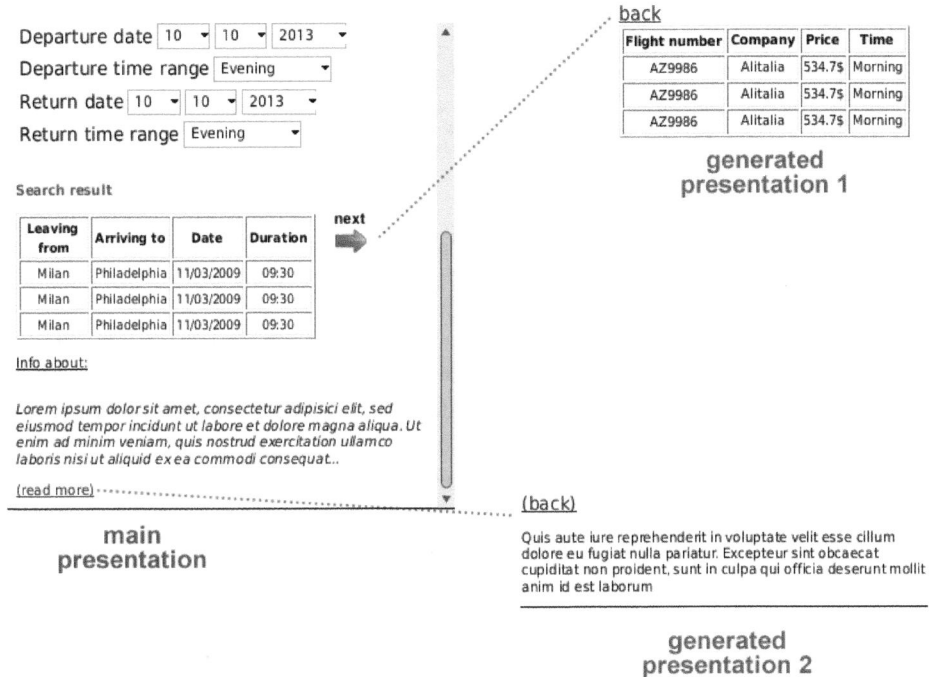

Fig. 10. The presentation generated by the semantic redesign

7   Comparison with Other Approaches

We have conducted a study comparing our tool, in terms of adaptation results, with two publicly available tools for desktop-to-mobile adaptation: Mowser (http://mowser.com) and Skweezer (http://www.skweezer.com). Figure 11 shows an example form interface adapted using the three systems.

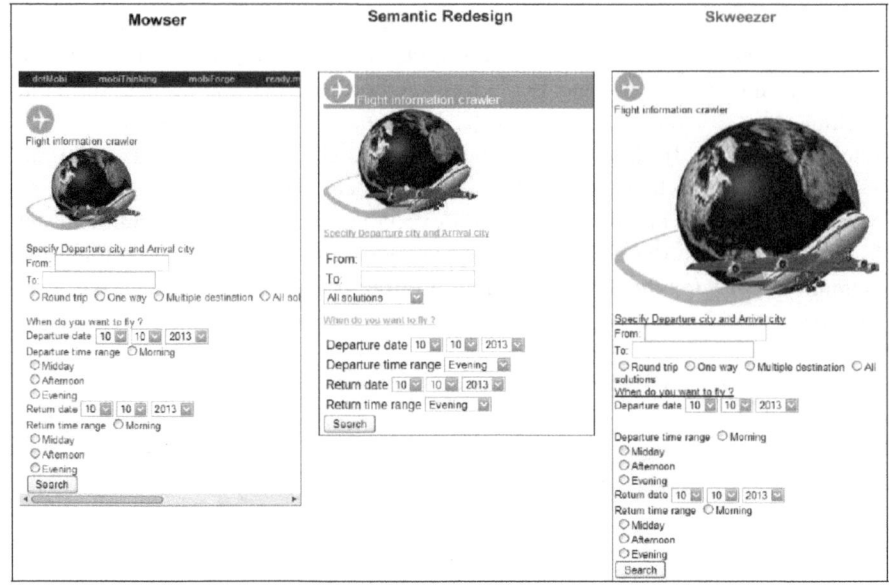

Fig. 11. Form adaptation comparison

By comparing the three versions we have noted that Mowser resizes only the images larger than 150 pixels, ignores style sheets and text attributes indicated in the pages because it associates them with predefined sheets. It provides no particular support for long texts, tables, or change of interactors. In addition, it aims to reduce vertical use of screen space, but this is obtained by requiring users to perform considerable horizontal scrolling.

Squeezer follows a different policy. It reduces the image quality but it does not change their dimensions. Like Mowser, it ignores the colours and the properties specified by the style sheets but it preserves some HTML tags (<b>, <i> and <u>) for the text formatting. Also Squeezers does not support long text transformations, table management (see Figure 12), or interactor changes. Differently from Mowser, Squeezer aims to reduce horizontal scrolling, which implies increasing the vertical one. It also aims to reduce the page download time by reducing the size of its content in terms of bytes.

The results of this comparison were encouraging because our tool has shown to be more flexible. Indeed, it allows end users to customize the adaptation parameters and is able to adapt a higher number of interface element types than the other two tools (e.g. tables and long texts do not receive specific adaptation transformations with the other two tools).

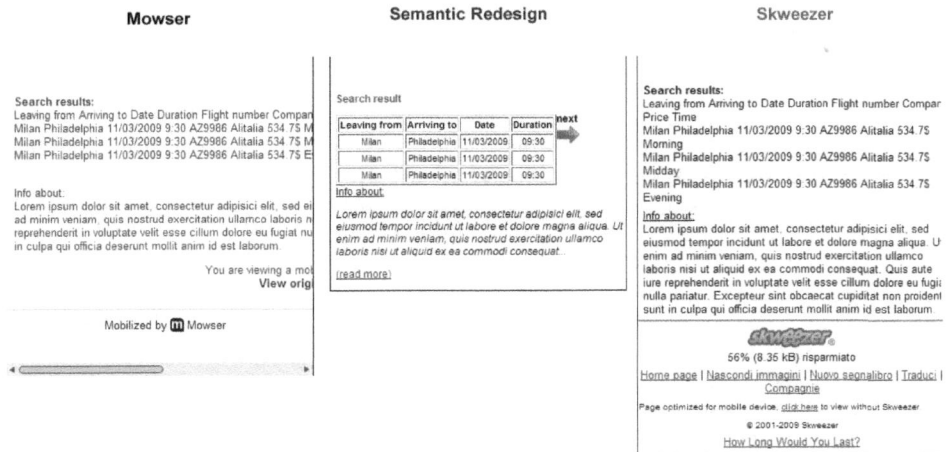

Fig. 12. Table adaptation comparison

8 Conclusions and Future Work

Ubiquitous environments call for adaptive systems in order to adapt to the varying interaction resources. Model-based approaches can provide useful support in this context. We propose a solution for desktop-to-mobile adaptation of Web user interfaces, which overcome limitations of previous ones.

The solution is able to dynamically handle Web pages and build the corresponding logical description through a reverse engineering module able to analyse all the HTML and CSS associated tags. In the adaptation interface elements can be replaced with others that are semantically equivalent but require less screen space. The scripts are preserved in the adapted version. Content such as Flash, Java applets are not currently adapted.

In addition, there is a need for providing users with more control on ubiquitous interfaces, according to the end-user development paradigm. In this paper we have presented a solution that also allows end-users to customize the desktop-to-mobile adaptation in order to change the results that can be obtained by automatic user interface generation.

We plan to further extend this work in various directions. The customization user interface can be improved in order to make the effects of the various customization parameters more understandable. In addition, in this work we have considered only desktop-to-mobile adaptation but other types of transformations can benefit from the approach proposed, e.g. graphical-to-vocal adaptation.

Acknowledgments

This work has been partially supported by the EU ICT STREP Project OPEN (http://www.ict-open.eu/).

References

1. Berti, S., Paternò, F., Santoro, C.: Natural Development of Ubiquitous Interfaces. Communications of the ACM, 63–64 (September 2004)
2. Bickmore, T., et al.: Web page filtering and re-authoring for mobile users. Computer Journal Special Issue on Mobile Computing 42(6), 534–546 (1999)
3. Calvary, G., Coutaz, J., Bouillon, L., Florins, M., Limbourg, Q., Marucci, L., Paternò, F., Santoro, C., Souchon, N., Thevenin, D., Vanderdonckt, J.: The CAMELEON reference framework. CAMELEON Project. Deliverable 1.1 (2002)
4. Buyukkokten, O., Kaljuvee, O., Garcia-Molina, H., Paepcke, A., Winograd, T.: Efficient web browsing on handheld devices using page and form summarization. In: TOIS, pp. 82–115 (2002)
5. Chu, H., Song, H., Wong, C., Kurakake, S., Katagiri, M.: Roam, a seamless application framework. Journal of Systems and Software 69(3), 209–226 (2004)
6. Laakko, T., Hiltunen, T.: Adapting web content to mobile user agents. IEEE Internet Computing 9(2), 46–53 (2005)
7. Kaikkonen, A., Roto, V.: Perception of narrow web pages on a mobile phone. In: Proc. Human Factors in Telecommunications (2003)
8. Lieberman, H., Paternò, F., Wulf, W. (eds.): End-User Development. Springer, Heidelberg (2006) ISBN-10 1-4020-4220-5
9. Melchior, J., Grolaux, D., Vanderdonckt, J., Van Roy, P.: A Toolkit for Peer-to-Peer Distributed User Interfaces: Concepts, Implementation, and Applications. In: EICS 2009, Pittsburgh, Pennsylvania, USA, July 15-17, pp. 69–78 (2009)
10. Ohnishi, K., Tajima, K.: Browsing large html tables on small screens. In: ACM Symposium on User Interface Software and Technology (UIST 2008) (2008)
11. Paternò, F., Santoro, C., Scorcia, A.: Automatically Adapting Web Sites for Mobile Access through Logical Descriptions and Dynamic Analysis of Interaction Resources. In: AVI 2008, Naples, pp. 260–267. ACM Press, New York (May 2008)
12. Paternò, F., Santoro, C., Spano, L.D.: MARIA: A Universal Language for Service-Oriented Applications in Ubiquitous Environment. ACM Transactions on Computer-Human Interaction 19(4), 19:1–19:30 (2009)
13. Sottet, J., Ganneau, V., Calvary, G., Coutaz, J., Demeure, A., Favre, J., Demumieux, R.: Model-Driven Adaptation for Plastic User Interfaces. In: Baranauskas, C., Palanque, P., Abascal, J., Barbosa, S.D.J. (eds.) INTERACT 2007. LNCS, vol. 4662, pp. 397–410. Springer, Heidelberg (2007)
14. Uemukai, T., Nishio, S., Arase, Y., Hara, T.: Opa browser: a web browser for cellular phone users. In: ACM Symposium on User Interface Software and Technology (UIST 2007), pp. 71–80 (2007)
15. Wang-Wei-Ying, C., Baudisch, P., Xie, X.: Collapse-to-zoom: Viewing web pages on small screen devices by interactively removing irrelevant content. In: ACM Symposium on User Interface Software and Technology (UIST 2004), pp. 91–94 (October 2004)
16. Weiser, M.: The Computer for the 21st Century. Scientific American Special Issue on Communications, Computers, and Networks (September 1991)

Extending UsiXML to Support User-Aware Interfaces

Ricardo Tesoriero[1,2] and Jean Vanderdonckt[1]

[1] Université catholique de Louvain
Place des Doyens, 1 (B-1348)
Louvain-la-Neuve, Belgium
[2] University of Castilla-La Mancha
Av. España S/N. Campus Universitario de Albacete (02071)
Albacete, Spain
`ricardo.tesoriero@uclm.es, jean.vanderdonckt@uclouvain.be`

Abstract. Mobile and portable devices require the definition of new user interfaces (UI) capable of reducing the level of attention required by users to operate the applications they run to improve the calmness of them. To carry out this task, the next generation of UIs should be able to capture information from the context and act accordingly. This work defines an extension to the UsiXML methodology that specifies how the information on the user is modeled and used to customize the UI. The extension is defined vertically through the methodology, affecting all layers of the methodology. In the Tasks & Concepts layer, we define the user environment of the application, where roles and individuals are characterized to represent different user situations. In the Abstract UI layer, we relate groups of these individuals to abstract interaction objects. Thus, user situations are linked to the abstract model of the UI. In the Concrete UI layer, we specify how the information on the user is acquired and how it is related to the concrete components of the UI. This work also presents how to apply the proposed extensions to a case of study. Finally, it discusses the advantages of using this approach to model user-aware applications.

1 Introduction

In 1994, Mark Weiser introduced the notion of Calm Technology in [16]. The aim of Calm Technology is to reduce the "excitement" of information overload by letting the user select what information should be placed at the center of their attention and what information should be peripheral. A way to support Calm Technology is the use of the context information to reduce users' work.

According to [11], context-aware applications [4] are characterized by a hierarchical feature space model. At the top level, there is a distinction between human factors, in the widest sense, and the physical environment. Both, the human factors and the physical environment, define three categories of features each. While, the human factors are defined in terms of features related to (a) the information on the user (knowledge of habits, emotional state, bio-physiological

R. Bernhaupt et al. (Eds.): HCSE 2010, LNCS 6409, pp. 95–110, 2010.

conditions, ...); (b) the user's social environment (co-location of others, social interaction, group dynamics, ...); and (c) the user's tasks (spontaneous activity, engaged tasks, general goals, ...); the physical environment are defined in terms of features related to (a) the location (absolute position, relative position, co-location,...), (b) the infrastructure (surrounding resources for computation, communication, task performance, ...) and (c) physical conditions (noise, light, pressure, ...).

This article explores the development of multi-modal UIs that are affected by human factors. Concretely, it focuses on those features related to the information on the user (i.e. emotional state, bio-physiological conditions, skills, experience, ...) and the user's tasks (i.e. , defined by the role played in the society).

The proposal is based on an extension to the UsiXML [14] methodology based on the social model of CAUCE methodology defined in [13]. While UsiXML provides a model-based approach to design multi-modal UIs based on the Cameleon reference framework [2], the social model provide designers with the ability express how user features affect the application UI.

The paper is organized as follows. In Section 2, we present the most relevant related works on the development of multi-modal UIs. Then, the UsiXML extension to support user awareness is exposed in Section 3. Afterwards, the extension is applied to a case of study in Section 4. Finally, in Section 5 we expose conclusions and future works.

2   Related Work

Teallach tool and method [1] exploit three models: a task model, a domain model as a class diagram, and a presentation model both at logical and physical levels. Teallach enables designers to start building a UI from any model and maps concepts from different models one to each other. However, the tool does not support the development of context-aware UIs. Moreover, from the user modeling point of view, Teallach does not support any type of user profile nor awareness.

The approach exposed in [3] describes a toolkit of interactors, which are designed to develop UIs that handle both input and output using multiple mechanisms. The toolkit supports adaptation for a change in the resources available to the widgets, or a change in the context the platform is situated in. However, the approach does not support any model to capture user information from external sources that are not directly related to the platform or the widget contents defined in the interface.

XIML [5] is a more general UIDL than UIML as it can specify any type of model, any model element, and relationships between. The predefined models and relationships can be expanded to fit a particular context of use. The term context is interpreted as the platform of the application is running and not the application is adapter to such platform, instead of the information that affects, or is relevant, to the application. No other issue related to the context awareness is taken into account by the model.

SeescoaXML [8] supports the production of UIs for multiple platforms and the run-time migration of the full UI. However, the development does not take into account the definition of the user-aware behavior of the UI.

The CTTE (ConcurTaskTrees Environment)[9] is a development environment to support the development and analysis of task models for interactive systems. Based on these models, the TERESA (Transformation Environment for inteRactivE Systems representAtions) [10] produce different UIs for multiple computing platforms by refining a general task model. Thus, various presentation and dialog techniques are used to map the refinements into XHTML code adapted for each platform such as the Web, the PocketPC, and mobile phones.

Although CTT (the language used to describe the task model of the applications developed using TERESA) supports the role definition and the definition of different task models for each role, the task and role concepts are so coupled that the definition of similar interfaces derive in different models (one for each role). Besides, this approach does not take into account the attributes of role definitions, although CTT allows designers to assign values to standard attributes. Thus, the definition of custom attributes is not supported directly.

RIML [12] consists of an XML-based language that combines features of several existing markup languages (e.g., XForms, SMIL) in a XHTML language profile. This language is used to transform any RIML-compliant document into multiple target languages suitable for visual or vocal browsers on mobile devices. Although RIML provides the ability to specify multi-modal UI, RIML is focused on the view of the application independently of the context it is being executed. Therefore, no context or user awareness is taken into account.

3   The User-Aware UsiXML Extension

UsiXML defines a development process based on the Cameleon Reference Framework [2] to build multi-device interactive applications. The development process is divided into four layers.

The Task & Concepts (T&C) layer describes users' tasks to be carried out, and the domain-oriented concepts required to perform these tasks.

The Abstract User Interface (AUI) defines abstract containers and individual components [7] (two forms of Abstract Interaction Objects [15]) by grouping subtasks according to various criteria (e.g., task model structural patterns, cognitive load analysis, semantic relationships identification), a navigation scheme between the container and selects abstract individual component for each concept so that they are independent of any modality. Thus, an AUI is considered as an abstraction of a CUI with respect to interaction modality.

The Concrete User Interface (CUI) concretizes an abstract UI for a given context of use into Concrete Interaction Objects (CIOs) [15]. It also defines the widget layouts and the interface navigation. It abstracts a FUI into a UI definition that is independent of any computing platform. Therefore, a CUI can also be considered as a reification of an AUI at the upper level, and an abstraction of the FUI with respect to the platform.

Finally, the Final User Interface (FUI) is the operational UI running on a particular computing platform either by interpretation (e.g., through a Web browser) or by execution (e.g., after compilation of code in an interactive development environment).

These layers are defined by the UIModel depicted in Figure 1. Each model that is part of the UIModel represents an aspect of the UI to be developed. Thus, the proposal defines the User Model to represent how the features of the user that affect the UI.

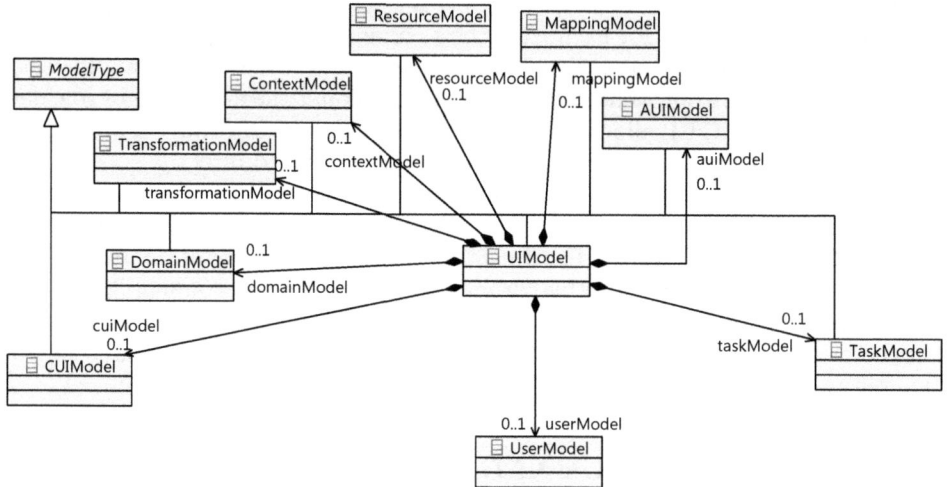

Fig. 1. UIModel models defining the UI

3.1   The Task and Concepts Layer Extension

The User Model is the core of the user-awareness modeling. It is defined in the T&C layer of the UsiXML methodology. The goal of this model is the representation of the user features that affect the UI.

To carry out this task, the model represents this information in two levels of abstraction: the user feature level and the user profile level.

- The user feature level defines the features of the user that affect the UI. Thus, designers are able to represent the user features that are relevant to the application domain providing flexibility when describing user profiles.
- The user profile level is based on the information defined at the user feature level. It characterizes the features according to runtime situations. Thus, designers are able to identity different groups of individuals that share the same characteristics.

Both, the user feature level and the user profile level are rooted in the UserModel metaclass, as depicted in Figure 2. It represents the user characteristics that affect the UI at both levels of abstraction.

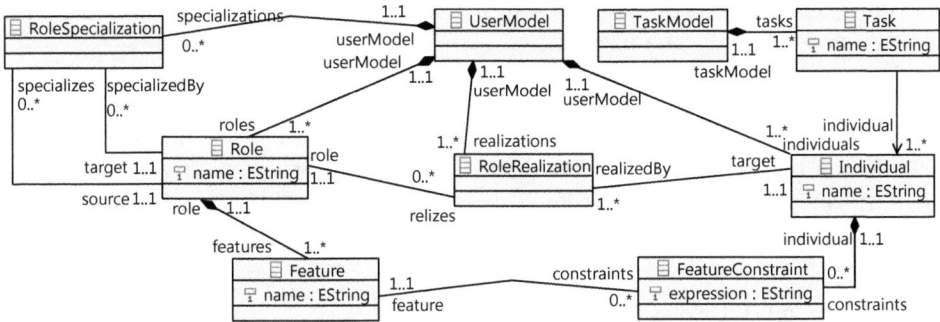

Fig. 2. The UserModel metamodel

The user feature level defines the user characteristics in terms of *Roles* and *Features*. We have defined *Role* as a set of user *Features* where a *Feature* represents an attribute related to the user playing this role in the system. For instance, a Patient *Role* may define the age, cardiac pulse, temperature and glucose level *Features*.

In order to represent *Roles* that have common *Features*, we have defined the *RoleSpecialization* relationship between *Roles*. It is a directional relationship defined by the *source* and the *target* attributes. The semantic meaning of the *RoleSpecialization* relationship is defined as follows:

Let A and B be instances of the *Role* metaclass; Let $FwoS(R)$ be the function that takes the *Role* R as parameter and returns the set of *Features* defined by R *Role* **without taking into account the *RoleSpecialization* relationship**. Let $F(R)$ be the function that takes the *Role* R as parameter and returns the set of *Features* defined by R *Role* **taking into account the *RoleSpecialization* relationship**. Finally, let $S(A, B)$ be the *RoleSpecialization* relationship that defines A as the *source* and B the *target* of the relationship.

Then,

$$F(B) = FwoS(B)$$

$$F(A) = FwoS(B) \cup FwoS(A)$$

The user profile level defines user characteristics in terms of *Individuals* and *FeatureConstraints*

Users are characterized according to the *Features* defined by the *Roles* they play in the system. The characterization at this level is defined by the *FeatureConstraints* metaclass that is related to an *Individual* playing a *Role*. Thus, the *RoleRealization* metaclass defines the relationship between the *Role* and the *Individual*. Then, the *Individual* defines a set of *FeatureConstraints* that are related to the *Features* defined by the *Role* it plays in the system.

For instance, following the example exposed on the user feature level, the Patient *Role* may be realized by the *aPatientWithFever Individual* that defines a *FeatureConstraint* where the *temperature Feature* is higher than 38 Celsius Degrees.

Thus, the same user may be a *aPatientWithFever* or not, according to the body *temperature* of the user.

Finally, the *UserModel* is related to the *TaskModel* by the means of reflecting how the characteristics defined by the *UserModel* are propagated to the UI in the T&C layer of the UsiXML methodology. Each *Task* defined in the *TaskModel* is affected by an *Individual* that describes the user situation in which the *Task* is performed. Therefore, in order to perform a *Task*, all the *FeatureConstraints* defined by the *Individual* that is related to the task must be satisfied.

3.2   The AUI Layer Extension

The AUIModel is part of the AUI layer of the UsiXML methodology. Although the user awareness extension does not affect the AUIModel definition directly, it introduces some modifications in the AUI layer by the means of the definition of new inter-model relationships in the MappingModel.

These relationships are established between Abstract Interaction Objects (*AIOs*) and *Individuals*. However, they do not affect Abstract Individual Components *AICs* in the same way they affect Abstract Containers *ACs*.

On the one hand, *ACs* are directly affected by *Individuals*. On the other hand, *AICs* are affected through *Facets* that are affected by *Individuals*.

The Figure 3 shows the extensions of the MappingModel and how it affects the AUIModel.

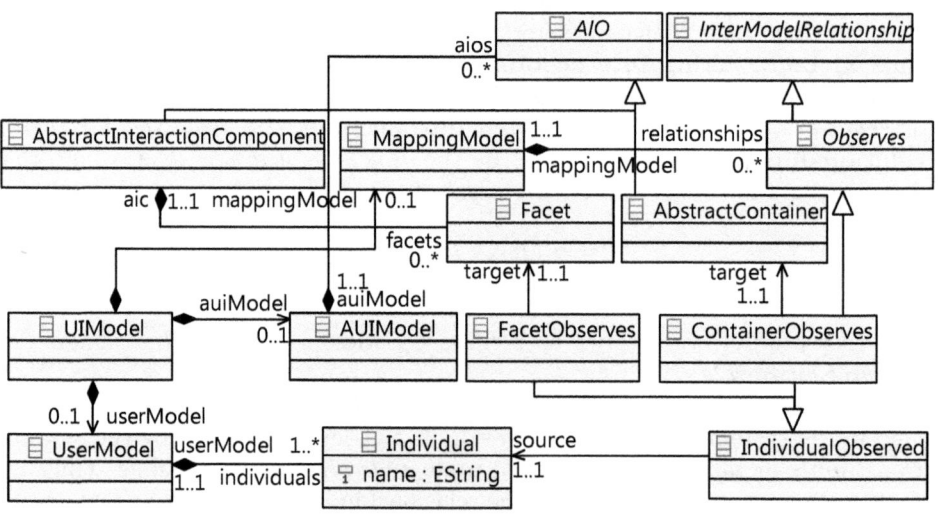

Fig. 3. MappingModel extensions in the AUI layer

Let suppose that an *Individual* is related to an *AC*. If all the *FeatureConstraints* of the *Individual* are satisfied, then the *AC* is "active", "enabled" or "available". Otherwise, the *AC* is "inactive", "disabled" or "unavailable".

*AIC*s define *Facets*. These *Facets* are manipulated by the *FeatureConstraints* defined by the *Individual* they are attached to.

Let suppose that an *Individual* is related to a *Facet*. If all the *FeatureConstraints* of the *Individual* are satisfied, then the *Facet* is "active", "enabled" or "available". Otherwise, the *Facet* is "inactive", "disabled" or "unavailable".

Therefore, the behavior of the UI is affected by profiles defined in the Tasks & Concepts layer of the UsiXML methodology. This relationship is defined by the *FacetObserves* and *ContainerObserves* submetaclasses of the *Observes* metaclass, which belongs to the MappingModel.

Thus, as an *AC* or a *Facet* can "observe" many *Indivuduals*, a conflict among *FeatureConstraints* may arise. Therefore, we enable the *Facet* or *AC* when any of the *Individuals* match the user state.

Depending on the development path, these relationships can be derived from the TaskModel and the *IsExecutedIn* inter-model relationships defined in the MappingModel using transformation rules defined in the TransformationModel.

3.3   The CUI Layer Extension

The extension to support the user awareness in the CUI layer is depicted in Figure 4.

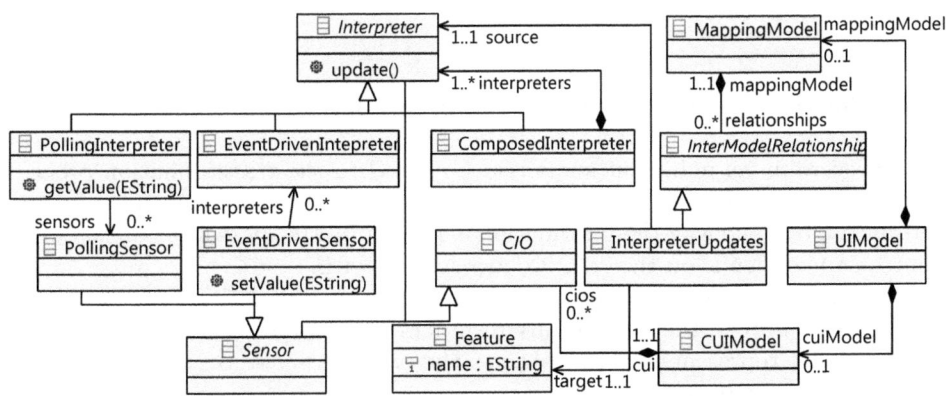

Fig. 4. Relating Sensors and Interpreters to Features

The metamodel is divided into two parts:

- The CUI model extension
- The mapping model extension

The CUI extension goal is the description of the system is aware of the information on the user. To carry out this task, we have introduced the *Sensor* and the *Interpreter* entities that are in charge of capturing, interpreting and providing information to be processed by the system.

The information can be perceived in different ways according to the sensor it is used to capture it. Therefore, we have defined two types of *Sensors*: *EventDrivenSensors* and *PollingSensors*. The information that is perceived by sensors should be interpreted accordingly. To perform this task, we have defined *Interpreters*. *Interpreters* are in charge of transforming information that comes from *Sensors* into information that is compatible with the user environment definition.

We have defined three types of *Interpreters*: the *PollingInterpreter* that deals with information coming from a *PollingSensor*, the *EventDrivenInterpreter* that is in charge of interpreting information from an *EventDrivenSensor*, and the *ComposedInterpreter* that is responsible for the interpretation of information coming from several sensors. The *Interpreter* hierarchy is an implementation of the Composite design pattern [6].

The information processed by the CUI extension is propagated through the rest of the model by the mapping model extension. Therefore, the connection between the *CIO*s and the rest of the models is performed through the *interpreterUpdates* submetaclass of the *intermodelRelationship* defined by the MappingModel. This relationship is used to define the relationship between *Features* defined in the user environment model and the *Interpreters*.

Thus, *Individual*s are notified of the changes of the information on the user through *FeatureConstraints*.

3.4   The Transformation Process and the FUI

In this section, we point out some issues related to the transformation process that takes place between the abstract user interface *AUI* and the concrete user interface *CUI*. The way the information captured by the models is translated to source code depends on the *AIO* we are dealing with.

If we are dealing with *abstractContainers*, the translation of an *Individual* that matches the state of the user usually results in the modification of a property in the *CIO* that represents it. For instance, the *visible*, *enabled* or *opaque* property of the *CIO* is set to `true`.

However, the mechanism used by *AIC*s is not the same because *Individual*s are related to *Facets*. Therefore, some aspects of the *AIC*s may match some *Individual*s and some of them may not.

Suppose that an *AIC* defines the following *Facets*: *Input*, *Output* and *Navigation*. In addition, each *Facet* is related to different *Individual*s: $I_1 \leftrightarrow input$, $I_2 \leftrightarrow output$ and $I_3 \leftrightarrow navigation$.

Thus, if I_1 is the unique *Individual* that matches the user environment, then the *AIC* may be represented by a `TextField`. However, if I_2 is the unique *Individual* that matches the user environment, then the *AIC* may be represented by a

Label. Finally, if I_3 is the unique *Individual* that matches the user environment, then the *AIC* may be represented by a `Button` or a `Link`.

Therefore, the same *AIC* can be turned into different *CIO*s, at runtime, according to the user state. The Figure 5 represents the possible results of the transformation, according to the interface specification taking into account the user environment.

The situation is solved using different mappings for the same *AIO*. Thus, the user state defines which component is available according to the user environment.

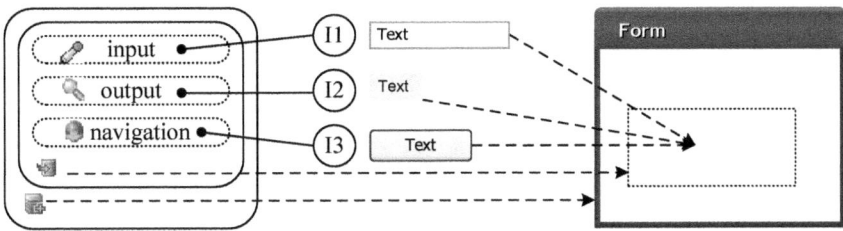

Fig. 5. Possible results on the Final User Interface

4   Case of Study

The application that will serve as case of study is the "Healthy Menu". The goal of the application is the presentation of dishes according to the role and the biophysical state of the user. Thus, views and controls are customized to provide the user with Calm UIs.

The explanation is focused on issues related to the definition of the user environment and the relationships between this environment and the UI. Other issues are left behind for the sake of clarity.

4.1   The User Model

The application defines five roles: Users, Patients, Doctors, Nurses and Visitors.

The Users of the application are identified by the *idNumber*, *roleName* and *userName* features.

As all other roles are specializations of the User role, these roles inherit User features. Besides these features, Patients are characterized by the *age*, *temperature* and *glucose* features; Doctors by the *specialty*; Nurses by the *experience* (in years); and Visitors by the patient they are visiting (the *patientId* feature).

As we will focus on the Patient role, we have defined five *Individuals* for this role (aPatient, NormalPatient, PatientWithHyperGlycemia, PatientWithHipoGlycemia and PatientWithFever); and only one for each remaining role (anUser, aPatient, aNurse, aDoctor and aVisitor).

Each *Individual* is defined by a set of *FeatureConstraint*s. For instance, we say that a Patient is normal, if the body temperature is between 36.5 and 38 Celsius degrees and the Sugar level in blood is between 70 and 110 millimoles/liter.

The Figure 6 shows the user model of the application. Rounded rectangles represent Roles, the dashed rectangles defined inside them represent features, the specialization of roles is represented by a triangle-ended arrow pointing to the role that is being specialized, circles represent instances and the rectangles on drawn on the right of these circles represent feature constraints.

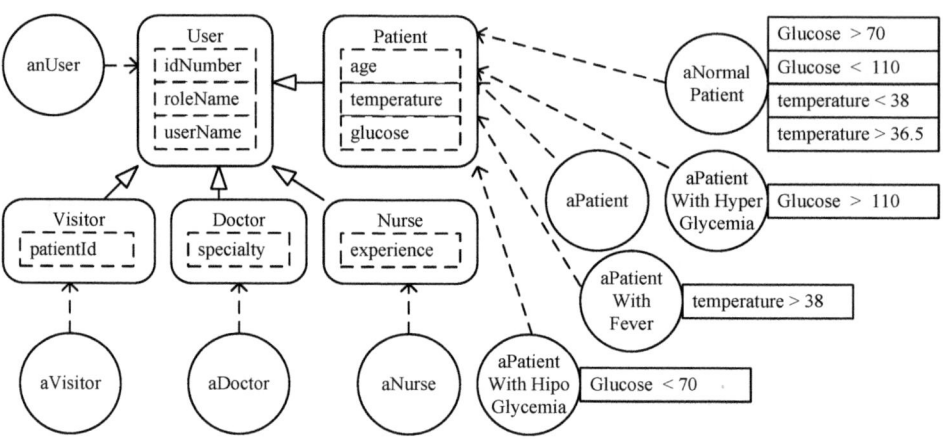

Fig. 6. Healthy screen user model

4.2 The Task Model

The simplified version of the task model for the Healthy screen application is defined in Figure 7.

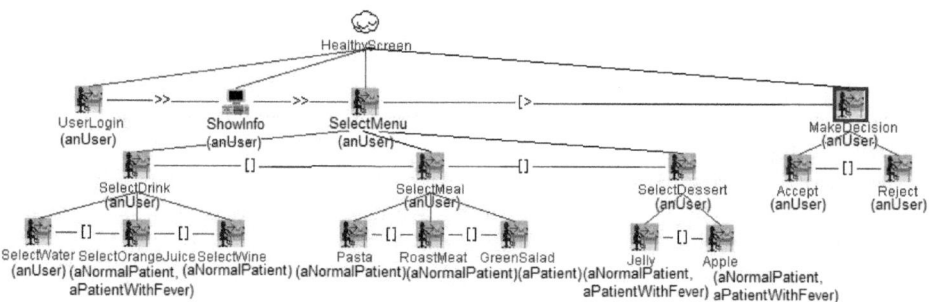

Fig. 7. Healthy screen task model

The *UserLogin* task allows the system to identify the user that is using the application. The information that is retrieved from the system is exposed to the user by the means of the *ShowInfo* system task. Then, the user is able to choose the menu (*SelectMenu* task). To improve task model readability, the menu is divided into three types of selection defined under the *SelectDrink*, *SelectMeal*, *SelectDesset* task. Each task represents a possible menu option. For instance, *SelectWater* (to select water as a drink) is available to all users. However, *SelectWine* (to select wine as a drink) is available for normal patients only. It is also possible to assign more than one individual for each task. Therefore, it is available if any of the involved individuals match the "user state".

4.3   The AUI Model

Once the user model was defined, we define the *AUI* model. The AUI model defines the UI without taking into account its modality.

Although the AUI layer introduced two new types of mappings to describe the relationship between *AIOs* and *Individuals*, the extension does not introduce new elements to AUIModel. Therefore, AUIs are described in the same way they are described traditionally.

The Figure 8 depicts a partial view of the *AUI* model focused on the Patient *Role*. On the left, we show an overview of the containers that are related to the roles defined in the user environment. On the right, we show a detailed view of the Patient role AUI.

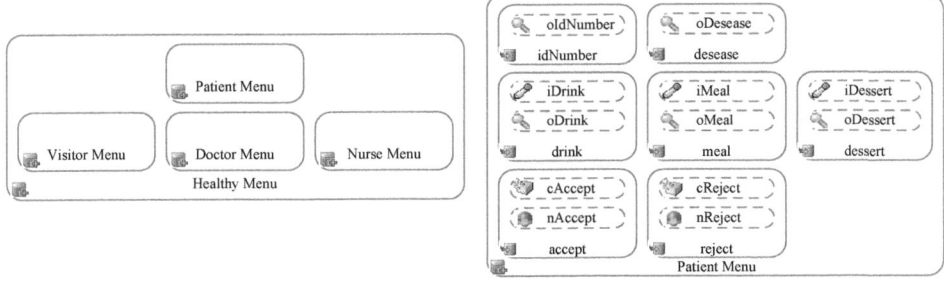

Fig. 8. Partial Healthy Menu AUI model

Then, these *AUIs* are linked to *Individuals* to reflect the modifications in the "user state" accordingly.

The Table 1 shows the *Observes* relationships that relate *ACs* and *Facets* to *Individuals* . These relationships are defined in the mapping model and described in terms of the $O_c(I, AC)$ and the $O_f(I, F)$ functions. While the O_c function represents the *ContainerObserves* relationship, which relates an *Individual* I to an *AbstarctContainer* AC, the O_f function represents the *FacetObserves* relationship, which relates an *Individual* I to a *Facet* F.

Table 1. AUI mappings

AUI mappings

Containers
$O_c(aPatient, PatientMenu)$
$O_c(aNurse, NurseMenu)$
$O_c(aDoctor, DoctorMenu)$
$O_c(aVisitor, VisitorMenu)$

Facets	
$O_f(anUser, nAccept)$	$O_f(anUser, oIdNumber)$
$O_f(anUser, cAccept)$	$O_f(anUser, oDesease)$
$O_f(anUser, nReject)$	
$O_f(anUser, cReject)$	
$O_f(aPatientWithHipoGlycemia, oDrink)$	$O_f(aPatientWithFever, iDrink)$
$O_f(aPatientWithHipoGlycemia, oMeal)$	$O_f(aPatientWithFever, oMeal)$
$O_f(aPatientWithHipoGlycemia, oDessert)$	$O_f(aPatientWithFever, iDessert)$
$O_f(aPatientWithHyperGlycemia, oDrink)$	$O_f(aNormalPatient, iDrink)$
$O_f(aPatientWithHyperGlycemia, oMeal)$	$O_f(aNormalPatient, iMeal)$
$O_f(aPatientWithHyperGlycemia, oDessert)$	$O_f(aNormalPatient, iDessert)$
$O_f(aPatientWithFever, oDrink)$	$O_f(aNormalPatient, oDrink)$
$O_f(aPatientWithFever, oMeal)$	$O_f(aNormalPatient, oMeal)$
$O_f(aNormalPatient, oDessert)$	

To conclude this section, we analyze the *drink AIC* defined in Figure 8 to show an example of how to define the AUI and how to link it to the *Individuals* defined in the user model.

From the AUI perspective, the *drink AIC* represents the component that is in charge of providing users with the information about drinks. This information may be input and output information (if the user is able to select the drink, i.e. *aNormalPatient*), or may be output information only (if the user is not able to select the drink, i.e. *aPatientWhyHyperGlycemia*). Therefore, two Facets (*oDrink* and *iDrink*) were defined for this *AIC*.

From the Mapping perspective, lets analyze the individual *aPatientWithHipo-Glycemia* and its relationship with the *drink AIC*. The O_f *(aPatient With Hipo Glycemia, oDrink)* is the only relationship between individuals and facets of the *drink AIC*. Therefore, the *drink AIC* is an output control. However, if we analyze the *aNormalPatient* individual, we see that the O_f *(aNormal Patient, iDrink)* and the O_f *(aNormal Patient, oDrink)* relationships define an input/output relationship.

4.4 The CUI Model

The *CUI* definition is based on two sensors: *PollingGlucoseSensor* and *Polling TemperatureSensor*. Both of them are instances of the *PollingSensor* metaclass. It also defines two instances of the *PollingInterpreter* metaclass, the *GlucoseInterpreter* and *TemperatureInterpreter*.

Table 2 shows the mapping between the Patient role features and sensors. The function $R_p(S_p, I_p)$ represents the relationship between a *PollingSensor* (S_p) and a *PollingInterpreter*(I_p). The function $U(I, F)$ represents an instance of the *InterpreterUpdates* submetaclass of *Updates*, which relates an *Interpreter* to a *Feature*.

Table 2. CUI mappings

CUI mappings
Sensors
$R_p(PollingGlucoseSensor, GlucoseInterpreter)$
$R_p(PollingTemperatureSensor, TemperatureInterpreter)$
Features
$U(GlucoseInterpreter, Patient.glucose)$
$U(TemperatureInterpreter, Patient.temperature)$

To illustrate the use of the elements defined in the CUIModel, we will expose how the *temperature* feature is related to the environment.

The temperature is captured from the environment through a *Polling Temperature Sensor*. To poll the sensor, we have to link it to a *Polling Temperature Interpreter* in charge of requesting the sensor status and propagating it to the rest of the system.

Finally, the *Polling Temperature Interpreter* is linked to the *temperature* feature of the Patient role to propagate the changes from the environment.

4.5   The HealthyScreen FUI

The result of the *FUI* of a Patient is depicted in Figure 9. The first capture shows the UI for a Patient whose vital parameters are considered normal, the second one shows the UI for a Patient whose body temperature is above normal, and the third capture shows the UI for patients affected with HipoGlycemia or HyperGlycemia.

Finally, we show how the elements defined by the user awareness extension work together in this case of study. To see the effect of the user awareness, we set the initial state of the individual as *aNormal Patient*. Then, we modify the *temperature* feature of the individual, and we set it to 39 Celsius degrees.

This change in the temperature is captured by the *Polling Temperature Interpreter* that is constantly polling the *Polling Temperature Sensor* to be aware of the changes in the environment (in this case the user). Once the interpreter captures the information, it is propagated to the *temperature* feature defined by the Patient role. All features are linked to the features constraints that reference them. Thus, the chance is captured by the individual that is defined by these constraints. If all the feature constraints that are defined by the individual are satisfied then the individual is able to propagate this information through the *IndividualObserves* mappings to the AUI. Consequently, the UI is aware of the changes produced by the change on the temperature level.

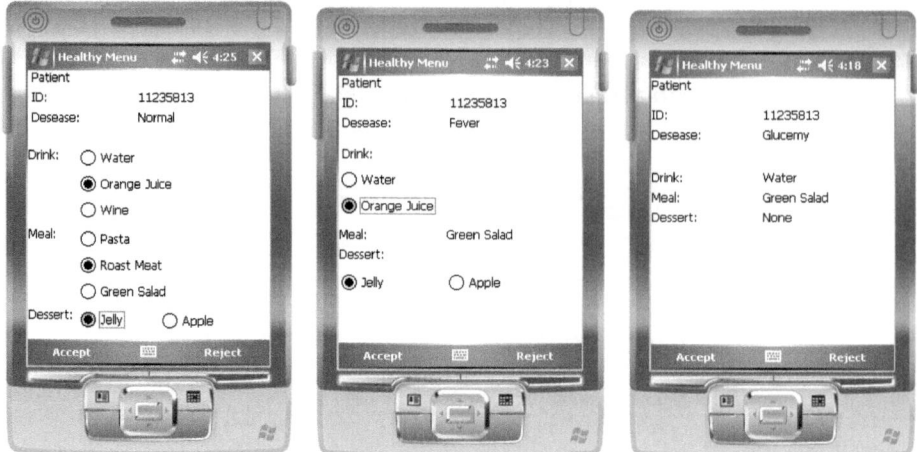

Fig. 9. Healthy Menu GUIs

5   Conclusions and Future Work

This work exposes a model-based approach to develop user-aware multi-platform and multi-modal UIs based on the UsiXML methodology. It encourages the separation of the user modeling from the application domain to improve the model reuse during the development of UIs.

The approach embraces all steps of the application. It means that covers from conceptual modeling of the user environment to the specification of the sensing infrastructure to support the different user profiles dynamically.

In the "Tasks & Concepts" step of the methodology, we introduced two levels to define custom characterizations of the users. While the first level allows designers to specify the user features that are taken into account by the application, the second one allows designers to quantify these characteristics in order to characterize a group of individuals that have common characteristics.

As consequence, designers are able to specify customized user characteristics instead of standard characteristics that are difficult to interpret because of their general nature. Besides, it provides designers the ability to characterize different groups of individuals that define the same characteristics, and so the user characterization can be easily reused.

This separation also allows the definition of static and dynamic characteristics at the same time in the same space of definition.

Finally, another advantage of using the UsiXML methodology is the separation of the definition of concepts and tasks from the definition of UIs. Thus, the characterization of users can be modified without having to modify the abstract user interface model, and vice versa.

As future work, we are actually working in the definition of an extension of the user awareness in order to model the social awareness of the user interfaces.

The social awareness allows the UI to be aware not only of the user is operating it; it makes the UI be aware of other users that are part of the system. Thus, we cover the description of the social environment of context aware applications.

Another issue we have considered as part of future works is the inclusion of the location awareness as part of the UI specification to cover other context aware characteristics of the UI, such as the infrastructure environment, user position, etc.

Finally, we are also working on the definition of a common feature-based framework allowing designers to express characteristics that are related to the combination of the social and location features of context-aware UIs, such as the co-location.

References

1. Barclay, P.J., Griffiths, T., McKirdy, J., Kennedy, J.B., Cooper, R., Paton, N.W., Gray, P.D.: Teallach - a flexible user-interface development environment for object database applications. J. Vis. Lang. Comput. 14(1), 47–77 (2003)
2. Calvary, G., Coutaz, J., Thevenin, D., Limbourg, Q., Bouillon, L., Vanderdonckt, J.: A unifying reference framework for multi-target user interfaces. Interacting with Computers 15(3), 289–308 (2003)
3. Crease, M., Gray, P.D., Brewster, S.A.: A toolkit of mechanism and context independent widgets. In: Palanque, P., Paternó, F. (eds.) DSV-IS 2000. LNCS, vol. 1946, pp. 121–133. Springer, Heidelberg (2001)
4. Dey, A.K.: Understanding and using context. Personal and Ubiquitous Computing 5, 4–7 (2001)
5. Eisenstein, J., Vanderdonckt, J., Puerta, A.R.: Applying model-based techniques to the development of uis for mobile computers. In: IUI, pp. 69–76 (2001)
6. Gamma, E., Helm, R., Johnson, R., Vlissides, J.: Design Patterns: Elements of Reusable Object-Oriented Software. Addison-Wesley, Reading (1995)
7. Limbourg, Q., Vanderdonckt, J., Michotte, B., Bouillon, L., López-Jaquero, V.: USIXML: A language supporting multi-path development of user interfaces. In: Bastide, R., Palanque, P., Roth, J. (eds.) DSV-IS 2004 and EHCI 2004. LNCS, vol. 3425, pp. 200–220. Springer, Heidelberg (2005)
8. Luyten, K., Laerhoven, T.V., Coninx, K., Reeth, F.V.: Runtime transformations for modal independent user interface migration. Interacting with Computers 15(3) (2003)
9. Mori, G., Paternò, F., Santoro, C.: CTTE: Support for developing and analyzing task models for interactive system design. IEEE Trans. on Soft. Eng. 28, 797–813 (2002)
10. Paternò, F., Santoro, C., Mäntyjärvi, J., Mori, G., Sansone, S.: Authoring pervasive multimodal user interfaces. Int. J. Web Eng. Technology 4(2) (2008)
11. Schmidt, A., Beigl, M., Gellersen, H.W.: There is more to context than location. Computers & Graphics 23(6), 893–901 (1999)
12. Spriestersbach, A., Ziegert, T., Grassel, G., Wasmund, M., Dermler, G.: A single source authoring language to enhance the access from mobile devices to web enterprise applications. In: WWW 2003 Developers Day Mobile Web Track, Springer, Heidelberg (2003) (not printed)

13. Tesoriero, R.: CAUCE: Model-driven Development of context-aware applications for ubiquitous computing environments. Ph.D. thesis, University of Castilla-La Mancha (December 2009)
14. Vanderdonckt, J.: A MDA-compliant environment for developing user interfaces of information systems. In: Pastor, Ó., Falcão e Cunha, J. (eds.) CAiSE 2005. LNCS, vol. 3520, pp. 13–17. Springer, Heidelberg (2005)
15. Vanderdonckt, J.M., Bodart, F.: Encapsulating knowledge for intelligent automatic interaction objects selection. In: Ashlund, S., Mullet, K., Henderson, A., Hollnagel, E., White, T. (eds.) Proc. of the Conf. on Human Factors in Computing Systems, pp. 424–429. ACM Press, New York (April 1993)
16. Weiser, M., Brown, J.S.: The coming age of calm technology. In: Denning, P.J., Metcalfe, R.M. (eds.) Beyond Calculation: The Next Fifty Years of Computing, pp. 75–85. Copernicus (1997)

The Secret Lives of Assumptions: Developing and Refining Assumption Personas for Secure System Design

Shamal Faily and Ivan Fléchais

Oxford University Computing Laboratory
Wolfson Building, Parks Road, Oxford OX1 3QD UK
{shamal.faily,ivan.flechais}@comlab.ox.ac.uk

Abstract. Personas are useful for obtaining an empirically grounded understanding of a secure system's user population, its contexts of use, and possible vulnerabilities and threats endangering it. Often, however, personas need to be partly derived from assumptions; these may be embedded in a variety of different representations. Assumption Personas have been proposed as boundary objects for articulating assumptions about a user population, but no methods or tools currently exist for developing and refining these within the context of secure and usable design. This paper presents an approach for developing and refining assumption personas before and during the design of secure systems. We present a model for structuring the contribution of assumptions to assumption personas, together with a process for developing assumption personas founded on this model. We also present some preliminary results based on an application of this approach in a recent case study.

1 Introduction

Personas are useful for obtaining a grounded understanding of a system's contexts of use, and communicating that understanding within a design team. Recent work on applying personas to help elicit and specify secure system requirements found that the data and analysis from which personas are derived also help identify threats and vulnerabilities [10]. Although adherents of personas argue that these should be primarily derived from real-world observations [7,14], the necessary resources for eliciting and analysing such data may not always be available. In these cases, it is necessary to rely on second-hand data about users and their contexts, much of which might be derived from assumptions.

Many usability professionals are familiar with analysing assumption-based usage data, but this may not be the case for software engineers. Engineers are usually employed for their technical expertise and domain knowledge; we cannot reasonably expect them to have a working knowledge of usability design techniques as well. They do, however, have tacit knowledge of the problem domain and a sensitivity to the values at play within its contexts of use. The challenge is to not only trace assumptions made about personas to their source, but to

R. Bernhaupt et al. (Eds.): HCSE 2010, LNCS 6409, pp. 111–118, 2010.

explicate the claims these assumptions represent. By doing so, we also explicate tacit knowledge about users and their contexts. Like data directly elicited from real-world observations, this data also suggests hitherto unknown threats and vulnerabilities related to a system.

Techniques from Design Rationale research are useful for tracking the refinement of assumptions to architectural components and software. Such techniques may also be useful for tracking the same assumptions to less refined concepts used in security analysis. Security design has the same needs for discharging potential ambiguity grounded in assumptions; these may be sources of attack vectors if the vulnerabilities they expose are exploited. In this paper, we present an approach for developing assumption personas for secure system design, and describe how this approach can be embedded into an existing design process and associated tool-support. In section 2, we briefly introduce personas and describe the related work motivating our approach. In section 3 we present an overview of our approach, and in section 4 we report on some preliminary findings which arose when applying this approach in a recent case-study.

2   Related Work

2.1   Personas and Assumption Personas

Personas are behavioural specifications of archetypical users. These were introduced by Cooper [6] to deal with programmer biases arising from the word *user*. These biases lead to programmers bending and stretching assumptions about users to meet their own expectations; Cooper called this phenomena *designing for the elastic user*. Personas are now a mainstay in User-Centered Design, with articles, book-chapters, and even a book [14] devoted to developing and applying them in practice. Personas have also been applied to Requirements Engineering, an area of intersection between HCI and Software Engineering [4].

Accepting that data-driven personas are an ideal rather than a norm, Pruitt & Adlin [14] proposed *Assumption Personas*: persona sketches created to articulate existing assumptions about an organisation's user population. These personas are grounded in assumptions contributors hold about users, and the context of investigation. These assumptions may be derived from interpreted or misinterpreted experiences, and coloured by individual and organisational values. Assumption Personas help people see the value of personas in design, and how different assumptions shape them. As a result, when exposed, they can guide subsequent analysis or data collection for data-driven personas.

Personas are not, however, without their critics. Chapman & Milham argue that, as fictional archetypes, personas are difficult to verify as there is no way to falsify them [5]. They further argue that questions remain about how personas should be reconciled with other information, understanding what data underpins their characteristics, and what happens when different interpretations are made from the same persona.

2.2   Integrating Personas with Secure Software Engineering

Chapman and Milham's criticism about the stand-alone nature of personas can be addressed by integrating them into the software engineering process. This has been the subject of our recent work on the IRIS (Integrating Requirements and Information Security) framework, which integrates usability into the design of secure software systems [8]. As part of this work, a meta-model for usable secure requirements engineering was devised, which integrates the persona with other concepts in usability, security, and software engineering. From this model, we have developed CAIRIS (Computer Aided Integration of Requirements and Information Security): a tool for managing information about personas and other design elements, and evaluating the effect to security and usability of different design decisions [1]. CAIRIS manages requirements, task, and risk data, and automatically generates different types of visual model to represent the ongoing analysis. We demonstrate this approach in [9] by illustrating how categorical information about a task performed by a pre-defined persona is associated with the results of risk analysis, and how the usability of this task can be visually represented before and after a related risk is mitigated.

In [10], we presented a process for developing personas for secure systems; this is based on collecting and analysing empirical data from qualitative and contextual interviews. The personas derived from analysing this data were validated and further refined in participatory requirements and risk analysis workshops. We also found that empirical data used to derive personas could be re-used for other analysis.

Even though personas may be grounded in empirical data, the quandary about the validity of personas remains. It may be possible to verify the quality of the empirical-data or the robustness of the methodology to develop them, but we cannot easily falsify the representativeness of personas. The vision of the system may be tentative enough that what may have been valid working assumptions at the beginning of the persona development process may be invalid by the time the personas are presented to project stakeholders. It is, therefore, useful to understand how characteristics about personas track back to their assumptions, and why.

2.3   Toulmin's Model of Argumentation

Codifying the rationale underpinning assumption personas guides analysis and decision making, but the *rationale capture problem*, characterised by the reluctance of those involved in design activities to record their rationale, cannot be ignored [3]. Although the Design Rationale community has proposed several different approaches for building rationale capture into the design process, the Security and Requirements Engineering community has taken a recent interest in capturing rationale using the vehicle of informal argumentation. These approaches are founded on Toulmin's Argumentation Model: a logical structure for reasoning about the validity of arguments [15], the elements of which are defined in table 1.

Table 1. Elements of Toulmin's Argumentation Model

Element	Description
Claim	A proposition representing a claim being made in an argument.
Grounds	One or more propositions acting as evidence justifying the Claim.
Warrant	One or more rules of inference describing how the Grounds contribute to the Claim.
Backing	The knowledge establishing the Grounds for believing the Warrant.
Modal Qualifier	A phrase qualifying the degree of certainty in the argument for the Claim.
Rebuttal	One or more propositions challenging the validity of the Claim.

Alexander & Beus-Dukic describe a number of simple rationale models for Requirements Engineering based on this structure [2]. From a security standpoint, Haley et al. have proposed using Toulmin's model to support arguments for security requirements [11]. In their approach, an argument for a system satisfying its security requirements is presented for analysis. Each proposition within this argument is treated as a Claim, and argued accordingly. Rebuttals represent *Trust Assumptions*; these can be countered as part of another security argument, or examined in subsequent threat modelling activities.

3   Approach

We have chosen to embrace, rather than ignore, the contribution assumptions make to assumption persona design. We propose a novel approach to structuring the contribution of assumptions to persona specifications, and integrating this conceptual structure into an existing approach for secure systems design.

3.1   Developing Assumption Personas

Personas are usually represented as a narrative describing the behaviour of an archetypical user. Authoring these narratives remains a creative exercise, but we propose augmenting these by structuring the assumption data contributing to them. We have aligned this structure to Toulmin's Model of Argumentation, introduced in section 2.3. Adopting this approach allows us to treat assumptions directly contributing to part of the narrative as a Claim. The task of justifying this Claim both strengthens the foundations of the persona, and guides subsequent elicitation and analysis activities. These Claims are represented conceptually using one of more *Characteristics*; these are propositions about a specific aspect of a persona's behaviour. Characteristics are categorised according to one of the behavioural variable types defined by IRIS personas; these are based

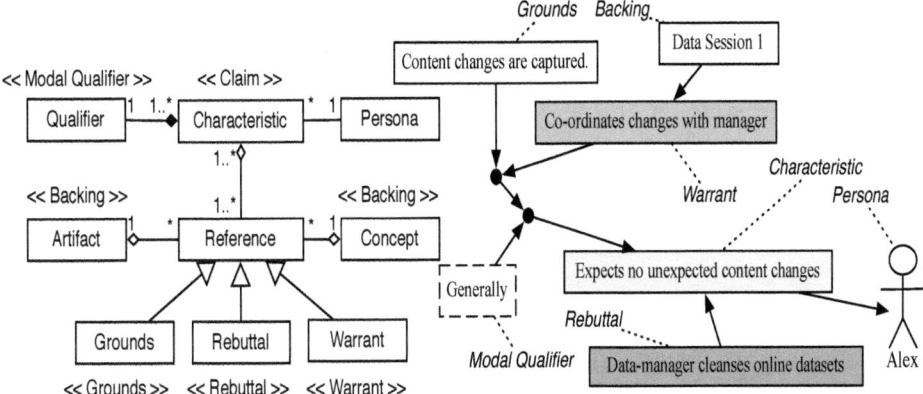

Fig. 1. Conceptual model of assumption persona data (left), and Toulin model visualisation based on an individual characteristic (right)

on the behavioural variable types proposed by Cooper [7]: activities, attitudes, aptitudes, motivations, and skills. Also associated with a Characteristic is a qualifying phrase representing the strength of belief in the Characteristic; this qualifying phrase aligns with the Modal Qualifier in Toulmin's model.

Persona Characteristics originate from one of two sources. The first source is some form of *Artifact*: a document related to the problem domain or the system being specified, such as a specification, or a transcript from an interview or design workshop. The second is a design *Concept*: an instance of an object defined within the work-in-progress IRIS analysis, such as a description for an asset, a goal or requirement, or even another persona. Because an individual source may give rise to multiple Characteristics of the same or different behavioural categories, a *Reference* is associated with a given source and Characteristic. The contents of a Reference will depend on the source type. In the case of an Artifact, a reference contains information tying an attributable piece of information or comment to a source document or verbal comment, e.g. page number, document version, or person. In the case of a Concept, a Reference contains the name and type of the contributing concept. In both cases, the Reference will contain as much textual attribution information as necessary to justify the persona's Characteristic. The name of the Reference object is a synoptic proposition of this attribution information. With regards to Toulmin's model, References align to either Grounds, Warrants, or Rebuttals. Where a Reference represents a Warrant, the corresponding Artifact or Concept acts as the Warrant's Backing.

The meta-model in figure 1 (left) summarises these concepts and their relationships. The stereotypes adjacent to each class represent the corresponding concept name from Toulmin's model.

3.2   Applying and Refining the Assumption Personas

Before assumption personas are used, they are presented to a workshop or focus group containing representative system stakeholders. Following this workshop, the remaining steps of the process are carried out in the context of smaller design sessions, as described by [10]. These sessions entail requirements and risk analysis activities, where, rather than referring to users, personas are used in their place. In both the workshop and design sessions, new assumptions about personas may be identified, or existing assumptions challenged. Armed with the proposed meta-model, tool-support can be developed to elicit the structural elements of the assumption persona argumentation model. Aside from guiding and structuring the elicitation of assumption data, the structured argument of Characteristics can be cross-checked with the persona narrative. If it becomes difficult to write a believable narrative based on the Characteristics identified, then these need to be re-evaluated.

We modified the CAIRIS tool introduced in section 2.2 to illustrate how tool-support can take advantage of this approach. As well as allowing Characteristics associated with a persona to be quickly reviewed against the narrative, we found that Characteristics could be quickly created or modified when assumptions are introduced or challenged during design sessions. Structuring the data according to the meta-model also facilitates the automatic generation of visual Toulmin models for persona Characteristics. An example of such a model for a specific Characteristic is provided in figure 1 (right).

Unsubstantiated Claims and Rebuttals are also an additional source of risk analysis information. In the case of the latter, obstacles – conditions representing undesired behaviour preventing an associated goal from being achieved [12] – can be elicited from these, and its placement guided by the related Characteristic negated by the Rebuttal. This placement guidance is possible because a persona invariably participates in tasks operationalised by one or more goals or requirements.

4   Preliminary Results

We used this approach to help specify requirements for an online portal for a medical research project. The nature of this project was such that eliciting empirical data from representative users during the study was impossible. During the course of the project, an assumption persona – Alex – was developed to embody the assumptions held by the project team about the researchers expected to use the portal. The assumptions underpinning this persona were initially derived from a high-level requirements specification document developed by a different team within the same project; as such, Alex represented the assumptions that team had made about the expected user population. After developing this persona, a half-day workshop was held with the complete project team to agree the scope for a subsequent requirements and risk analysis of the portal. During this workshop, Alex was presented to the team. The team both agreed and disagreed with the characteristics of Alex. Where there was disagreement, the structured nature of the assumption data was used to track the questionable characteristic to its originating source, which was discussed in more detail within the team. Following the workshop, a number of new assumptions were elicited, which formed the basis of new characteristics about Alex.

After the workshop, three 2-hour design sessions were held with team members to carry out requirements and risk analysis relating to two specific tasks carried out by Alex. As part of this analysis, scenarios were developed describing how Alex would carry out these tasks with the aid of the portal. During these sessions, Alex's characteristics evolved; by the end of the 3rd session, 23 different Characteristics about Alex had been captured. Some of these were modifications to assumptions captured in the initial stages of persona development, but several were derived from assumptions which surfaced while eliciting other concepts, such as tasks and goals. In all cases, these characteristics were justified by Grounds, and in many cases, a Warrant and Backing were also elicited.

Haley & Nuseibeh [13] observed that experts provide essential domain knowledge about the subtleties of threats, but non-experts ask journalist questions challenging implicit assumptions assumed by the domain expert. Our preliminary results during the design sessions concur with this observation. When the tasks carried out by one of the personas was modelled during one session, one non-expert participant raised pertinent points about implicit assumptions in the task description; these were not accounted for by the personas, and led to the rebuttal of one Characteristic.

Although identifying Grounds for Characteristics was found to be straightforward, identifying Warrants provided to be more difficult. In particular, we found that, prior to their initial validation, many of the Characteristics were based exclusively on Grounds, rather than Warrants as well. As such, value judgements about the source data and the context were directly reflected in these Characteristics. Although the initial workshop surfaced a number of these issues, it was usually not until the personas were directly used to model tasks in design sessions that many invalid Characteristics were identified. Applying the personas within a specific context did, however, help identify missing inferential data, or guide the refactoring of the argumentation structure for affected Characteristics.

5   Conclusion

Personas are a mainstay in User-Centered Design, yet there is a dearth of guidance on how to build and refine these from assumptions, as opposed to empirical data. We believe this guidance, and corresponding tool-support, may contribute to a wider adoption of personas in secure software engineering, and a better understanding of how to use these in a secure software engineering context. This paper makes three contributions towards these ends. First, we have presented a model for structuring the assumptions contributing to personas; to help guide subsequent analysis, this model has been aligned these with Toulmin's Model of Argumentation. Second, we have illustrated how tool support reifies this structured model, and guides subsequent risk analysis. Finally, we have reported some of the preliminary results validating our approach in a recent case study. A more detailed report of this study will appear as a future publication.

Acknowledgements

The research described in this paper was funded by EPSRC CASE Studentship R07437/CN001. We are very grateful to Qinetiq Ltd for their sponsorship of this work.

References

1. CAIRIS web site, http://www.comlab.ox.ac.uk/cairis
2. Alexander, I., Beus-Dukic, L.: Discovering requirements: how to specify products and services. Wiley, Chichester (2009)
3. Burge, J.E., Carroll, J.M., McCall, R., Mistrik, I.: Rationale-Based Software Engineering. Springer, Heidelberg (2008)
4. Castro, J., Acua, S., Juristo, N.: Integrating the personas technique into the requirements analysis activity. In: Mexican International Conference on Computer Science, ENC 2008, pp. 104–112 (October 2008)
5. Chapman, C.N., Milham, R.P.: The persona's new clothes: Methodological and practical arguments against a popular method. In: Proceedings of the Human Factors and Ergonomics Society 50th Annual Meeting (2006)
6. Cooper, A.: The Inmates Are Running the Asylum: Why High Tech Products Drive Us Crazy and How to Restore the Sanity, 2nd edn. Pearson Higher Education (1999)
7. Cooper, A., Reimann, R., Cronin, D.: About Face 3: The Essentials of Interaction Design. Wiley, Chichester (2007)
8. Faily, S., Fléchais, I.: A Meta-Model for Usable Secure Requirements Engineering. In: ICSE Workshop on Software Engineering for Secure Systems, SESS 2010, pp. 126–135. IEEE Computer Society Press, Los Alamitos (May 2010)
9. Faily, S., Fléchais, I.: Analysing and Visualising Security and Usability in IRIS. In: Fifth International Conference on Availability, Reliability and Security, ARES 2010 (2010)
10. Faily, S., Fléchais, I.: Barry is not the weakest link: Eliciting Secure System Requirements with Personas. In: Proceedings of the 2010 British Computer Society Conference on Human-Computer Interaction BCS HCI 2010 (to appear, 2010)
11. Haley, C.B., Laney, R., Moffett, J.D., Nuseibeh, B.: Arguing satisfaction of security requirements. In: Mouratidis, H., Giorgini, P. (eds.) Integrating Security and Software Engineering, ch. 2, pp. 16–43. Idea Group, USA (2007)
12. van Lamsweerde, A., Letier, E.: Handling obstacles in goal-oriented requirements engineering. IEEE Transactions on Software Engineering 26(10), 978–1005 (2000)
13. Nuseibeh, B., Haley, C., Foster, C.: Securing the skies: In requirements we trust. Computer 42(9), 64–72 (2009)
14. Pruitt, J., Adlin, T.: The persona lifecycle: keeping people in mind throughout product design. Elsevier, Amsterdam (2006)
15. Toulmin, S.: The uses of argument. Cambridge University Press, Cambridge (2003) (updated edn.)

Dazed and Confused Considered Normal: An Approach to Create Interactive Systems for People with Dementia

Nasim Mahmud[1], Joël Vogt[2], Kris Luyten[1], Karin Slegers[3], Jan Van den Bergh[1], and Karin Coninx[1]

[1] Hasselt University - tUL - IBBT, Expertise Centre for Digital Media, Wetenschapspark 2, B-3590 Diepenbeek, Belgium
{nasim.mahmud,kris.luyten,jan.vandenbergh,karin.coninxg}@uhasselt.be
[2] Department of Informatics, University of Fribourg, Boulevard de Pérolles 90, CH-1700 Fribourg, Switzerland
joel.vogt@unifr.ch
[3] Centre for User Experience Research (CUO), IBBT / K.U. Leuven Parkstraat 45 bus 3605, B-3000 Leuven, Belgium
karin.slegers@soc.kuleuven.be

Abstract. In Western society, the elderly represent a rapidly growing demographic group. For this group, dementia has become an important cause of dependencies on others and causes difficulties with independent living. Typical symptoms of the dementia syndrome are decreased location awareness and difficulties in situating ones activities in time, thus hindering long term plans and activities. We present our approach in creating an interactive system tailored for the needs of the early phases of the dementia syndrome. Given the increasing literacy with mobile technologies in this group, we propose an approach that exploits mobile technology in combination with the physical and social context to support prolonged independent living. Our system strengthens the involvement of caregivers through the patient's social network. We show that applications for people suffering from dementia can be created by explicitly taking into account context in the design process. Context dependencies that are defined in an early stage in the development process are propagated as part of the runtime behavior of the interactive system.

1 Introduction

In Europe, at least half of the elderly population who suffer from dementia, have mild form of dementia [24]. Elderly citizens who are suffering from any form of dementia, are increasingly dependent on their social environment. Although people in early stages of dementia, are often able to perform everyday tasks without help. Their dependence on caregivers and need for assistance increases as the dementia syndrome progresses. This dependency puts strains on both the patients and their caregivers. As a patient's dependency on caregivers grows, patients feel reluctant to leave their home for the fear of getting lost, losing track

R. Bernhaupt et al. (Eds.): HCSE 2010, LNCS 6409, pp. 119–134, 2010.

of time or forgetting their goals. While the person with dementia is outside on his own, caregivers are burdened by worrying for the patients' safety.

In sum, during the course of the dementia syndrome, patients are likely to be *less autonomous*. They increasingly *depend on caregivers* with respect to their everyday tasks and activities. Most of the cases, in the early or mild stages of dementia, the caregiver is a family member or friend [30], thus part of the informal social network of the patient. A solution to this problem might both increase patients independence and relieve caregivers from (parts of) the stress they experience while taking care of their relative with dementia. A potential solution might be found in the realm of virtual *connectedness* to the social context.

In this paper we show how to map two of the main issues with dementia on the design of a mobile interactive systems. Roughly, people with dementia suffer from being *lost in time and lost in space*. Space and time are two important aspects that are taken into account in typical context-aware user interfaces [10,1]. Besides these typical contextual parameters, the social network itself is also considered as part of the context in our approach. This implies that these contextual parameters (time, space and social network) should be part of the design process for building an interactive systems for people with dementia.

In order to validate our concept, we have developed a prototype of an interactive system, which is an aiding tool for persons with dementia. The prototype was built taking into account the important factors for independence of persons with dementia as mentioned above time, location and social network of a person with dementia to provide context aware help. It offers help only when it is necessary, without patronizing the user all the time.

2   Background

2.1   Dementia

Dementia is a term for a syndrome related to the loss of cognitive functions. It is usually the result of conditions that cause dysfunction of the brain. Draper [12] defines the dementia syndrome as an acquired decline in memory and thinking (cognition) due to brain disease that results in significant impairment of personal, social or occupational function. He explains that other brain functions such as orientation, language, reasoning and language processing are also affected. Dementia progresses over time. However the progression of dementia is individual and different brain functions do not decline at the same rate, some symptoms develop later in the course of the disease than others. The progression of dementia can be roughly classified according to the degree of severity. For example, by applying the scale developed by Leonard Berg [20]. The focus of this paper is on questionable and mild dementia. Further stages require increasing personal caring, which is outside the scope of our work. Dementia also puts enormous strains on the patients social context, especially as dementia progresses [12]. In most cases, the caregivers are spouses and when they can no longer care for the patient, their children take over [30]. In a comparative study between caregivers for dementia and caregivers for non-dementia people, Ory et al. [26] found that the former was in almost all aspects more demanding than the latter.

2.2   Assistive Social Navigation

As mentioned earlier a person with dementia needs help with memory, spatial and temporal orientation. A context aware reminder and navigation system can help to partly regain independence by providing focused navigation information when necessary.

People often make decisions about their actions based on what other people have done in the past or on what other people have recommended them. This process is referred to as everyday social navigation [11]. When people need clue about some actions or things, they mostly base their decisions and actions on recommendations by people they know or people who share at least some common ground (e.g. person buying a book may also want to see what other people bought, who bought the same book). The process of finding the required information source and identifying the relevant information requires a lot of effort when it has to be performed in situ. An alternative method is to gather information by asking other people for advice [21]. Identifying the appropriate person for answering questions in a particular context and in suitable time is not a straightforward task [19], it is difficult even for people who do not suffer from dementia.

This becomes more difficult for a person with dementia, especially when he is spatially or temporally disoriented. Because of the disorientation, he becomes frustrated and it gets more difficult for him to formulate his enquiry. Assistive social navigation is *tailor made* information provided as suggestion for a particular end user. The suggestion is produced by a familiar person e.g. caregiver. In our case, the end user is the elderly person with dementia who needs information or help to complete any tasks by himself. When a person with dementia is lost in time or space (e.g. forgets where he is, where he is going or what he is supposed to do), he usually cannot get back to his normal state immediately. A person with dementia is often aware that he is lost, or he forgot his goal [29]. In this kind of frustrating situation he is unable to carry out his normal activity. Often he can recall his goal with some clues. But only his informal caregiver (e.g. spouse), who is aware about him and his tasks, can easily provide that targeted clues. Thus the caregiver can assist the person with dementia to navigate to complete his tasks only when it is needed; maintaining his autonomy when he is not disoriented.

2.3   Technologies for Dementia Aid

The need for independence for both people with dementia and their caregivers is commonly agreed on by researchers in the field [31,29,14]. Mulvenna et al. [24] conducted a study to analyze the need of people with dementia and their caregivers. They chartered the needs for more independence by means of *memory assistance* and by providing more context such as *spatial and temporal orientation, social contact and, social interaction.* The person(s) who are in early stages or in mild stages of dementia are capable of living independently, and have occasional need for help [2]. A context-aware system can exert such support without patronizing the user. Based on these findings, the context-of-use will be explicitly taken into account in our approach to create an *interactive systems* that prolog independent living of elderly people with early and mild dementia.

Over the last decade, numerous IT-based support system for elderly people with dementia have been proposed [22,17,29]. One of the main objectives of those was to ensure helping elderly people live a safe and independent life. Providing cognitive support as a way of improving quality of life in general [16] has also been proposed. There are different ways in which such system offered support for independent living in some extent such as, tele-monitoring, reminding important activities [13], such as time to take medication etc. Reminder is a form of usually short message that helps people remember what is to be done. It consists of two independent features, signal and description [28]. An alarm clock could be a signal only reminder whereas an email notification is both visual signal and text description of the task to be done. Dey et. al. [9] proposed context-aware reminder system, other reminder system taking into account time, location, user present in the vicinity, user's activity.

Robinson et al. [29] developed a prototype to facilitate independent living for patients with light dementia that includes a communication platform for patients with dementia and their families. Hettinga et al. [16] evaluated the safety of navigation aid for people with mild dementia. The authors conclude that there is no evidence suggesting that the use of navigation devices for people with mild dementia are unsafe. Miskelly used a tracking system to define safe zones for persons with dementia. When the dementia person left the safe zone, the caregiver would receive a notification with name of person, location and cause [23]. Social awareness has been studied to enrich context information to provide context aware and appropriate help for nomadic persons [19,5], and limited social awareness such phone book with the picture of social contact for persons with light or mild dementia has been proposed [8]. In our approach, we combine navigation aid and tracking system along with reminder service and social awareness as a mediator, to provide a tool to plan and assist activities of daily living to regain independence.

3   Scenario

This section motivates the use of an assistive application for a person with dementia. We use the COMuICSer approach presented by Haesen et al. in [15]. This approach uses a storyboard to reveal important information on the context of the user and helps to elicit the requirements to be taken into account. Furthermore, based on [18] it provides us with context information for usage in other models instantaneously.

A storyboard illustrating a regular day for a person with mild dementia is shown in Fig. 1. The storyboard depicts the sequence of activities that the person with dementia performed during that day. At one point, the person with dementia loses his orientation and cannot perform his task without help. At this point, the storyboard introduces other roles, such as a caregiver, that support the target user of our system. This information will be fed in the construction of the social network underpinning the target application.

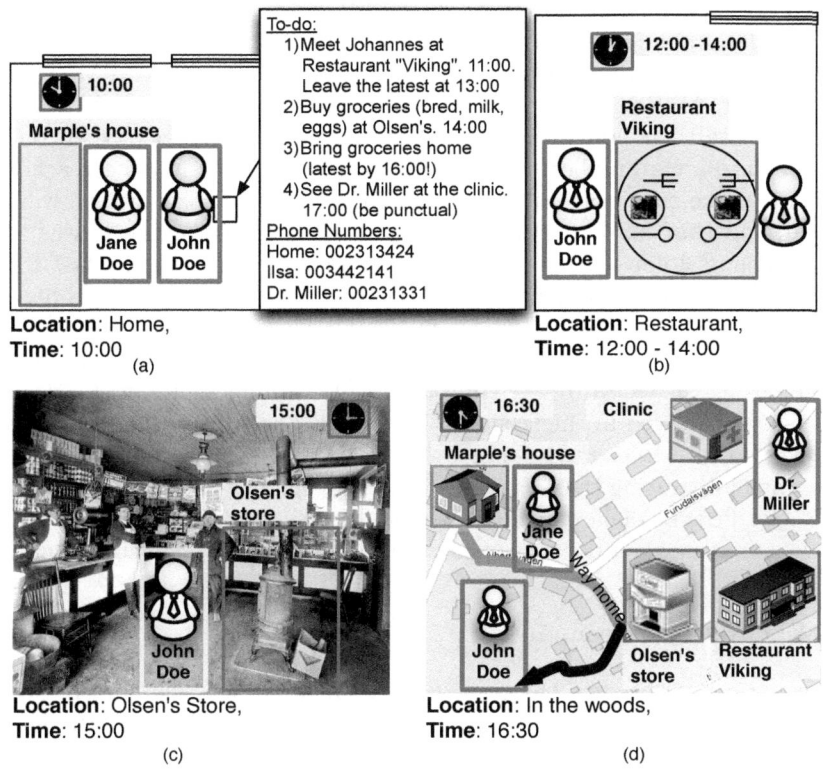

Fig. 1. A day in Mr. John Doe's life, a) Jane helps John to plan his day, b) John meets his friend at the restaurant, c) John buys groceries and d) John is lost

The depicted scenario of Fig. 1 goes as follows: John is in his early seventies, married to Jane. They have been living in a small village for more than three decades. Their daughter Ilsa is married and lives in the same village. John is a retired school teacher. He is an enthusiastic bird watcher and spends a lot of his time on this hobby. Since his retirement, he enjoys reading books and hiking. Lately he started forgetting things but managed to hide it from Jane by taking notes or blaming it on others. But now he started having difficulties to find his way back home. This happens even when he is in familiar places he has known for years. Initially he took this very lightly and did not pay attention. Until one day it took John an exceptionally long time to arrive back home; he was lost and came back with the help of nomadic foresters. Jane became highly worried after this incident. She started watching her husband more closely and noticed that her husband forgets small things on a regular basis as well. After talking to the family doctor and friend, Dr. Miller, he was diagnosed as having early stage of dementia. This diagnosis was made two months ago. Since then, John has been quite sad. He often worries about his future and gets angry a lot when he cannot remember things.

Today, John planned to go to local restaurant, and to the grocery shop afterwards. Next, he will come back home. In the late afternoon at 5PM he is going to the see Dr. Miller. In the morning, Jane made a simple to-do list on paper. She also wrote their home phone number, the phone number of their daughter Ilsa and the phone number of Dr. Miller, in case she cannot be reached. She wanted to make sure that John does not forget all his tasks that he wanted to perform, and that he does not feel afraid of getting lost again. It was already after 4PM and John did not come back home yet (shown in the last frame of Fig. 1). Jane started worrying, should she call him to check everything is OK and remind him where he needed to go?

Besides having the sequence of actions crystallized and overview of the context of use by using the COMuICSer approach, it also provides support for describing the personas involved in the scenario. Next in our approach, these personas will be converted into roles in the user interface. The personas can also be used as filters when integrating the social network, i.e. when the patient requires support from a specific type of caregiver the persona can be used as an indication for this type. In our scenario a doctor acts as the caregiver in the depicted situation.

3.1 Elicited Requirements

The scenario presented in the previous section describes the current situation and reveals the requirements for an interactive system for persons with dementia. We want to emphasize the following context of use especially plays an important role for our target application:

- the dementia person's time and location
- the caregivers' time and location
- the social context and the participants' states, e.g. a caregiver is busy or available

Time and location deserve special attention, since these are two parts of the context of use that a person with dementia has the most difficulties with. This means a mismatch between the time and location of the person with dementia with the time and location on which a specific task should be executed needs to be explicitly handled by the resulting interactive system. A task and dialog model provide more insight in how the system can actually support the user.

The scenario further hints at the computing devices and communication services that should be available to support an improved scenario. For our purpose, a smartphone is sufficient to support the tasks and activities at hand.

4   Approach

4.1   User Interface Design Considerations for People with Dementia

Based on the scenario outlined in the previous section and related work in Sect. 2.3, it is clear that the design of an interactive system for elderly people with symptoms of early or mild dementia poses a number of challenges. Besides typical physical age-related impairments, such as reduced eye sight, decreasing motor skills or hearing difficulties, dementia adds further requirements to the interface design. The *deteriorating short term memory, spatial and temporal orientation* and the increasing difficulties with performing complex tasks make traditional user interfaces very difficult to use for dementia patients. Newell et al. [25] make several recommendations for the design of information technology for people with cognitive impairments. These are classified based on the type of impairment:

- *Mitigate memory impairment.* The interface should be simple and limit the possibilities for error. Users should be able to recognize errors and correct them. The system can assist by providing feedback and asking, where appropriate, the user to confirm an action and offer sensible reminders and prompts. Additionally, the user interface can assist the user's memory by providing navigation in the interaction.
- *Avoid cognitive overload.* The interface should limit options and be simple. Whenever possible, the dialog flow should be linear and parallel tasks possibly avoided.
- *Take into account individual characteristics of dementia.* Systems for patients with cognitive impairments must be adaptable to the patient's personal conditions that change over time.

The first two guidelines are appropriate for every end user and are especially desirable for people with dementia. Due to their cognitive decline, persons with dementia have difficulties performing parallel tasks and recalling the flow of task even if they are familiar with the task.

Context-awareness is a key feature to achieve personalized, situation-aware adaption of services, which is in accordance with the guidelines described above. Context-aware interactive systems are able to adapt according to the situational context in which they are executed. The context includes characteristics of the user, the device, the environment or a combination of these. Context can be used as input in the design process (for the parts that are known beforehand) and processed during runtime usage of an interactive system [6]. The latter ensures adaptability of the system while it is being used.

4.2   A Model Driven Design Approach

As appropriate handling of context is crucial to our application, we explored ways to effectively take all the relevant context influences into account from the start of the development process. Task models, such as the ConcurTaskTree (CTT) [27], are established starting points in the development process of interactive systems, such as the reference framework proposed by [6]. We explored the usage of the Contextual ConcurTaskTrees [4]. This allowed us to effectively represent influences of context changes on the tasks. However, the high-level of abstraction and the restricted set of information proved too limited to effectively create the application.

We thus looked for a more concrete notation that helped in clarifying the overall picture. Robinson et al. [29] developed applications for people with dementia and suggest eliciting the users requirement into the design by using storyboards. This improves the involvement of all stakeholders in the elicitation process. A storyboard is also a useful tool to capture the context of use. It clearly helps to highlight the social context of the persons who are communicating.

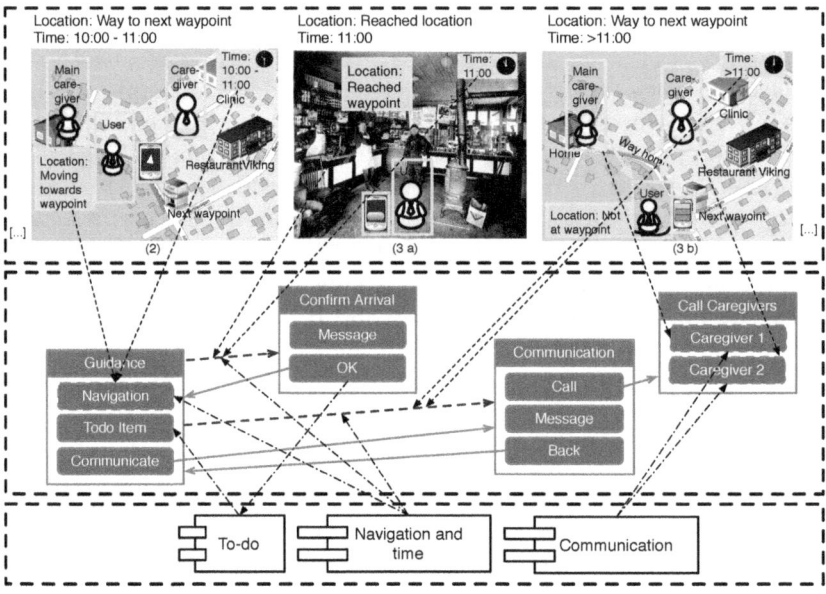

Fig. 2. Relation between the models used to develop the system. On the top, part of the storyboard showing the actors and their context. In the middle, the dialog model and arrows pointing the involvement of context and at the bottom, application model arrows showing influence on the dialog and the presentation model.

Section 3.1 and 4.1 discussed the requirements for the interactive system for a person with dementia. A storyboard is drawn that described the person with dementia and the caregivers using the system that fulfills the requirements in Sect. 3.1. The storyboard shows a sequence of scenes depicting the situations and context in which the interactive system needs to operate. A scene shows the person with dementia and his mobile device and other (secondary) users (e.g. caregivers). We also add the time and place of a scene. Each scene is also accompanied by a textual description that further specifies the details. We used the COMuICSer tool [15] to annotate important characteristics in the storyboard (e.g. actors, location, time) and textual scene description.

The storyboard depicts the caregivers and the location and time when the user performs an activity. For example, one scene shows the user visiting the doctor at a certain time and place. The last scene shows the person with dementia getting lost. This scene hints at an incident were the person with dementia may require help. The context information time and location are associated with events that occur when certain predefined context rules are triggered. For example, the user is not at a given location at a predefined time or the user has reached the location for this task on time. The specific rules that are triggered by this context information are discussed into detail in Sect. 5.5. We further used low fidelity prototyping by sketching the user interfaces that would be shown to the user in the different scenes of the storyboard.

Based on the specifications captured by the storyboard (top of Fig. 2), we defined a dialog model (middle of Fig. 2) that describes the behavior of the application. The sequence of scenes indicates the states in the dialog model and how they are connected. The visual nature of the COMuICSer storyboard allows to easily identify all aspects of the context that are relevant for each state in the dialog model. Context events that are related to time and location trigger affect the flow of the dialog. The dotted arrows in Fig. 2 indicate this influence. In contrast with typical behavior of context-aware systems, the system does not adapt its presentation according to the context of use but tries to figure out how it can help the user to accomplish the tasks at hand. This means the context is not used to automate the system but rather the system works in a mixed initiative approach, the goal is to empower the user by pro-actively providing information cues and making suggestions.

Next, we need to create the presentation that exposes the behavior described in the previous paragraph. First, we have the presentation based on the sketches done in the earlier stage of the development. The presentation model and dialog model link is established by sketching the interfaces for the different scenes and clearly relating them with each other. There is also a link between the social context and the presentation model that needs to be taken into account. The availability states of caregivers are represented differently; we chose distinct colors for that purpose.

In the last step, the components of the system and their functionality are defined. This is taken as well from the requirements captured at the start of the development process. We identified a component for the to-do list manager, the social network, a component for location-based events and for time-based events. These components are described with the application model (bottom of Fig. 2).

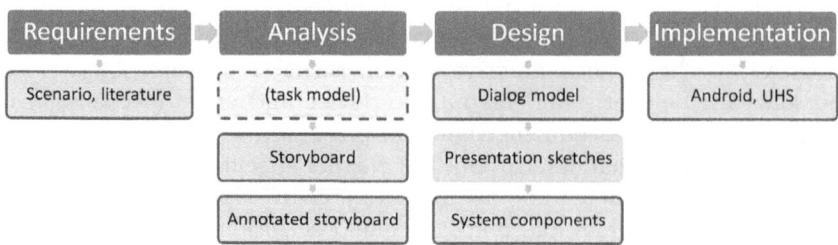

Fig. 3. The development process, fine grained steps in which context, and context influences are explicitly described have borders with full lines

The application model is then linked to the dialog and presentation model for orchestrating the behavior of the overall system.

The links between the application model and the dialog model are bi–directional: from the dialog model, functions described in the application model can be called. Dialog changes that are initiated by the application logic are triggered through time and location related events. Section 5.5 provides more details about these events. The link between the application model and presentation model determines how objects that are returned by an application are displayed. For example, depending on the availability status, a caregiver is displayed differently.

Figure 3 summarizes the different steps taken to develop our application. It clearly shows the mix informal and abstract formal notations during the development process and the explicit definition of context (influences) in almost all steps from the start of the development process. The task model step has a dashed border because the information it provided was not complete enough and could be completely replaced by the storyboard.

5   The Resulting System

5.1   Overview

Our system consists of three main building blocks: the user interface, context rules and the application logic. The user interface layer consists of three parts, namely 1) the to-do list and navigation module that is used by the person with dementia, 2) The to-do list manager that is the interface for the primary caregiver to manage the to-do list of the person with dementia and 3) the communication module that connects the person with dementia with the caregivers. The application logic consists of 1) the context module that receives time and location information, 2) the to-do list repository that stores the plans for the person with dementia and 3) the social network that connects the person with dementia with his or her social context. Between the user interface and the application logic reside the context rules. The rules use the current time and location, and assigned time and location for the current task to change the dialog.

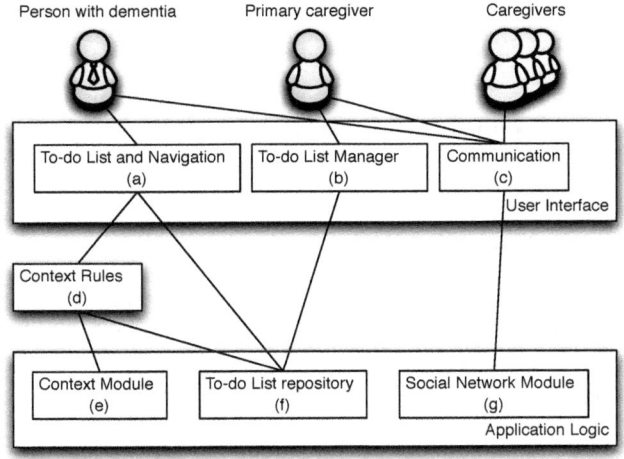

Fig. 4. System overview

The system runs on different communicating devices: the person with dementia uses a smart phone that runs Google Android. The communicating caregivers can use any Java enabled communicating devices that can connect to the phone network and the Internet. In the prototype described in this paper, the behavior of the system is presented in Java. The description of the user interface presentation uses the native XML user interface description language of the Google Android platform.

5.2 To-Do List and Navigation

The to-do list and navigation (see Fig. 4(a)) is used by the person with dementia to navigate through his plan. It receives the plan from the to-do list repository. The main navigation display shows information about the current task that is relevant to the user. This is an arrow indicating the direction where the user is expected to go, the name and time of the current task and a button that takes switches to the communication interface. An example of the to-do list and navigation interface is shown in Fig. 5(b). The to-do list and navigation module receives the location information from the context module through the context rules. This corresponds to the linking between the dialog model and the application model (see Fig. 2). The rules initiate intra and inter-dialog changes in response to the current time and location, and time and location associated with the current task.

5.3 To-Do List Manager

The to-do list manager (see Fig. 4(b)) is used by the primary caregiver, in most cases the spouse, to compile a plan for person with dementia. A plan is a set of tasks that is uploaded to the to-do list repository which is accessed by the to-do list navigator of the person with dementia. For each new task the caregiver defines the name and description of the task, the time and location associated with this task and possible relevant caregivers (e.g. daughter, brother, personal physician). To avoid confusing the user, the list of the caregivers defined at this stage are always displayed in the communication screen (see 5(c)).

5.4   Communication Module

The communication module (see Fig. 4(c)) offers a communication channel between the person with dementia and his caregivers. The person with dementia can choose between selecting predefined text messages or making a phone call. The list of available caregivers is provided during run-time via an XML-RPC connection from the social network module, discussed in Sect. 5.7. The caregivers are marked in a color that depicts their availability status. This is shown in Fig. 5(c). It also contains an option to return to the navigation screen.

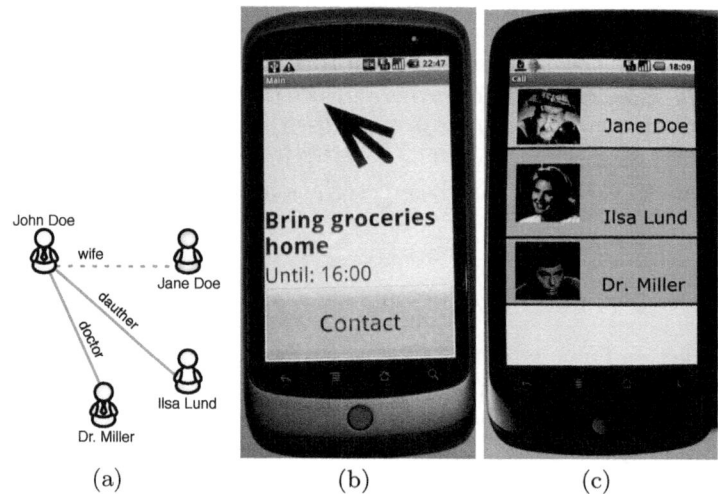

(a)   (b)   (c)

Fig. 5. The system in action, 5(a) visualization of the social network, dashed line represents unavailable user 5(b) navigation screen showing the navigation arrow pointing towards the location of the current task to perform, as well as information about the task and 5(c) communication screen showing list of caregivers, their availability status is distinguished by colors

5.5   Context Module and Context Rules

The context module (see Fig. 4(e)) listens for time and location information. These are passed to the context rules (see Fig. 4(d)). The context module is implemented as a location listener that is registered with the the Google Android platform Location Manager to receive location updates. It further contains a local thread that queries the current time in predefined intervals. The context rules are executed after each time interval.

Context rules mediate between the context events sent by the context module, the current task and the dialog model. Based on time and location, intra or inter-dialog changes can occur.

- Intra-dialog changes occur for example when the user has reached the location for the task but is early or when the user is on time. In this case, the person with dementia is notified with an alert that pops up on the screen.
- Inter-dialog changes are triggered when a disorientation of the user is suspected. This is measured when the user has not reached the location for the task at the expected time. In this case, the user interface is changed to the communication screen. The user can at any time switch back to the to-do list and navigation screen.

5.6   To-Do List Repository

The to-do list repository is a database that stores the lists of tasks that the person with dementia wants to perform. This database is accessed by the primary caregiver to create the to-do list (i.e. the plan). The rest of the time, it is accessed by the to-do list and navigation module to inform the user about the current task.

5.7   Social Network Module

The social networking module exploits the Ubiquitous Help System (UHS) [19] as a basis for the social networking communication platform. The UHS is based on a client-server architecture. An HTTP/XML based communication framework is used to facilitate a UHS client to communicate with other UHS clients. The UHS client can send and receive plain text and attached files such as a regular email. When a user needs help and asks query, the controller of the UHS sends the query to other clients via server. The controller of the receiving client initiates processing for profile and availability status matching, and replies with the appropriate information.

In the prototype we developed, a user is identified by a Friend-Of-A-Friend (FOAF) profile. This contains information about the social relations of the user and traditional information that identifies the user (such as name, address). FOAF is a Resource Description Framework vocabulary (RDF) [3] for describing people and social networks.

6   Discussion

In this paper we presented an interactive system and showed that applications for people with dementia can be created by explicitly taking context into account in the design process. In our approach, context dependencies are defined in an early stage in the development process. We utilized the COMuICSer storyboarding tool to elicit our design requirements. This tool supports annotation of context information (time, location, social context) and proofed to be more informative than task models.

Typical context aware user interfaces consider space and time as important aspects. In addition, our approach includes the social context of the users involved in a communication process. The inclusion of social factors goes further than simply using internal context of the user. We have exploited the Ubiquitous Help System (UHS), introduced in earlier work, to empower social networking feature into our prototype. This completes the different types of context that need to be supported for applications that target people with early-stage dementia.

However, in our current prototype, the interaction from the caregivers' perspective has not been fully explored yet. Our aim was mainly to present an appropriate approach that addresses the three different types of context (location, time, social) that are important for these users explicitly during the development of such a system. In our future work, this issue will be addressed in order to have a system, which can be tested with real users.

The development of this prototype learned us that informal notations play an important role in the development of context-sensitive interactive systems, such as the one described in this paper. The explicit relations between the informal description and the formal models, such as the dialog model, inspire us to explore potential automation or consistency checks between the informal specifications offered by the scenario model and the presentation sketches, especially since there are already existing formalizations of both notations [18,7].

Acknowledgments

The authors are pleased to thank Mieke Haesen of EDM for her help in utilizing the storyboard [1] tool. Part of the research at EDM is funded by EFRO (European Fund for Regional Development) and the Flemish Government. Funding for this research is also provided by the Research Foundation – Flanders (F.W.O. Vlaanderen, project CoLaSUE, number G.0439.08N) and one of the authors is funded by the Hasler Foundation (LoCa project).

References

1. Balme, L., Demeure, A., Barralon, N., Coutaz, J., Calvary, G.: CAMELEON-RT: A software Architecture Reference Model for Distributed, Migratable, and Plastic user Interfaces. Ambient Intelligence 3295, 291–302 (2004)
2. Baumgarten, M., Mulvenna, M.: The Role of Context-aware Computing in Support of People with Dementia. In: Supporting People with Dementia Using Pervasive Health Technologies, pp. 131–143. Springer, Heidelberg (2010)

---

[1] StoryBoardML: `http://research.edm.uhasselt.be/~kris/research/projects/StoryBoardML/storyboards.html`

3. Beckett, D., McBride, B.: RDF/XML Syntax Specification (Revised). Tech. rep., W3C (February 2004), http://www.w3.org/TR/rdf-syntax-grammar/
4. Van den Bergh, J., Coninx, K.: Contextual concurtasktrees: Integrating dynamic contexts in task based design. In: PerCom Workshops, pp. 13–17. IEEE Computer Society, Los Alamitos (2004)
5. Bilandzic, M., Foth, M., De Luca, A.: CityFlocks: designing social navigation for urban mobile information systems. In: DIS 2008: Proceedings of the 7th ACM Conference on Designing Interactive Systems, pp. 174–183. ACM Press, New York (2008)
6. Calvary, G., Coutaz, J., Thevenin, D., Limbourg, Q., Bouillon, L., Vanderdonckt, J.: A unifying reference framework for multi-target user interfaces. Interacting with Computers 15(3), 289–308 (2003)
7. Coyette, A., Kieffer, S., Vanderdonckt, J.: Multi-fidelity Prototyping of User Interfaces. In: Baranauskas, M.C.C., Palanque, P.A., Abascal, J., Barbosa, S.D.J. (eds.) INTERACT 2007. LNCS, vol. 4662, pp. 150–164. Springer, Heidelberg (2007)
8. Davis, R., Nugent, C.D., Donnelly, M.: Prototyping Cognitive Prosthetics for People with Dementia. In: Mulvenna, M.D., Nugent, C.D. (eds.) Supporting People with Dementia Using Pervasive Health Technologies, pp. 145–163. Springer, Heidelberg (2010)
9. Dey, A.K., Abowd, G.D.: CybreMinder: A Context-Aware System for Supporting Reminders. In: Thomas, P., Gellersen, H.-W. (eds.) HUC 2000. LNCS, vol. 1927, pp. 172–186. Springer, Heidelberg (2000)
10. Dey, A.K., Häkkilä, J.: Context-Awareness and Mobile Devices. User Interface Design and Evaluation for Mobile Technology 1, 205–217 (2008)
11. Dourish, P., Matthew, C.: Running out of space: Models of information navigation. Presented at HCI 1994, Cambridge, UK, NA, p. 134 (1994)
12. Draper, B.: Dealing with dementia: a guide to Alzheimer's disease and other dementias / Brian Draper. Allen & Unwin, Crows Nest (2004)
13. Du, K., Zhang, D., Zhou, X., Mokhtari, M., Hariz, M., Qin, W.: HYCARE: A Hybrid Context-Aware Reminding Framework for Elders with Mild Dementia. In: Helal, S., Mitra, S., Wong, J., Chang, C.K., Mokhtari, M. (eds.) ICOST 2008. LNCS, vol. 5120, pp. 9–17. Springer, Heidelberg (2008)
14. Graff, M., Vernooij-Dassen, M., Thijssen, M., Dekker, J., Hoefnagels, W., Rikkert, M.: Community based occupational therapy for patients with dementia and their care givers: randomised controlled trial. British Medical Journal 333(7580), 1196 (2006)
15. Haesen, M., Luyten, K., Coninx, K.: Get Your Requirements Straight: Storyboarding Revisited. In: Gross, T., Gulliksen, J., Kotzé, P., Oestreicher, L., Palanque, P., Prates, R.O., Winckler, M. (eds.) INTERACT 2009. LNCS, vol. 5727, pp. 546–549. Springer, Heidelberg (2009)
16. Hettinga, M., De Boer, J., Goldberg, E., Moelaert, F.: Navigation for People with Mild Dementia. Studies in Health Technology and Informatics 150, 428 (2009)
17. Lauriks, S., Reinersmann, A., Roest, H., Meiland, F., Davies, R., Moelaert, F., Mulvenna, M., Nugent, C., Dröes, R.: Review of ICT-Based Services for Identified Unmet Needs in People with Dementia. In: Mulvenna, M.D., Nugent, C.D. (eds.) Supporting People with Dementia Using Pervasive Health Technologies, Springer, Heidelberg (2010)
18. Luyten, K., Haesen, M., Ostrowski, D., Coninx, K., Degrandsart, S., Demeyer, S.: Storyboard creation as an entrypoint for model-based interface development with UsiXML. In: UsiXML, pp. 1–8 (2010)

19. Mahmud, N., Luyten, K., Coninx, K.: Context Aware Help and Guidance for Large-Scale Public Spaces. In: SMAP 2009: Proceedings of the 2009 Fourth International Workshop on Semantic Media Adaptation and Personalization, pp. 105–110. IEEE Computer Society Press, Washington (2009)

20. Maj, M., Sartorius, N.: Dementia. WPA series, vol. 3. John Wiley and Sons, Chichester (2003)

21. McDonald, D.W., Ackerman, M.S.: Expertise recommender: A flexible recommendation system and architecture. In: Proceedings of the 2000 ACM Conference on Computer Supported Cooperative Work, pp. 231–240. ACM, New York (2000)

22. Mileo, A., Merico, D., Bisiani, R.: Support for context-aware monitoring in home healthcare. J. Ambient Intell. Smart Environ. 2(1), 49–66 (2010)

23. Miskelly, F.: A novel system of electronic tagging in patients with dementia and wandering. Age and Ageing 33(3), 304 (2004)

24. Mulvenna, M.D., Nugent, C.D., Moelaert, F., Craig, D., Dröes, R.: Supporting People with Dementia Using Pervasive Healthcare Technologies. In: Advanced Information and Knowledge Processing, pp. 3–14. Springer, London (2010)

25. Newell, A., Carmichael, A., Gregor, P., Alm, N., Waller, A.: Information technology for cognitive support. In: Sears, A., Jacko, J.A. (eds.) The Human- Computer Interaction Handbook: Fundamentals, Evolving Technologies, and Emerging Applications, ch. 41, 2nd edn., pp. 811–828. CRC Press, Boca Raton (2007)

26. Ory, M., Hoffman III, R., Yee, J., Tennstedt, S., Schulz, R.: Prevalence and impact of caregiving: A detailed comparison between dementia and nondementia caregivers. The Gerontologist 39(2), 177 (1999)

27. Paterno, F.: Model-Based Design and Evaluation of Interactive Applications (Applied Computing). Springer, Heidelberg (2000)

28. Ren, Y., Kiesler, S., Fussell, S.: Multiple group coordination in complex and dynamic task environments: Interruptions, coping mechanisms, and technology recommendations. J. Manage. Inf. Syst. 25(1), 105–130 (2008)

29. Robinson, L., Brittain, K., Lindsay, S., Jackson, D., Olivier, P.: Keeping In Touch Everyday (KITE) project: developing assistive technologies with people with dementia and their carers to promote independence. International Psychogeriatrics 21(03), 494–502 (2009)

30. Schulz, R., Martire, L.: Family caregiving of persons with dementia: prevalence, health effects, and support strategies. American Journal of Geriatric Psych. 12(3), 240 (2004)

31. Woods, B.: Promoting well-being and independence for people with dementia. International Journal of Geriatric Psychiatry 14(2), 97–105 (1999)

Supporting Multimodality in Service-Oriented Model-Based Development Environments

Marco Manca and Fabio Paternò

CNR-ISTI, HIIS Laboratory, Via Moruzzi 1, 5614 Pisa, Italy
{Marco.Manca,Fabio.Paterno}@isti.cnr.it

Abstract. While multimodal interfaces are becoming more and more used and supported, their development is still difficult and there is a lack of authoring tools for this purpose. The goal of this work is to discuss how multimodality can be specified in model-based languages and apply such solution to the composition of graphical and vocal interactions. In particular, we show how to provide structured support that aims to identify the most suitable solutions for modelling multimodality at various detail levels. This is obtained using, amongst other techniques, the well-known CARE properties in the context of a model-based language able to support service-based applications and modern Web 2.0 interactions. The method is supported by an authoring environment, which provides some specific solutions that can be modified by the designers to better suit their specific needs, and is able to generate implementations of multimodal interfaces in Web environments. An example of modelling a multimodal application and the corresponding, automatically generated, user interfaces is reported as well.

Keywords: Multimodal interfaces. Model-based design, Authoring tools.

1 Introduction

Multimodal user interfaces support various user input modes. Ongoing technological evolution is making such interfaces more and more affordable and is proposing them in the mass market as well. However, developing multimodal user interfaces is still difficult and there is a lack of authoring environments for this purpose.

Model-based approaches have received renewed attention in recent years because they can help developers in managing the complexity of designing and developing multi-device applications. Most of the proposed model-based approaches have focused on desktop and mobile applications, sometimes with support for vocal interfaces as well, but there has been little effort in applying them to multimodal user interfaces, and such rare studies have found limited applications, as results were still too preliminary to provide general solutions.

In this paper, we present a logical language and an associated authoring environment able to provide a useful and general solution to such issues, and which can be exploited by developers of multimodal user interfaces. In the paper after discussing related work we introduce our approach to modelling multimodal interaction; next we show how it has been formalized in an XML logical language to address composition

R. Bernhaupt et al. (Eds.): HCSE 2010, LNCS 6409, pp. 135–148, 2010.

of vocal and graphical modalities, and we present how such language is supported within an authoring environment. Then, the transformation from the logical description to implementation is discussed, and an example multimodal application obtained through this environment is presented as well. Lastly, some conclusions are drawn along with indications for future work.

2 Related Work

The problem of designing multi-modal interfaces has been addresses in some previous work but still needs more general and better engineered solutions. Damask [7] includes the concept of layers to support the development of cross-device (desktop, smartphone, voice) user interfaces. Thus, the designers can specify user interface elements that should belong to all the user interface versions and elements that should be used only with one device type. However, this approach can be useful in developing single modality versions (graphical or vocal) but does not provide particularly useful support when considering multimodal interfaces, which require specific support to indicate how to compose the involved modalities. XFormsMM [5] is an attempt to extend XForms in order to derive both graphical and vocal interfaces. In this case the basic idea is to specify the abstract controls with XForms elements and then use aural and visual CSS for vocal and graphical rendering, respectively. The problem in this case is that aural CSS have limited possibilities in terms of vocal interaction and the solution proposed requires a specific ad hoc environment in order to work. For this purpose we propose a more general solution able to derive different implementations for desktop and mobile devices. Obrenovic et al. [11] have investigated the use of conceptual models expressed in UML in order to then derive graphical, form-based interfaces for desktop or mobile devices or vocal ones. UML is a software engineering standard mainly developed for designing the internal software of application functionalities. Thus, it seems unsuitable to capture the specific characteristics of user interfaces and their software. In [15] there is a proposal to derive multimodal user interfaces using attribute graph grammars, which have a well-defined semantics but limitations in terms of performance. The possibility of deriving mutlimodal interfaces was addressed in [12] but using hardcoded solutions for the transformation and logical descriptions that were unable to describe typical Web2.0 interactions and access to Web services.

A different approach to multimodal user interface development has been proposed in [6], which aims to provide a workbench for prototyping them using off-the-shelf heterogeneous components. In that case model-based descriptions are not used and it is necessary to have an available set of previously defined components able to communicate through low-level interfaces, thus making it possible for a graphical editor to easily compose them.

To summarise, we can say that the few research proposals that have also considered multimodal interfaces have not been able to obtain a general solution in terms of logical descriptions and provide limited support in terms of generation of the corresponding user interface implementations. For example, in [12] the transformations were hard-coded in the Java implementation, while in [15] the transformations were specified using attributed graph grammars, whose semantics is formally defined but have considerable performance limitations.

In this paper we present a general logical language for multimodal interaction, which is included in an overall environment able to support development of multi-device user interfaces. The associated authoring environment includes a transformation tool able to derive X+V implementations from the logical specifications and satisfies the requirements for multimodal interface generation discussed in previous work [10], such as modality independence, support for specifying hierarchical grouping, etc.

3 Background

MARIA [13] is a recent model-based language, which allows designers to specify abstract and concrete user interface languages according to the CAMELEON Reference framework [2]. This language represents a step forward in this area because it provides abstractions also for describing modern Web 2.0 dynamic user interfaces and Web service accesses. In its first version it provides an abstract language independent of the interaction modalities and concrete languages for graphical desktop and mobile platforms. In general, concrete languages are dependent on the typical interaction resources of the target platform but independent of the implementation languages. In this paper we present a concrete language for multimodal interfaces, which has been designed within the MARIA framework.

In MARIA an abstract user interface is composed of one or multiple presentations, a data model, and a set of external functions. Each presentation contains: a number of user interface elements (interactors) and interactor compositions (indicating how to group or relate a set of interactors); a dialogue model, describing the dynamic behaviour of such elements and connections, indicating when a change of presentation should occur. The interactors are classified in abstract terms, e.g. edit, selection, output, control. Each interactor can be associated with a number of event handlers, which can change properties of other interactors or activate external functions. While in graphical interfaces the concept of presentation can be easily mapped on that of a set of user interface elements perceivable at a given time (e.g. a page in the Web context), in the case of a vocal interface we consider a presentation as a set of communications between the vocal device and the user that can be considered as a logical unit, e.g. a dialogue supporting the collection of information regarding a user. In defining the vocal concrete language [14] we have refined the abstract vocabulary for this platform. This mainly means that we have defined vocal refinements for the elements defined in the abstract language: interactors (user interface elements), the associated events and their compositions. The multimodal support has been built on top of such parts following an approach discussed in the next section.

4 Approach to Modelling Multimodal Interaction

In this paper we present a multimodal environment able to support composition of graphical and vocal interactions. There are many ways to compose such modalities. The goal is to provide a structured support that aims to identify the most suitable solutions at various granularity levels. In order to indicate how to combine the modalities, we have considered the well-known CARE properties (CARE: Complementarity, Assignment, Redundancy, Equivalence) [4] at various granularity levels. We apply such properties in the following manner:

1   *Complementarity*: the considered part of the interface is partly supported by one modality and partly by another one;
2   *Assignment*: the considered part of the interface is supported by one assigned modality;
3   *Redundancy*: the considered part of the interface is supported by both modalities;
4   *Equivalence*: the considered part of the interface is supported by either one modality or another.

How such properties will be applied to the user interface elements depends on the modalities and platforms considered. In the following, how these properties are applied to mixed vocal+graphical interfaces in both desktop and mobile devices is described, but the approach presented can be applied to other types of modalities.

Since we want to provide a flexible environment, the possibility of applying such properties is supported in the definition of the various aspects characterising our logical descriptions: the composition operators, the interaction and the only-output elements. In addition, in order to have the possibility of controlling multimodality at a finer level, the interaction elements are structured into three phases (each of them can be associated with a different CARE property):

5   Prompt: represents the interface output indicating that it is ready to receive an input.
6   Input: represents how the user can actually provide the input.
7   Feedback: represents the response of the system after the user input.

In practise, not all the CARE properties can be applied to all the three phases of an interaction. In particular, equivalence can be applied only to input: when two modalities are available and either one or the other can be used to enter the input. Vice versa, redundancy can be applied to prompt and feedback, but not to input, since a redundant input would mean that the same input is provided through different modalities, which does not seem useful or efficient. Complementarity could be applied to all three phases. However, in the case of input it can meaningfully be applied when structured input are considered. Indeed, atomic inputs that require simple actions (e.g. button selection) can hardly be obtained through a complementary use of two modalities.

By default the tool provides some specific solutions in terms of possible CARE properties, which can be modified by the designers to suit their specific needs. Figure 1 shows the control panel to define the CARE properties that are made available or the refinement of the main abstract concepts (there is one tab for each of them). The CARE properties that have been deemed not meaningful appear greyed out. Designers can freely select those properties that seem more appropriate for their multimodal applications, and then the authoring environment will be able to generate user interfaces accordingly following transformations that will be introduced in the next sections. Thus, our environment allows the designers to customize what multimodal support to provide in user interface development.

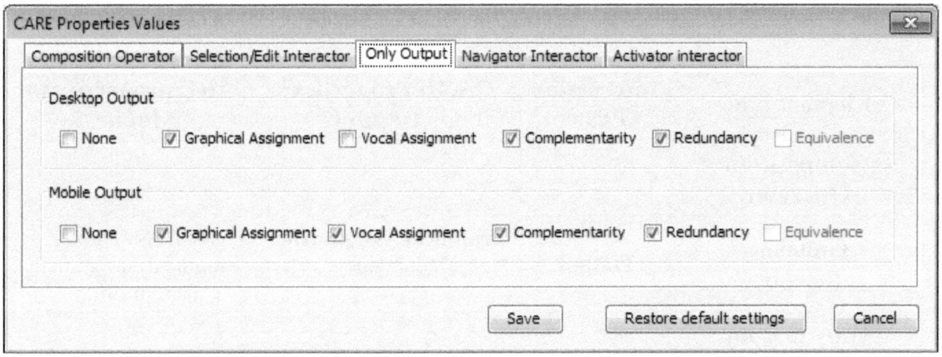

Fig. 1. Control panel for customizing CARE properties

While the CARE properties made available are similar for the two types of platforms that we consider (multimodal desktop and multimodal mobile), there are differences in the default properties proposed by the environment, taking into account the richer set of graphical resources of the desktop platform and that the mobile device can often be used on the move. Thus, in the case of the multimodal desktop, which has rich graphical resources, the composition operators are supported graphically. The interaction elements are structured in such a way that the prompt is graphical, input can be either graphical or vocal, and feedback is in both modalities. The only-output elements are graphical. In the case of a multimodal mobile, which has less rich graphical resources, the composition operators are supported both graphically and vocally, and the interaction elements are supported in such a way that the prompt is both vocal and graphical, the input either graphical or vocal, and the feedback is expressed in both modalities. The only-output elements can be both graphical and vocal or they use the two modalities in a complementary way, if they take a lot of resources.

Table 2 provides details on how the CARE properties are initially proposed by the environment to then generate graphical and vocal interfaces in both desktop and mobile platforms. Thus, it shows what properties have been deemed meaningful in the case of graphical and vocal interfaces, and these are made available in the authoring environment. We indicate in bold the specific properties that are initially pre-selected by default in the system. Thus, the properties in bold are those applied if the designer does not change anything in the tool. In particular, the first column indicates the element of the abstract interface considered. Different interaction phases (input, prompt, feedback) have to be considered depending on the interaction element in question.

In the case of only-output elements for the multimodal desktop platform the graphical assignment is proposed, while for the mobile one redundancy is suggested. For the interactive elements, in the desktop case we suggest equivalence for input and graphical assignment for prompt and feedback, while in the mobile case we prefer redundancy for prompt and feedback and still equivalence for input.

The composition operators aim to put together some interface elements in such a way that logical closeness or hierarchy of importance or some ordering is highlighted. Thus, usually there is some output information to indicate the involved elements (for example, it could be a graphical container or a sound at the beginning and the end of the grouped elements).

Table 2. How CARE Properties are made available for graphical+vocal desktop and mobile

Element type	Interaction Phase	CARE Properties for Desktop	CARE properties for Mobile
Composition Operator			
Grouping Relation	Output	**Graphical Assignment** Redundancy	Vocal Assignment Graphical Assignment **Redundancy**
Only Output Interactor			
Description, Object, Feedback, Alarm, Table	Output	**Graphical Assignment** Redundancy Complementarity	Vocal Assignment Graphical Assignment **Redundancy** Complementarity
Interaction Interactor			
Single/multiple selection Text Edit Numerical Edit	Input	Graphical Assignment **Equivalence**	Graphical Assignment **Equivalence** Vocal Assignment
	Prompt	**Graphical Assignment** Redundancy	Graphical Assignment **Redundancy** Vocal Assignment
	Feedback	**Graphical Assignment** Redundancy	Graphical Assignment **Redundancy** Vocal Assignment
Activator	Input	Graphical Assignment **Equivalence**	Graphical Assignment **Equivalence** Vocal Assignment
	Prompt	**Graphical Assignment** Redundancy	Graphical Assignment **Redundancy** Vocal Assignment
	Feedback	**Graphical Assignment** Redundancy	Graphical Assignment **Redundancy**
Navigator	Input	Graphical Assignment **Equivalence**	Graphical Assignment **Equivalence** Vocal Assignment
	Prompt	**Graphical Assignment** Redundancy	Graphical Assignment **Redundancy** Vocal Assignment
	Feedback	Vocal Assignment **None**	Vocal Assignment **None**

The navigator allows the user to move from one presentation of the application to another. This type of element usually has no immediate feedback because the actual feedback is given by the change of the application presentation loaded. However, it is possible to have some kind of vocal feedback to indicate that a change of presentation is under way.

5   A Logical Language for MultiModality

In the MARIA framework the concrete languages are derived from the abstract one by refining the abstract vocabulary taking into account the considered platform and the associated interaction modality. In the case of a multimodal concrete language we have to consider refinements for multiple modalities and indicate how to compose them. In particular, the MARIA concrete language for composing graphical and vocal modalities is based on the two previously defined concrete languages (one for the graphical [13] and one for the vocal modality [14]). It adds the possibility to specify how to compose them through the CARE properties.

As we introduced before the MARIA abstract language structures a user interface in terms of a number of presentation. Each presentation has composition operators (usually groupings). The composition elements contain interactors that can be either interaction or only-output interface basic components, which can have events handlers associated to them indicating how they react to events. Each of these components of the language, ranging from the presentations to the elementary interactors, have different refinements for the graphical and the vocal modality and in the multimodal concrete language we indicate how to compose them. Thus, a multimodal presentation has associated both graphical settings (such as background colour or image or font settings) and vocal settings (such as speech recogniser or synthesis attributes). A grouping in the multimodal concrete language can exploit both visual aspects (using attributes such as position, dimension, border backgrounds) and vocal techniques (for example inserting keywords or sounds or pauses or changing synthesis properties). The interactors are enabled to exploit both graphical events (associated with mouse and keyboards) or vocal-specific events (such as no input or no match input or help request).

In order to better understand how this approach works, we can take an example abstract interactor, the text edit. At the abstract level there is no assumption regarding the modality that should be used to perform this interaction. In Figure 2 there is a graphical representation of how this abstract interactor is refined into two parts depending on the modality, and then there are the possible CARE properties that have deemed meaningful for this interactor (in the top part of Figure 2). In the graphical case we have either a text area or a text field interactor as possible refinement, while in the vocal case we obtain a vocal textual input, which is composed of a request, a grammar to specify possible inputs and the associated feedback. Thus, the multimodal language includes both the vocal and the graphical refinements of the interactor, and adds attributes associated with instances of the CARE properties, which indicate the possible ways to compose them in the various interaction phases (input, prompt, feedback).

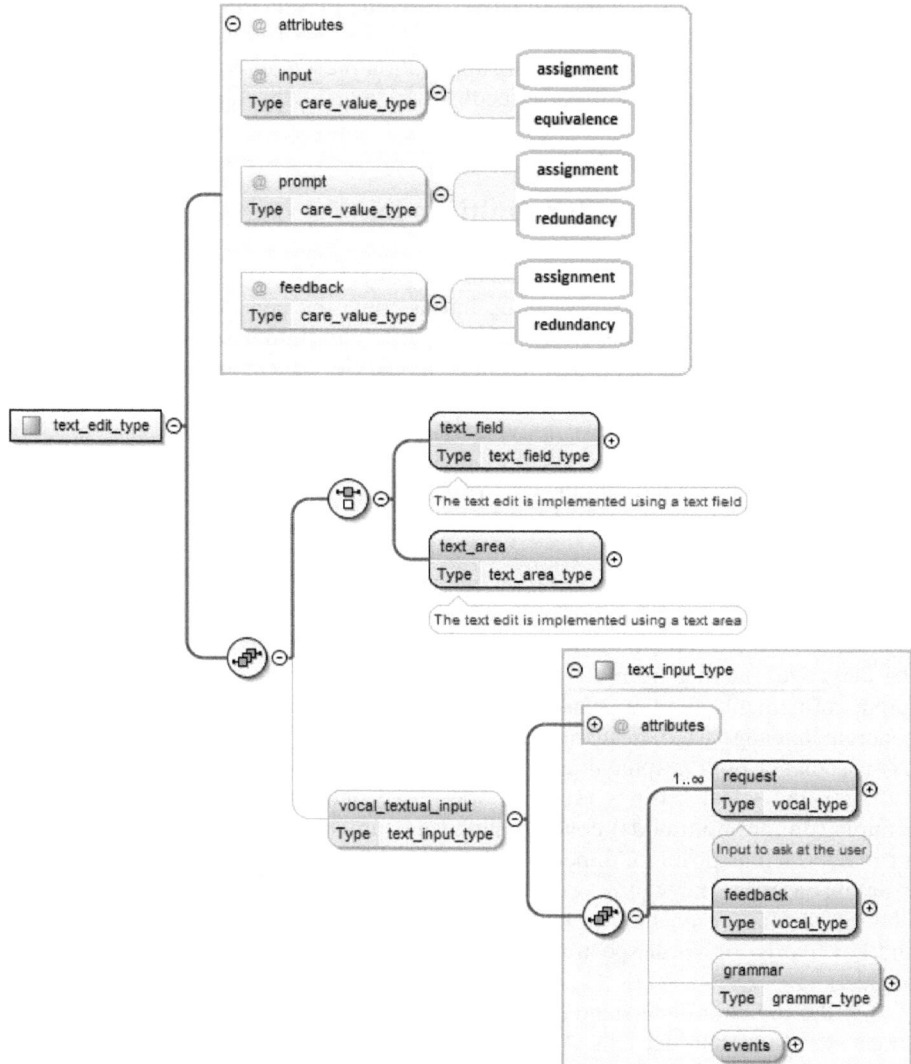

Fig. 2. An example of multimodal interactor derived from the graphical and vocal ones

6 The Transformation into an Implementation

In terms of target implementation languages, we have considered X+V [1] because it supports multimodality through the Web, which is the most common interaction environment, it is a standard and currently some publicly available browsers (such as Opera) support it, thus allowing developers to immediately test the resulting interfaces. X+V is an integration of HTML and VoiceXML. The VoiceXML part is included in the head of the X+V document, while the HTML is in the body part. Thus, there is a clear distinction between these two parts in an X+V implementation. The connection between the two parts is obtained through the events and the associated handlers. For example, the expression:

<input type =" text " id =" from " name =" departure_city " ev: event =" inputfocus " ev: handler ="# voice_city "/>

indicates that when the input focus event occurs in the from element of the graphical form then the voice_city event handler (which is managed in the vocal part) should be performed. In an X+V specification the synchronization between the values in the vocal and graphical part are obtained through the sync elements:

<xv: sync xv: input =" departure_city " xv: field ="# departure_city_field "/>

This sync element associates the value of an input element in the HTML part (departure_city) with the indicated field VoiceXML element (departure_city_field). This means that when an element is entered vocally then it is associated with both the vocal field and the input HTML element. The same result is obtained if the element is entered graphically. In addition, if the user changes the focus in the graphical part, then the corresponding vocal element, if any, is enabled. The sync element is not located in the VoiceXML form but it is a direct child of the HEAD element.

User interface generation is obtained through XSLT transformations [3]. They are obtained through stylesheets that transform an XML document into a new one in the target language (in our case the XML languages involved are the multimodal concrete MARIA language and X+V). The transformation is composed of a set template rules, which are defined by patterns indicating the source nodes conditions that should be verified, and templates indicating what corresponding element in the target document should be included. For example:

```
<xsl:template match=" c u i : p r e s e n t a t i o n ">
<html>
<head><t i t l e>Pr e s ent a t i on t i t l e</ t i t l e></head>
<body>Pr e s ent a t i on cont ent</body>
</html>
</xsl:template>
```

Indicates that a presentation in the source concrete language should be associated with the indicated elements in the corresponding HTML code.

The value of the CARE properties for the various user interface parts determines what should be generated. Assignment indicates whether only the vocal or only the graphical part is generated. Equivalence means that input in both modalities are generated, in particular for the vocal part a VoiceXML field is generated, for the HTML part an input element and then also a X+V element to synchronise the two parts. Complementarity and redundancy require generation of both the graphical and the vocal parts, even if they differ in the actual content that is generated.

The transformation is composed of three stylesheets: one for the graphical part and two for the vocal part, one to generate elements that are in already existing forms and one is for elements that require the creation of forms in which to put the currently generated element.

Thus, the transformation creates an X+V page for each presentation in the concrete description in such a way that in the head tag there is the call of the template to generate the X+V elements to synchronise the vocal and the graphical inputs and the templates to generate the vocal elements, while in the body tag there are the templates for generating the graphical elements. The X+V sync element is created only for the implementation of those interactors that are associated with the equivalence property for the input phase.

The transformation is also able to handle complex data structures such as tables. In the case tables must be rendered vocally, then it is possible to support either linear browsing (the elements are rendered line by line) or intelligent browsing, in which the corresponding header is rendered for each data element as well.

7 Authoring an Example Application

Tool support for the method presented has been implemented and integrated in the MARIAE environment, which is publicly available at http://giove.isti.cnr.it/tools/Mariae/. In order to see how it works we can consider an example application. We consider a home application, which allows users to control a number of domestic appliances.

The application is composed of four presentations: one for the user login, one showing the rooms that it is possible to monitor, one showing the appliances in the room selected, and one to change the settings of the appliance selected, if any.

Figure 3 shows the authoring environment in which the login presentation is being edited. The designer has specified a grouping element (*login_form*), which includes the input fields. It also contains a vocal element *grouping_start,* which is used to render a vocal message "Start login form!". On the right-top part of the environment there is a panel for setting the multimodal attributes (the CARE properties) of the currently selected element. In the main central part there are the elements that compose the currently selected presentation. They are graphically represented as the XML syntax of the specification may be not easy to read and manage. The currently selected element highlighted in red is a text edit interactor for the entering of the user name. Since the CARE properties indicate the use of both graphical and vocal modality it has a graphical part with a text edit interactor and a vocal one with a vocal textual input interactor. The vocal part has two request elements with the count attribute, which allows developers to implement the tapered prompting technique. The first request asks for 'Insert your username'. In the case the user does not provide an input within a given time or the input is not recognised then the second request provides a more detailed indication of what has to be entered. The vocal textual input also allows the specification of a grammar for which the grammar options represent the possible inputs.

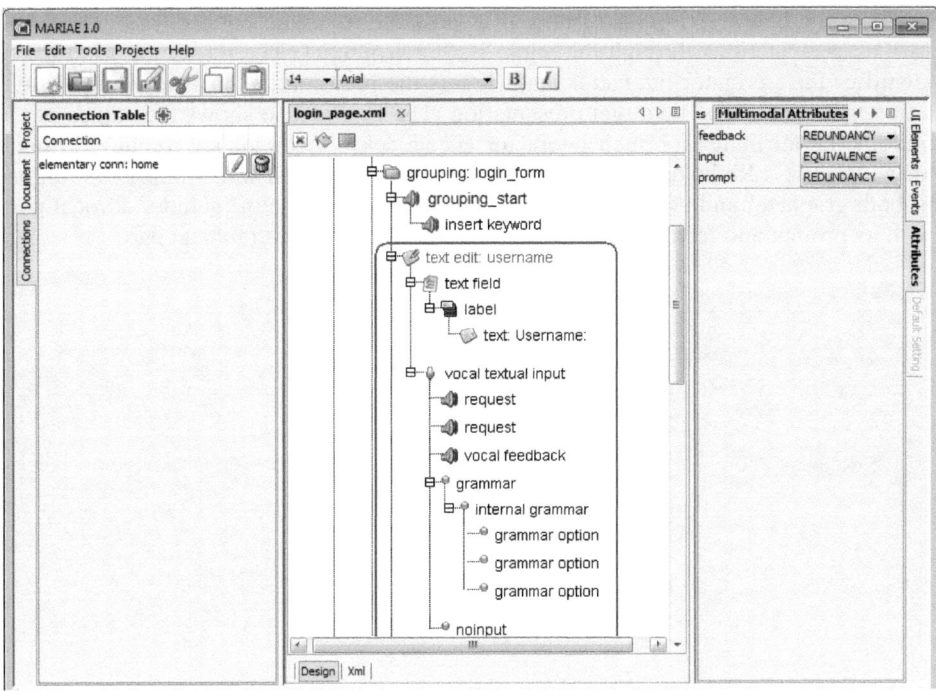

Fig. 3. Authoring a multimodal concrete presentation

Figure 4 shows the multimodal implementation rendered through an Opera browser of the login presentation.

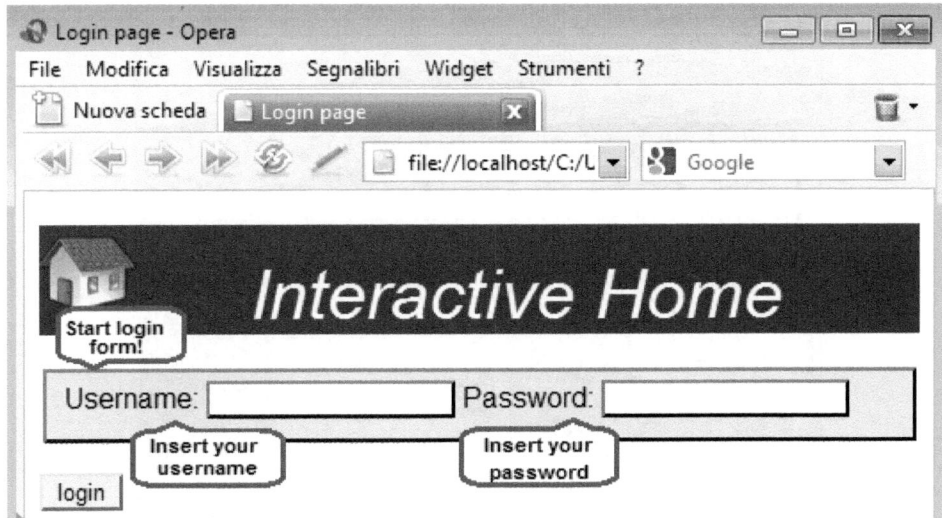

Fig. 4. The multimodal user interface corresponding to the previous presentation

Then, we can see (Figure 5) how it is possible to create connections among the
various presentations through the authoring environment. The interactor_id attribute
identifies the navigator interactor that triggers the presentation change, while presentation name indicates the target presentation. The Figure also shows the values of the
multimodal attributes for such interactor (Feedback = Redundancy, Input = Equivalence, Prompt = Redundancy). By assigning such properties, which imply the full use
of both graphical and vocal modalities, the navigator interactor includes a vocal part,
with its prompt and feedback, and uses an image link for the graphical part.

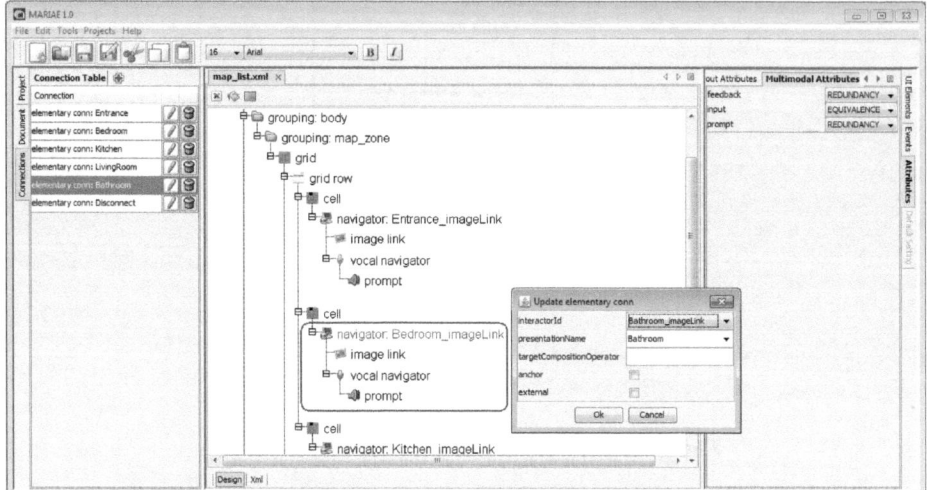

Fig. 5. Editing connections among multimodal presentations

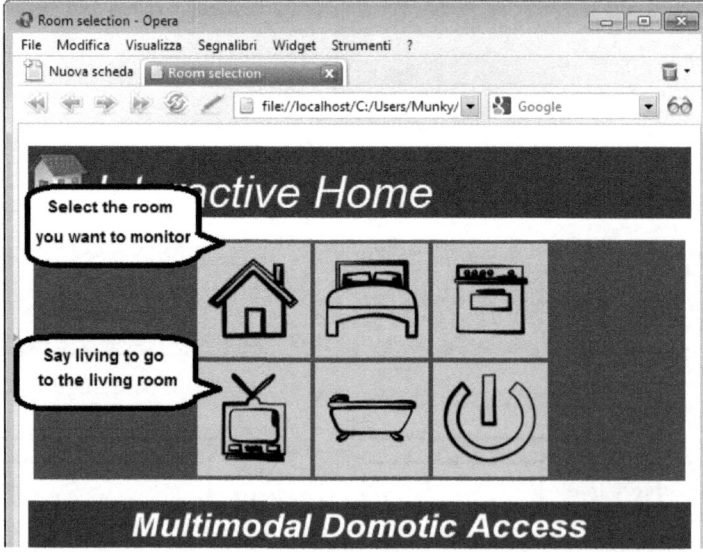

Fig. 6. The multimodal user interface implementation supporting the multiple connections

Once the new presentation has been completed we obtain a presentation for the room selection. It contains a grouping with an initial vocal message 'Select the room you want to monitor' to introduce the navigator elements associated with each select-able room. For each navigator there is a vocal prompt that indicates what vocal input to enter to select the corresponding room (e.g. 'Say living to go to the living room'). Figure 6 shows the corresponding user interface implementation.

8 Conclusions and Future Work

This work introduces a novel logical language for multimodal interfaces and the asso-ciated environment, which allows designers to easily compose multimodal interfaces and derive X+V implementations. It provides designers with the possibility to work through logical descriptions of the user interface and support for choosing the most suitable combination of various modalities at different granularity levels and for the various parts of the user interface.

This has been integrated in an environment for multi-device interface design and development, thus facilitating the implementation of multiple versions adapted to the various target modalities because of the use of a common abstract vocabulary, which is then refined according to the target platforms. This avoids requiring developers to learn a plethora of details of the many possible implementation languages

This result has been validated through the development of some multimodal appli-cations (one of them is briefly described in the paper), which can be rendered through publicly available browsers (Opera). The authoring environment is publicly available for download of the executable code.

Future work will be dedicated to empirical tests in order to better assess how the development process is facilitated with this approach, especially when multi-device interfaces should be developed (e.g. desktop, mobile, vocal and multimodal versions of the same application).

We also plan to develop an automatic system able to support graphical-to-multimodal user interface content adaptation. Future work will be also dedicated to extending the environment in order to provide support for additional modalities, such as tactile and gestural interaction, in several possible combinations, still for both sta-tionary and mobile devices.

Acknowledgments

This work has been supported by the EU ICT STREP Project ServFace (http://www.servface.eu/)

References

1. Axelsson, J., Cross, C., Lie, H.W., McCobb, G., Raman, T.V., Wilson, L.: XHTML+Voice Profile 1.0. Recommendation, World Wide Web Consortium, W3C (2001), http://www.w3.org/TR/xhtml+

2. Calvary, G., Coutaz, J., Bouillon, L., Florins, M., Limbourg, O., Marucci, L., Paternò, F., Santoro, C., Souchon, N., Thevenin, D., Vanderdonckt, J.: The CAMELEON reference framework. CAMELEON project, Deliverable 1.1 (2002)
3. Clark, J.: Xsl Transformations (XSLT) version 1.0. Technical Report, W3C (1999)
4. Coutaz, J., Nigay, L., Salber, D., Blandford, A., May, J., Young, R.: Four Easy Pieces for Assessing the Usability of Multimodal Interaction: the CARE Properties. In: Proceedings INTERACT 1995, pp. 115–120 (1995)
5. Honkala, M., Pohja, M.: Multimodal interaction with XForms. In: Proceedings ICWE 2006, pp. 201–208 (2006)
6. Lawson, J., Al-Akkad, A., Vanderdonckt, J., Macq, B.: An open source workbench for prototyping multimodal interactions based on off-the-shelf heterogeneous components. In: Proceedings ACM EICS 2009, pp. 245–254 (2009)
7. Lin, J., Landay, J.A.: Employing Patterns and Layers for Early-Stage Design and Prototyping of Cross-Device User Interfaces. In: Proc. CHI, pp. 1313–1322 (2008)
8. Myers, B.A., Hudson, S.E., Pausch, R.: Past, Present and Future of User Interface Software tools. ACM Trans. Comput. Hum. Interact. 7, 3–28 (2000)
9. Multimodal Interaction Activity (W3C), http://www.w3.org/2002/mmi/
10. Nichols, J., Myers, B.A., Higgins, M., Hughes, J., Harris, T.K., Rosenfeld, R., Pignol, M.: Generating remote control interfaces for complex appliances. In: Proceedings ACM UIST 2002, pp. 161–170 (2002)
11. Obrenovic, Z., Starcevic, D., Selic, B.: A Model-Driven Approach to Content Repurposing. IEEE Multimedia, 62–71 (January/March 2004)
12. Paternò, F., Giammarino, F.: Authoring interfaces with combined use of graphics and voice for both stationary and mobile devices. In: AVI 2006, pp. 329–335 (2006)
13. Paternò Santoro, C., Spano, L.D.: MARIA: A Universal Language for Service-Oriented Applications in Ubiquitous Environment. ACM Transactions on Computer-Human Interaction 16(4), 19:1-19:30 (2009)
14. Paternò, F., Sisti, C.: Deriving Vocal Interfaces from Logical Descriptions in Multi-Device Authoring Environments. In: Benatallah, B., Casati, F., Kappel, G., Rossi, G. (eds.) ICWE 2010. LNCS, vol. 6189, pp. 204–217. Springer, Heidelberg (2010)
15. Stanciulescu, A., Limbourg, Q., Vanderdonckt, J., Michotte, B., Montero, F.: A Transformational Approach for Multimodal Web User Interfaces based on UsiXML. In: Proc. ICMI, pp. 259–266 (2005)

RTM*E*: Extension of Role-Task Modeling for the Purpose of Access Control Specification

Birgit Bomsdorf

University of Applied Science Fulda, Marquardstraße 35, 36039 Fulda, Germany
`bomsdorf@hs-fulda.de`

Abstract. Interactive systems are often developed without taking security concerns into account. We investigated a combination of both HCI models and access control specifications to overcome this problem. The motivation of a combined approach is to narrow the gap between different modeling perspectives and to provide a coherent mapping of modeling concepts. The general goal is a systematic introduction and tool support of security concerns in model-based development of interactive system. In this paper we report results of our work currently concentrating on the early design steps. The focus of this presentation is on the specification of task and role hierarchies, conflicting privileges and related tool support.

Keywords: Task modeling, Role modeling, Role task assignment, Tool support, Access control.

1 Introduction

Task and domain models are commonly used for the purpose of conceptual modeling. The combination of the two describes how users may manipulate objects while performing tasks. Access control management requires similar information, i.e. detailed specifications of the users' privileges to access objects and to perform operations on them. Security, however, is often postponed until the end of the design cycle or until the implementation of a system [4], [12]. Interactive systems are therefore developed without taking **authorization** concerns into account.

An access control model defines the permissions of users (e.g. human users, processes, computers) to access system resources (e.g. on an object, data base content, a file). Role is the central concept of prevalent access control models (Role-Based Access Control, RBAC [10]). Approaches such as [6], [8], [15] extending RBAC as well as the task-modeling approach TADEUS [13] have been showing the demand of differentiating between roles based on the structure of an organization (organizational roles) and roles based on the privilege to perform tasks (task-grouping roles).

In HCI this distinction exists but is hardly introduced into the kernel concepts of tools supporting task-based modeling. In some tools an explicit role model does not exist (K-MADe [1], Diane+/Tamot [7], TaskArchitect [14]). In contrast to this, in CTTE [9] separate task models are created per role defining all tasks that can be performed by that role. The role specification, however, does not support inheritance of

R. Bernhaupt et al. (Eds.): HCSE 2010, LNCS 6409, pp. 149–157, 2010.

privileges. This is supported in WSDM [3] but resulting role hierarchies are not formally integrated with task models. All in all, concepts such as agent, actor, role, and group are used equivocally and ambivalently even within a single HCI approach. Furthermore, (semi-) automatic support in modeling the group, role, and task hierarchies taking care of their mutual dependencies is hardly supported. These facts complicate the combination of HCI modeling with security concerns.

Guo [5] has been showing in his work how the complexity of the three hierarchies and their relationships may be handled in the context of access rights. Based on his proposal we extended our modeling approach [2]. The extensions are also combined with MAD [1] aiming at modeling extensions in general. Therefore, for the remaining of the paper we refer to it by the abbreviation RTME (Role-Task Model Extension). In the following, as indicated by the name, the focus is on tasks, roles and their mutual dependencies. The approaches reported in [12] and in [4] are comparable with our work. They aim at the integration of access control specifications with models known from Software Engineering and Web-Engineering, respectively. However, privileges are formulated by means of roles and system functionality, not considering the context of users performing tasks to reach goals.

2   RTME: Integrative Modeling

Fig. 1 depicts an overview of the model and the interrelations of our integrative approach. It enables the explicit specification of organizational roles, named *groups*, as well as of task-oriented *roles* to define privileges. Users (individual persons) are specified as well. They are members of groups whereby, because of *adopts* relations, they are enabled to perform tasks (*performs* relation) and hence to act on objects (*involves* relation), i.e. to invoke methods. Our current tool, which is based on these concepts, supports the creation of group, role, and task hierarchies taking into account their interdependencies. Underlying functions check consistency violations and support to solve them. Hereby they contribute to the reduction of modeling complexity and to avoid modeling errors.

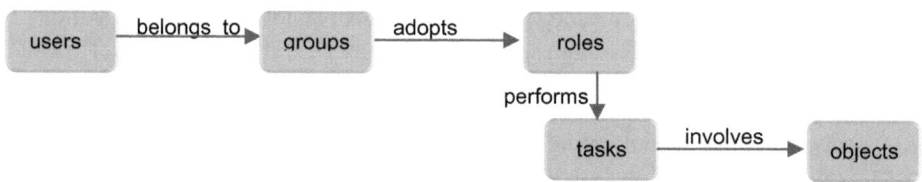

Fig. 1. Overview of modeling concept

2.1   Task Model

Figure 2 depicts a task model example by means of the notation as introduced in MAD [1]. The simplified task model consists of three unconnected task trees. The task *online shopping* is a composition of the subtasks *rate seller* and *buy product*, which is further refined. The task *sell online* is subdivided into two subtasks, whereas *administrate website* simply consists of a single task. Additional concepts are commonly in use to specify the order of task execution, such as temporal relations, and conditions constraining task performance, e.g. pre- and post-conditions. These concepts are not detailed here since the subsequent considerations reference only the task hierarchy. The following remarks are added only to complete the description of the example: The sequencing of the direct subtasks of *online shopping* as well as of *sell online* is open because of the *No order* declaration in each case. The option *enabling* defines that subtasks are to be performed one after the other, in which the sequence is given by the graphical order from left to right in the diagram. *Elementary* is used for leaf tasks, i.e. for tasks without subtasks. The label *OPT* denotes optional task execution.

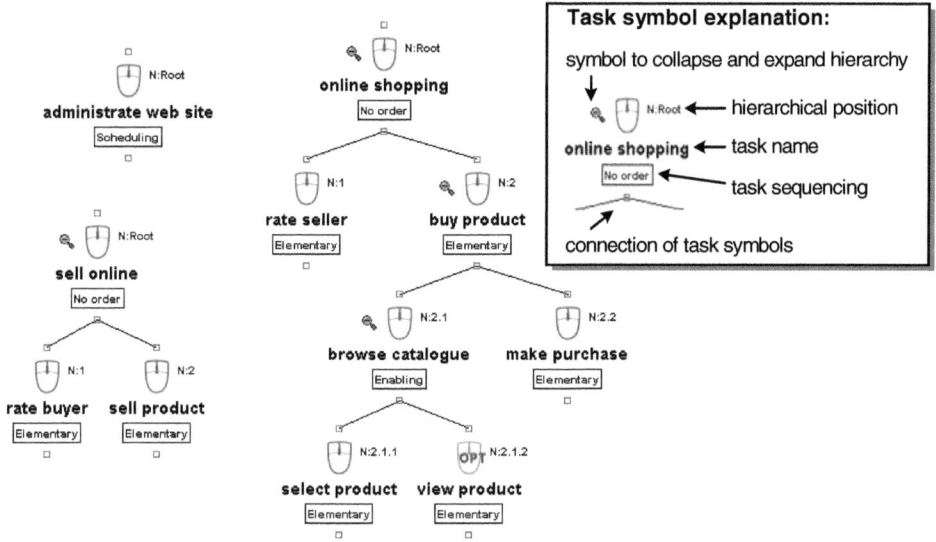

Fig. 2. Example of a task and a role model

2.2 Role Model

A role-task-mapping "r *performs* t" (see figure 1) means that the user who has taken role r possesses the privilege to perform t. The set of all privileges of a role r is denoted by *privileges*(r). Roles are structured by a so called poly-hierarchy that is given by a graph. While the task hierarchy expresses composition relations, the role hierarchy describes inheritance of privileges. An edge from a role r1 to a role r2 indicates that the privileges assigned to role r1 are a proper subset of the privileges of r2, i.e. *privileges*(r1) $\subset$ *privileges*(r2). For this kind of relation it is said that r1 is junior to r2 and that r2 is senior to r1 [10].

In our example we want to allow each person to browse the catalogue. However, only persons adopting a role *buyer* should be enabled to buy a product and to rate a seller. First of all we create a role *everyone* and assign to it the task *browse catalogue*. Fig. 3 left hand shows the result of this editing step. Inserting the first role is done easily. It is positioned between *minRole* and *maxRole* as shown in the example with *privileges*(*minRole*) $\subset$ *privileges*(*everyone*) $\subset$ *privileges*(*maxRole*).

Each graph posses a minimal and a maximal role that are introduced for the purpose of computing a role model's hierarchy and taking care of conflicts. A detailed description is provided in [5]. Please note that the set of privileges of *minRole* is always empty while *maxRole* possesses all the time all privileges defined by the task model.

Now we create a role *buyer* and assign the task *online shopping* and hereby also all of its subtasks to the role (see *Inherited role task(s)* in the role editor window). This step results in a model (see Fig. 3 bottom), in which *buyer* is positioned into the role hierarchy according to the privileges added to the role as well as to the hierarchy existing so far. The task *browse catalogue* is part of *online shopping*, i.e. *privileges(everyone)* ⊂ *privileges(buyer)* holds true, based on which the position is determined. Similarly the roles *seller* and *administrator* are inserted to define privileges for *administrate web site* and *sell online*. These two tasks are not connected to the tasks taken into account so far. Hence, both roles are inserted separately into the role hierarchy (see figure 5 right hand). Explanations of more complex cases can be found in [5] and [11].

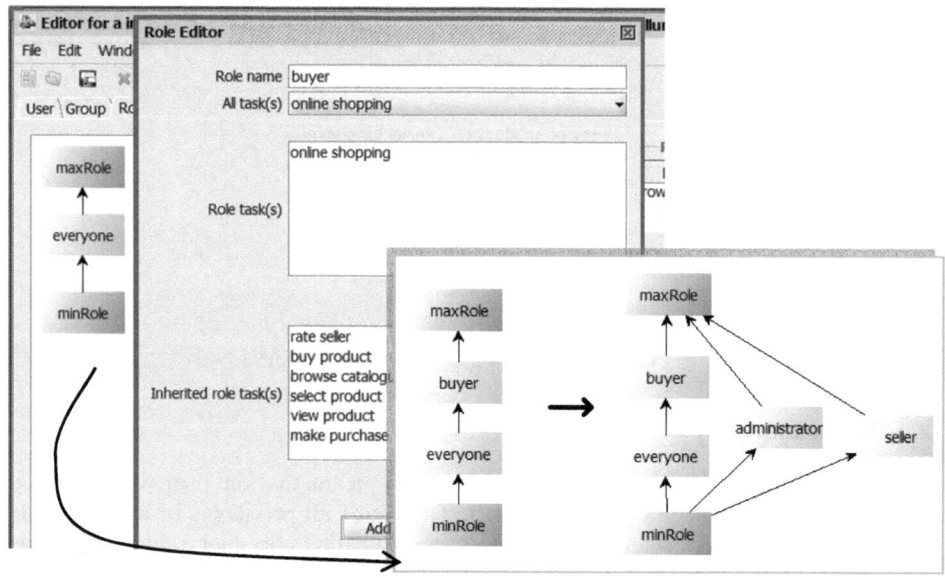

Fig. 3. Inserting the role *buyer*

2.3 Conflicts

Task models as well as role models mostly lead to complex hierarchical structures. Complexity is increased by their mutual dependencies. Thus, different conflicts within a specification may result from assigning roles and tasks to each other. The existing hierarchical structures of both the tasks and the roles are to be considered. It is not allowed to assign more tasks to a junior role than to one of its senior roles. This would result in an *assignment conflict* because in such a case *privileges(senior role)* ⊂

privileges(junior role) would hold true. This, however, is conflicting with the definition of the role hierarchy (given above). A strategy for avoiding such modeling errors is incorporated in RTME. Each time a user of our role editor selects a task that would cause a conflict a warning is shown and the user is prompted to perform a correction. Similarly RTME evaluates editing steps while the task model is under construction or is being modified.

In addition to such *assignment conflicts* RTME enables to define explicit cases of conflicts, named *privilege conflicts* and *role conflicts*, which are checked during modeling.

2.3.1 Role Conflicts

A *role conflict* is defined for two roles r1 and r2, formally denoted by r1 $\leftrightarrow$ r2. It specifies that roles are mutually exclusive. In such a case a user must not take both roles; it is also forbidden to assign the two roles to the same group. Hence, either r1 can be assigned to a group g or r2 can be assigned to g. Furthermore, for r1 $\leftrightarrow$ r2 it must hold true that no path exists between r1 and r2 in the role graph.

Basically, the two roles r1 and r2 must be independent from each other, i.e. the only common junior is *minRole* [5]. (A role is a common junior role of two roles if it is junior of both.) In addition, *maxRole* must be the only senior role of the two conflicting roles r1 and r2 [5]. Thus, a role conflict can only exist if r1 is neither senior nor junior to r2. Otherwise, r1 and r2 would have at least a common privilege violating the mutual exclusiveness.

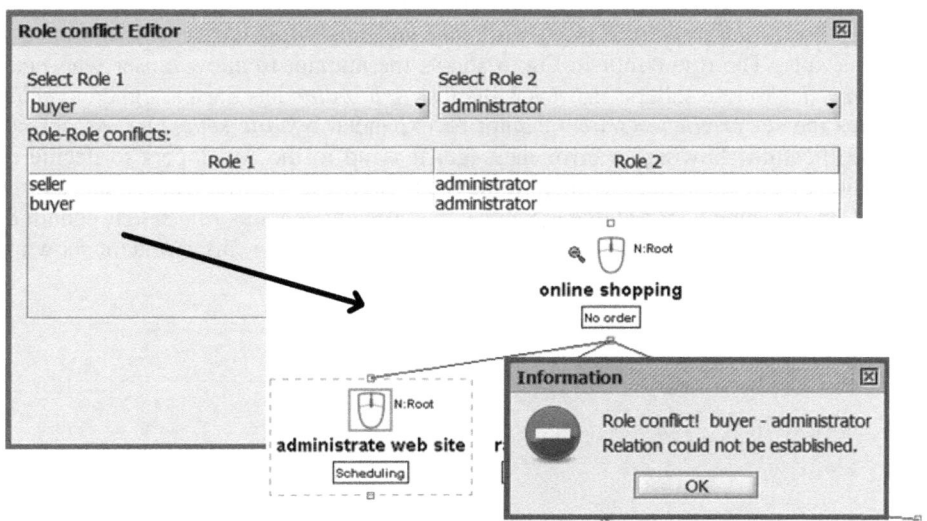

Fig. 4. Role conflict example

Obviously, a defined role conflict does not only impact group but also task modeling. Fig. 4 shows two role conflicts specified for the example given above: *seller* $\leftrightarrow$ *administrator* and *buyer* $\leftrightarrow$ *administrator*. Hence, common privileges of the roles *seller* and *administrator* as well as of the roles *buyer* and *administrator* are mutually exclusive. The attempt, for example, to define the task *administrate web site* as a subtask of *online shopping* results in an error now. Please note that the task *online shopping* is assigned to the role *buyer* while *administrate web site* is assigned to *administrator*. In the case *administrate web site* should become a subtask of *online shopping*, the role model would have to be modified as well so that a junior relation exists between *buyer* and *administrator*.

2.3.2 Privilege Conflicts
In addition to formulating conflicts between roles RTM*E* enables to define conflicts of privileges. A *privilege conflict* specifies two tasks t1 and t2, noted by t1 < > t2, that must not be assigned to a role r at the same time. The role *maxRole* is an exception to this rule as it comprises all privileges existing in the model. However, this exception causes no problem since *maxRole* cannot be assigned to any user or group of users.

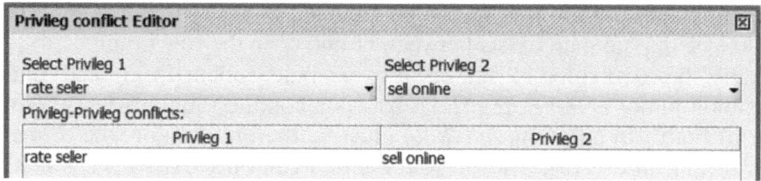

Fig. 5. Specification of a privilege conflict

Fig. 5 shows a privilege conflict defined for the tasks *rate seller* and *sell online* (*rate seller* < > *sell online*). Hence, *rate seller* and *sell online* must not be assigned to the same role. The role editor in Fig. 6 shows the attempt to allow a user who takes the role *seller* to rate sellers. However, the task *sell online* has been assigned to *seller* and thus the set *privileges(seller)* cannot be expanded by *rate seller*. RTM*E* forbids the modification showing an error message. It is up to the developers to decide on corrections. For example, they might remove the privilege conflict (*rate seller* < > *sell online*). In the same way *privileges(buyer)*, that already contains *rate seller*, cannot be extended with *sell online* (see for privileges of buyers the role editor content shown in Fig. 3).

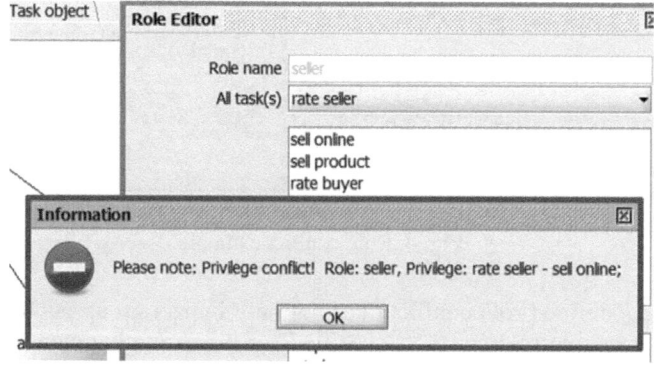

Fig. 6. Privilege conflict impacting role modeling

The defined privilege conflict has a similar impact on task modeling. The task *sell online* cannot be specified as a subtasks of *rate seller* (see Fig. 7). If the *rate seller-sell online* conflict is not specified the role seller would become a junior role of *buyer* because of the automatic role structure computation.

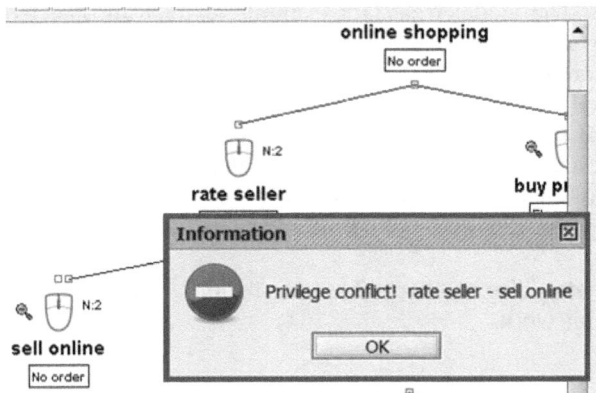

Fig. 7. Privilege conflict impacting task modeling

3 Conclusion

The modeling steps presented in this paper basically consist of privilege definitions. Hereby the groups a person belongs to, the roles a person may adopt, the tasks a person can perform, and the objects a person is allowed to access are specified. The definition of group structures, similarly to role modeling as presented above, is done by subset relations (also resulting in an acyclic graph with directed edge). RTM*E* handles the specification of group hierarchies and dependencies on role models in a very similar way as role-task modeling.

The underlying theory combines our own work on task modeling [2] with the work on conflict handling by [5]. Hence, our approach provides not only a sound theoretical basis but contributes also to integration of HCI with Access Control. The extensions with respect to our previous work are twofold: On the one hand the differentiation of organizational groups and roles defining privileges is incorporated. On the other hand RTM*E* implements an integrative group, role and task modeling approach. RTM*E* assists in structuring the model taking into account model properties defined so far. Each time a modeler inserts an additional assignment the resulting hierarchies are determined and the new assignment is inserted only if it causes no conflicts. This technique allows, for example, assigning roles and tasks to each other without performing required restructuring of the hierarchies. RTM*E* evaluates instead the new graph models considering resulting and explicitly defined rules of conflicts. This approach meets the fact that the model hierarchies result from the groupings of privileges.

Construction of model hierarchies and conflict control is based on the rules defined for the meta-model (assignment conflicts) together with the conflict rules defined by the modeler, namely role conflicts and privilege conflicts.

In the examples modeled so far by means of RTM*E* the underlying algorithms have proven to be very useful. However, the models were relatively small. We are aware that in the context of real projects more support is needed to reduce complexity and mental load. A common technique is to provide various views on a model in conjunction with filtering mechanisms. The first implementation of RTM*E* [11] provides such view generation. The modeler can, for example, extract all objects a special person has access to or all persons that are allowed to take a specific role. The interactive extracted views are presented by a diagram similarly to those used during editing.

The RTM*E* editor is in the state of a prototype. It possesses import and export functions (on the basis of XML) enabling the exchange of models with other tools. Currently our own task modeling approach and MAD are supported. Generally, RTM*E* can be combined with task models in which a super task is the sum of its sub-tasks, i.e. the superior task does not define additional functionality.

Acknowledgments. The author likes to thank Andreas Reitschuster for his contribution to this work.

References

1. Baron, M., Scapin, D.: K-MADe User Manual (2006), http://kmade.sourceforge.net (accessed 22.8.2010)
2. Bomsdorf, B.: The WebTaskModel Approach to Web Process Modelling. In: Winckler, M., Johnson, H., Palanque, P. (eds.) TAMODIA 2007. LNCS, vol. 4849, pp. 240–253. Springer, Heidelberg (2007)
3. Casteleyn, S., De Troyer, O.: Structuring Web Sites Using Audience Class Hierarchies. In: Arisawa, H., Kambayashi, Y., Kumar, V., Mayr, H.C., Hunt, I. (eds.) ER Workshops 2001. LNCS, vol. 2465, pp. 198–211. Springer, Heidelberg (2002)
4. Díaz, P., Aedo, I., Sanz, D., Malizia, A.: A model-driven approach for the visual specification of Role-Based Access Control policies in web systems. In: Visual Languages and Human-Centric Computing, VL/HCC 2008, pp. 203–210 (2008)
5. Guo, Y.: User/Group Administration for RBAC. The University of Western Ontario (1999)
6. Kang, M.H., Parker, J., Forscher, J.N.: Access Control Mechanisms for Inter-Organizational Workflow. In: Symposium on Access Control Models and Technologies, pp. 66–74 (2001)
7. Lu, S., Paris, C., Vander Linden, K.: Tamot: Towards a Flexible Task Modeling Tool. In: Proceedings of Human Factors, pp. 878–886 (2002)
8. Osborn, S., Nyanchama, M.: The Role Graph Model and Conflict of Interest. The University of Western Ontario (1999)
9. Paternò, F., Santoro, C., Tahmassebi, S.: Formal Models for Cooperative Tasks: Concepts and an Application for En-Route Air Traffic Control. In: Design, Specification, and Verification of Interactive Systems, pp. 71–86. Springer, Abingdon (1998)
10. RBAC Standard (2003), http://csrc.nist.gov/rbac/rbac-std-ncits.pdf (accessed 22.8.2010)
11. Reitschuster, A.: Realization of an Editor supporting an integrative Modeling of Groups, Roles and Tasks (Realisierung eines Editors zur integrativen Gruppen-, Rollen- und Aufgabenmodellierung, in German), Masterthesis, University Hagen (2008)

12. Romuald, T., Stéphane, C.: Integration of Access Control in Information Systems: From Role Engineering to Implementation. Informatica 30, 87–95 (2004)
13. Stary, C.: Role-Adapted Access to Medical Data: Experiences with Model-Based Development. In: Universal Access in Health Telematics, pp. 224–239 (2005)
14. Stuart, J., Penn, R.: TaskArchitect: taking the work out of task analysis. In: 3rd Annual Conference on Task Models and Diagrams, TAMODIA 2004, pp. 145–154 (2004)
15. Zhang, C., Hu, Y., Zahng, G.: Task-Role Based Dual System Access Control Model. International Journal of Computer Science an Network Scurity 6(7B), 211–215 (2006)

Web Applications Usability Testing with Task Model Skeletons

Ivo Maly and Zdenek Mikovec

Czech Technical University in Prague, Faculty of Electrical Engineering,
Karlovo namesti 13, 121 35 Prague, Czech Republic
{malyi1 xmikovec}@fel.cvut.cz

Abstract. Usability testing is technique for analysis of the usability problems of applications, but it requires significant effort to prepare the test and especially to analyze data collected during the test. New techniques such as usage of task models were introduced to improve and speed up the test analysis. Unfortunately, only few applications provide the task model. Therefore, we propose a method and tools for partial reconstruction of the task list and the task model called skeleton. This reconstruction is done from the usability expert's application walkthroughs. The task model skeleton is generated automatically, but it should provide similar information during the usability data analysis as manually created full-scaled task model. In order to evaluate usage of the task model skeleton we conducted a usability study with the web e-mail client Roundcube. Results show that the task model skeleton can be used as a good substitution for the manually created task model in usability testing when full-scaled task model is not available.

Keywords: Usability testing, Task list, Task model, Web applications.

1 Introduction and Motivation

Incorporating usability testing into software application development process, as presented e.g. in [2], can significantly increase the efficiency of the development process and the acceptance of the final application by the users. The problem is that usability testing is not an easy and straightforward process. It consists of several steps, see steps rectangles in Fig 1, which are time consuming. In each step of the usability test wide range of supportive data and documents are created, e.g. task list, screener, various questionnaires and forms for annotations, test logs. Also, additional data can be recorded like audio/video recordings or status log of the tested application. This information is not always interconnected, e.g. task list and audio/video recordings collected during the execution of the usability test. These not properly interconnected data is hard to analyze in the Step 4 of the usability testing process. If the data is interconnected sufficiently (e.g., usage of task model to create relations between collected data seem to be a very promising approach), we can use more sophisticated analytical methods, e.g. statistical [6] or visual analysis [1], to find usability problems of the tested application.

R. Bernhaupt et al. (Eds.): HCSE 2010, LNCS 6409, pp. 158–165, 2010.
© IFIP International Federation for Information Processing 2010

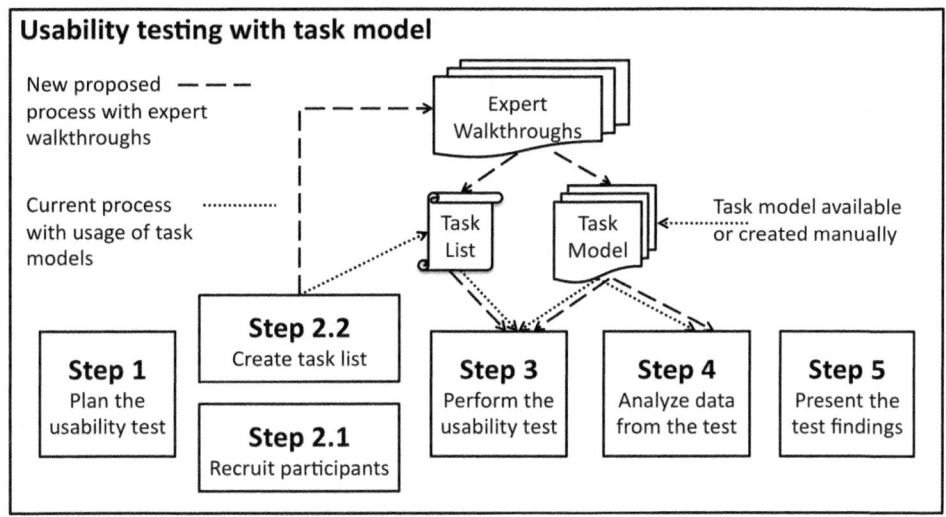

Fig. 1. Schematic diagram of the usability testing process with the task model. In the lower part there are steps of the usability testing process and in the upper part there are the task list and the task model incorporated into the process of usability testing.

1.1 Usability Testing with Task Models

In order to interconnect the collected data the task model can be used. In Fig. 1 we can see that the task model is created prior the start of the usability test and it is used in Step 3 during the execution of the usability test and mainly in Step 4 during the analysis of the data collected from the usability test. In Step 3, we also use task list, which is the foundation of the usability test. Usually, the task list and the task model are created separately, even though there is relation between them. During the execution of the usability test the task model can be used for interconnection of observer's annotations with the task, as presented in [1]. It can be also used for post-test interconnection of log records generated during the remote usability test with the task from the task model, as presented in [6].

Main benefits of the task model usage can be found in the analysis (Step 4), where it is used as an interconnection between the task list and the collected data. For each user interaction collected we can judge whether it belongs to the currently solved task or not without any time consuming search in the video recording or in other data sources. Several usability test analysis tools, which take advantage of task models, were introduced in [1], [4] and [5]. They show collected data in the form of timelines visualizations in order to present the length of each task, length of the interaction and they give information whether the interaction was expected in the current task.

1.2 Issues of Usability Testing with Task Models

Problem of usage of task models in the usability tests is the necessity to have the task model at disposal during the test. There are 2 typical scenarios that may happen:

- **Task model is available.** This is typical for applications that were generated automatically or semi-automatically based on the task model. Therefore the task model was created during the design of the application.
- **Task model is not available**. If we want to use the task models, we need to create them. Creation of the task model may not be an easy process, due to the often complexity of the task or the tested application. Creation of the task model is also additional activity that must be performed before the test begins.

For the majority of applications the task model is not available at the time of the usability testing. Therefore, we were looking for the possibility of automatic or semi-automatic generation of the task model or similar data structure, which would have similar properties like the task model during the usability test execution and during the analysis of the data from the test (Step 3 and Step 4 in Fig. 1). Our solution, depicted by dashed lines in Fig 1, is based on the expert walkthroughs that are created during the task list creation step (Step 2.2 in Fig. 1). From these walkthroughs the *task list skeleton* and the *task model skeleton* are created instead of the task list and the task model. The task list skeleton is a template for the task list with the list of expected steps. Details of the task list skeleton are in chapter 2.3. The task model skeleton is a sequence of expected user interactions. Compared with the task model, the task model skeleton is much simpler, without task relations or without hierarchical structures. Details of the task model skeleton are in chapter 2.4.

2   Creation of Task List Skeleton and Task Model Skeleton for Web Applications

Presented approach of creation of the task list and task model skeletons is on one hand generic but on the other hand it may differ on each application platform (e.g. web, desktop). In this paper, we will focus on the tools for the web application testing and on creation of the task list and the task model skeletons for web applications.

2.1   Related Work

Similar approach of automatic task model creation was presented by Paganelli et al. [8]. Authors parsed the HTML structure of each web page and created a Concur Task Tree (CTT) task model for the whole web application. Problem of the presented approach is that it generates quite big task models even for quite simple web applications, e.g. application with about 10 web pages is represented by CTT task model with 181 states. Such huge tree is good for computer processing but will be complicated for human expert. Another drawback is that it follows the HTML interactive objects only. Current rich web applications are using JavaScript to provide interaction with the user. Therefore the presented algorithm will not detect parts of the interactions and task model states based on the JavaScript. While our approach is based on recording of interactions executed by an expert walkthrough we are able to record all of them. Also the task model is containing much smaller number of states that make it easily understandable.

2.2 Interaction Log Recorder

Our approach of automatic task list and task model reconstruction is dependent on logging of user interaction (log record). Logging is used to detect and save both expert walkthroughs in Step 2.2 and user interactions during usability test (Step 3). Each log record must provide sufficient information about the type of interaction performed and about the new state into which the application had moved. In this work we were focused on implementation of a log recorder for web applications. Our recorder is based on Selenium IDE (http://seleniumhq.org/projects/ide/), which is a browser plug-in using JavaScript to listen to mouse clicks and key presses and records the data about interaction. Recorder is application independent so we do not have to install custom JavaScript code into the tested application in order to record interaction log. The structure of the log record is standard Selenium IDE XML log format [9]. While the standard Selenium IDE plug-in does not store time stamps, we have implemented custom function to include them into the log record.

2.3 Task List Skeleton

The task list skeleton is a template of a task list with the list of expected steps. It is a rich text document where expected steps generated by the expert walkthrough are automatically inserted into task list template using XML transformations. If there are more walkthroughs for the particular task, these walkthroughs are transformed into separated lists of the expected steps. In the Table 1, there is an example of the task definition from the usability test of the Roundcube e-mail client. Details about the usability test are in the chapter 3. The task description (in italics) must be entered by the usability expert who prepares the usability test. When the missing parts of the document are filled in the document becomes finalized task list and can be used in usual way by the usability test moderator and logger.

2.4 Task Model Skeleton

The task model skeleton is a sequence of expected user interactions. Visual representation of the task model skeleton automatically generated for the Task 5 (expert walkthrough 5.1) is in Fig. 2. There are 3 interactions that must be executed in order to complete the task. In Fig 3, the manually created task model for the Task 5 is presented, which is based on two expert walkthroughs (walkthrough 5.1 and walkthrough 5.2). Compared with the full-scaled task model, the task model skeleton is much simpler, without task relations or without hierarchical structures. Each subtask of the task model skeleton reflects one step in the task list.

Each subtask of the task model skeleton contains the same information about the user interaction as was recorded by the interaction log recorder. Thanks to that we can perform comparison of the subtask in task model skeleton with particular interaction in user log record in order to match the interaction with the subtask. Task model skeletons are stored in XML file format in order to be easily loaded by the analytical applications used in analysis step (Step 4 in Fig 1).

162   I. Maly and Z. Mikovec

Table 1. Example of the task list skeleton for the task 5 from the Roundcube e-mail client usability test

	Task list skeleton
Task description	*Open first new message in inbox and read it. Add sender of the message to the address book.*
Expected steps	1. Click at the link "Info bulletin". 2. Double click at the link " Info bulletin". 3. Click at the image "add". -- or -- 1. Click at the link "Info bulletin". 2. Double click at the link " Info bulletin". 3. Click at the "rcmbtn101". (Address book) 4. Click at the "rcmbtn105". (New contact) 5. Type "Info" into field " rcmfd_name ". 6. Type "info@lkom.cz" into field " rcmfd_ email". 7. Click at the "rcmbtn100".

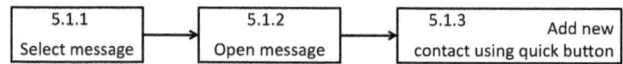

Fig. 2. Visual representation of task model skeleton 5.1 for task 5

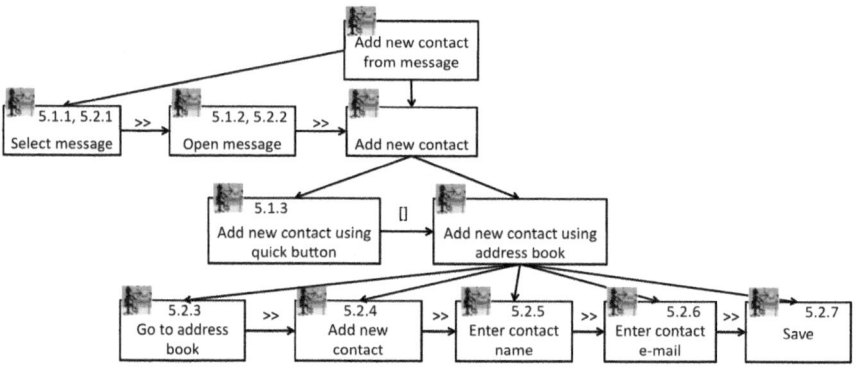

Fig. 3. Task model for task 5 representing possible task model created from the task model skeletons 5.1 (in Fig 2) and skeleton 5.2

4   Use Case: Web E-Mail Client Roundcube

In order to evaluate our proposal of the web application usability testing with the task model skeletons, we executed the usability test of the web e-mail client Roundcube (http://roundcube.net). At the beginning, we have analyzed the application and created the expert walkthroughs using the interaction log recorder (see chapter 2.2). Task list and the task model skeleton were created using XML transformations and the task descriptions in the task list were added. During the test we have recorded the user interaction using the interaction log recorder and then we have analyzed the data using Interactive Visualization Environment (IVE) tool [7]. IVE is an interactive tool for visual analysis of data from usability studies. IVE uses an internal object database and convertor plug-ins to convert collected usability test data into the internal database. Usability expert uses set of interactive visualization views to analyze the data. Each interactive visualization view is developed as a plug-in that has access to the IVE internal database and it can communicate with other plug-ins through a simple message dispatching system

3.1 Test Setup, Task Model and Task List Skeleton Creation

According to a minimal required number of participants for usability study [3] we selected 6 participants, both technically experienced and non-technical ones. None of them had a previous experience with the Roundcube client, but some of them had experience with other web e-mail clients, such as Gmail. The test was conducted in the usability lab and including pre- and post-test questionnaires it took from 30 to 40 minutes. Beside the data collected by the interaction log recorder we have also recorded an audio and video from each session.

During the application analysis we have selected 11 tasks and prepared the task model skeletons and the task list skeleton for them. Tasks were focused on typical e-mail activities like reading, sending and forwarding e-mails. We have also focused on e-mail folder management and work with address book. Each task in task list and task model skeleton was created using one expert walkthrough except the task 5, where we have recorded two walkthroughs. Creation of the task model skeleton and the task list skeleton generated only a small time overhead over the standalone task list generation, because we needed to save recorded interactions for every task, which has slightly broken the flow of recording process. Also recording of the alternative walkthrough for task 5 required rollback of the system to the previous state that took few minutes. Overall process of the task model skeleton generation and the task list skeleton generation was perceived positively.

3.2 Analysis of Usability Test Results with Help of Task Model Skeleton

In the Fig. 4, there are two timelines representing data collected during the usability study of the Roundcube e-mail client of the participant p7. The lower timeline shows length of each task. The upper timeline shows recorded log interaction combined with task model skeleton. Each rectangle represents one user interaction. The color of the rectangle highlight, whether the interaction was correct (green), incorrect (white) or it may be correct, because the interaction is expected in some moment in the task (yellow). The interpretation of the sequence of various colors is:

- **Sequence of green rectangles.** Such a sequence represents optimal execution of the task (e.g. Task 6). There may be white rectangles before the first green rectangle (e.g. Task 2), which represent unexpected interaction before the optimal execution started.
- **Sequence of green rectangles, which is interrupted by white rectangles and continues with green rectangles.** Such a sequence represents event, when participant performs optimal execution of the task, gets lost, but he/she is able to recover back.

- **Sequence of green rectangles, which turns into sequence of yellow rectangles.** Such s sequence represents same start as in previous example, but the participant recovers with interaction from the task but not the expected one (e.g. user starts from beginning).
- **Sequence of yellow rectangles.** Such a sequence (e.g. Task 3) represents situation when the participant starts the execution of the task with interaction that is part of the particular task model skeleton but is not the expected one. Example of such case is usage of browser navigation buttons or optional execution of first (or expected) interaction.

The interpretation of the timeline visualization allowed us to focus on the most problematic tasks, e.g. in task 3 we have found that the participant performed search action from different web page and in the task 5 the participant added wrong contact. In the task 2, the participant was not sure if he/she finished the task, so he/she performed last interaction again.

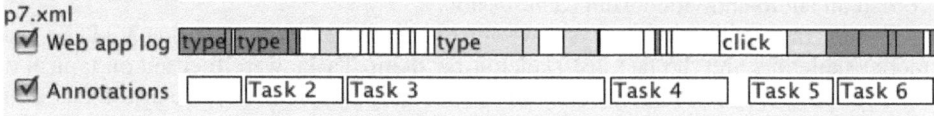

Fig. 4. Visualization of the timeline for participants 7

4 Conclusion

In this paper we have discussed the advantages of the usability testing with the task models. We pointed out that the biggest barrier of this method is the missing task model for the most of the tested applications. To overcome this barrier we have suggested the modification of the task list creation step be extended to create also the task model. The result is the automatically created task model skeleton and the task list skeleton. These are then used for task model based usability testing and analysis.

We have conducted the usability study of the web e-mail client Roundcube with 6 participants in order to evaluate our concept of the task model skeleton. The analysis of the data showed that we were able to match user's interactions with task model skeleton and to show which interaction belonged to which task. Then we showed the interpretation of data visualization and examples of usability problems that were found.

However, we found out that in the web environment the browser controls can influence the list of recorded interactions, e.g. the usage of the back navigation button. Therefore, the future work in this area should be addition of web browser interactions recording into the interaction log recorder. With this knowledge, we can introduce refinements to the user log record and better visualize user interactions as correct or incorrect. Sometimes it was hard to recognize, what was the object the participant interacted with. The example is click at "rcmbtn101" which means that the user clicked at the address book. As a future work, we should reflect this and design better identification of targets both during the interaction recording and data analysis.

Acknowledgments. This work has been partly supported by the Ministry of Education, Youth and Sports of the Czech Republic under the research program LC-06008 (Center for Computer Graphics) and by the Sucess project – Sun Center of Excellence for Accessibility & Usability (http://amun.felk.cvut.cz/coe/).

References

1. Maly, I., Slavik, P.: Towards Visual Analysis of Usability Test Logs. In: Coninx, K., Luyten, K., Schneider, K.A. (eds.) TAMODIA 2006. LNCS, vol. 4385, pp. 25–32. Springer, Heidelberg (2007)
2. Rubin, J.: Handbook of Usability Testing. John Wiley and Sons, New York (1994)
3. Nielsen's, J.: Why You Only Need to Test With 5 Users. Alertbox (March 19, 2000), http://www.useit.com/alertbox/20000319.html
4. Paterno, F., Russino, A., Santoro, C.: Remote evaluation of Mobile Applications. In: Winckler, M., Johnson, H., Palanque, P. (eds.) TAMODIA 2007. LNCS, vol. 4849, pp. 155–168. Springer, Heidelberg (2007)
5. Wurdel, M., Propp, S., Forbrig, P.: HCI-task models and smart environments. In: Forbrig, P., Paterno, F., Pejtersen, A.M. (eds.) 1st TC 13 Human-Computer Interaction Symposium (HCIS 2008). IFIP International Federation for Information Processing, vol. 272, pp. 21–32. Springer, Boston (2008)
6. Paganelli, L., Paterno, F.: Intelligent Analysis of User Interactions with Web Applications. In: Proceedings of ACM IUI 2002, pp. 111–118. ACM Press, New York (2002)
7. Maly, I., Mikovec, Z., Vystrcil, J.: Interactive Analytical Tool for Usability Analysis of Mobile Indoor Navigation Application. In: 3rd International Conference on Human System Interaction (HSI 2010), pp. 259–266. IEEE, Warsaw (2010)
8. Paganelli, L., Paterno, F.: Intelligent Analysis of User Interactions with Web Applications. International Journal of Software Engineering and Knowledge Engineering 13(2), 169–189 (2003)
9. Selenium IDE documentation, http://seleniumhq.org/docs/ (accessed on April 8, 2010)

Evaluating Relative Contributions of Various HCI Activities to Usability

Anirudha Joshi and NL Sarda

IIT Bombay, Mumbai 400076 India
{anirudha,nls}@iitb.ac.in

Abstract. Several activities related to human-computer interaction (HCI) design are described in literature. However, it is not clear whether each HCI activity is equally important. We propose a multi-disciplinary framework to organise HCI work in phases, activities, methods, roles, and deliverables. Using regression analyses on data from 50 industry projects, we derive weights for the HCI activities in proportion to the impact they make on usability, and compare these with the recommended and assigned weights. The scores of 4 HCI activities (user studies, user interface design, usability evaluation of the user interface, and development support) have the most impact on the Usability Goals Achievement Metric (UGAM) and account for 58% of variation in it.

Keywords: HCI activities, design process, weights.

1 Introduction

A human-computer interaction (HCI) design process is made up one or more phases, each of which may consist of one or more HCI activities. Each activity may be associated with one or more methods. A method may require specific skills. An activity may result in a specific deliverable that may be an end in itself, or may be an input for another activity in the HCI design process or the software development process.

For example, usability evaluation is an HCI activity that is a part of almost every HCI design process. Usability evaluation could be performed by several methods such as a think-aloud test, a performance test, a heuristic evaluation, a cognitive walkthrough, or an expert review. Performing each method requires a specific set of skills – e.g. the think-aloud test requires skills in prototyping, qualitative test design, user recruitment, interviewing users, and analysing data. The activity results in deliverables such as usability problems with the design, potential ideas to improve the design, and possibly a decision about the future course of development.

Several HCI activities are described in literature. One or more methods and deliverables are prescribed for each activity. Authors of HCI design processes often express their preference for one method over the other. However, it is not clear whether each HCI activity is equally important. In a specific project, some activities may happen with high level of fidelity, other activities may be cut short, and some activities may not happen at all. Given the context, skipping an HCI activity may have a significant impact on the usability of the product, while skipping or cutting short another activity may only have a marginal impact.

R. Bernhaupt et al. (Eds.): HCSE 2010, LNCS 6409, pp. 166–181, 2010.

In section 2, we review traditional design literature and HCI literature to articulate the characteristics relevant to design of interactive artefacts. In section 3, we identify 8 HCI activities that we believe are important in any HCI design process and organise them in a multi-disciplinary framework along with their associated methods, roles, and deliverables. In section 4, we propose a method to express the relative importance of these activities. In section 5, we describe a study that we conducted with 50 industrial projects in India to arrive at the relative importance of these activities empirically. In section 6, we present our conclusions.

2   Design Activities

2.1   Activities in Traditional Design Process

Archer defines design as a goal-driven problem-solving activity [1]. According to Jones [2], the effect of designing is to initiate a change in man-made things that in turn affect the manufacturers of those products, the distributors, the purchasers, the users, and ultimately the society. An important job of the designer is to predict each of those behaviours and responses at each stage in the life of the product.

One of the ways to understand design is to chart the design process [3]. Several authors agree that at its bare bones, a systematic design process comprises of three fundamental activities [1], [2], [3], [4]:

- Analyse the user needs, the problems and the opportunities to identify the goals and the constraints
- Synthesise alternative solutions
- Evaluate them against goals and redesign the product where necessary.

Authors also agree that the design processes are iterative. Problems found with the proposed design at the time of evaluation are fixed in a new design solution and this is done until the most appropriate solution is found. As iterations progress, the design also moves from generic to detailed. Designers have evolved many methods to carry out these activities. The main effect of the design methods is to externalise what good designers do intuitively to allow design of complex and innovative systems that might be beyond the experience of any one designer.

The need for expanding upon the design brief itself before converging to a solution has been expressed by several authors, including Jones [2] and Laseau [5]. Jones broadly divides design methods into three categories that correspond to the three stages of design – divergence, transformation, and convergence [2].

Divergence refers to the act of extending the boundary of the design situation to have a large search space in which to seek a solution. The aim of divergent search is to restate the original brief while identifying the features of the design situation that will permit a valuable and feasible degree of change. Key characteristics of the divergence stage are its tentativeness and instability. The objectives, the problem boundary, and the sponsor's brief are unstable, and evolve during this stage and evaluation is deliberately deferred so that nothing relevant is disregarded. Design methods related to this stage often require both rational and intuitive actions, and many of them require "legwork rather than armchair speculation"[2].

Transformation is the creative and the most interesting step of design when the objectives, the brief, and the problem boundaries are fixed, the critical variables are identified, the constraints are recognised, and the opportunities are taken. Jones warns that this could also be the stage where big blunders are made, and where experience and sound judgement are necessary. Design methods for searching for new ideas (such as brainstorming and synectics), and design methods to explore the problem structure (such as mind mapping, interaction matrix, and affinity) enable this transformation. Jones calls many of these methods as "black-box methods" as these depend on the chief designer's creativity and intuition 2].

In convergence, the designer's aim is to reduce the secondary uncertainties rapidly so that an optimum solution can be arrived at with minimal effort. During this stage, the designer is working with the most details in design and if he does not converge fast, the number of alternatives available can explode. Design methods related to convergence stage are related to evaluation, measurement, and analysis. Jones calls these as "glass-box methods" as these are very rational and analytical [2].

2.2 Activities in HCI Design Process

Many authors have prescribed process models specifically for the design of interactive products. Several of these (particularly the early authors) came from backgrounds in psychology, and their process models reflect a stronger emphasis on analysis, usability evaluation, and convergent thinking. Nevertheless, there are many overlaps with the traditional design processes, particularly in the later literature.

The basic ideas for design of interactive systems were already articulated by the 1980s. Gould and Lewis recommended three "principles" of design, which easily translate into the steps of a process: early focus on users and tasks, empirical measurement of user performance on prototypes, and iterative design to fix problems found during usability tests "as they will be" [6]. They also acknowledged the importance of the process to ensure meeting usability goals.

More detailed process models have been proposed by other authors. Nielsen suggests a 11-stage usability engineering lifecycle model [7]. Kreitzberg identifies a 6-stage design methodology [8]. Dix et al. relate the HCI design process to software development lifecycle [9]. Preece et al. emphasise the need to look "beyond HCI" into interaction design [10], [11].

Contextual Design process developed by Beyer and Holtzblatt explicitly brings in divergence and transformation in addition to convergence [12]. Divergence is enabled mainly by the technique of contextual inquiry, an interview technique that draws upon ethnography and allows designers to gain deep understanding of users' tasks, roles, artefacts, environment, and culture. Transformation is brought in by consolidating findings across users through techniques such as affinity and redesign of users' work with a vision of the design that drives changes to the organisational work practice.

Cooper and Riemann's goal-directed design process is driven by roles such as managers, designers, programmers, software testers and usability testers [13]. Their design process consists of steps that reflect divergence, transformation, and convergence: Research users and the domain; model users and use contexts (personas and their goals); define requirements of users, business, and technology; create a framework to define the design structure and flow through scenarios; refine the framework; design the interface details; and validate them.

Mayhew brings the perspective of an external usability consultant to the product development process 14]. Mayhew suggests a variety of techniques to carry out each task, but her approach is open and flexible – one may substitute a quicker / cheaper technique to do a task, but each task must be done. (Our approach to activity and method is similar to Mayhew's approach to task and technique). Garrett divides users experience of a website in five layers – surface, skeleton, structure, scope, and strategy [15]. Garrett's model of user experience is not a process model in itself, but it has important implications for the process. Decisions at lower layers affect the choices available at the higher layers. Therefore, a strategic decision will ripple through the scope, the structure, the skeleton, and the surface. Similarly, changes in the scope will affect the structure, the skeleton, and the surface. Therefore, one needs to consider as many alternatives as possible before freezing upon the strategy and the scope.

Gulliksen et al. review HCI literature and list key principles of user centred design 16]. One of the principles they emphasise is that the design should be holistic, considering all aspects including impact of design on the users' work, on the organisation, roles, etc. All parts of the product (task organisation, user interface, online help, user training, health and safety aspects etc.) should be influenced by common design thinking.

3 Framework for HCI Design

By combining the essential characteristics of the various processes discussed above, we propose a process framework for HCI design. In our framework, we prescribe 8

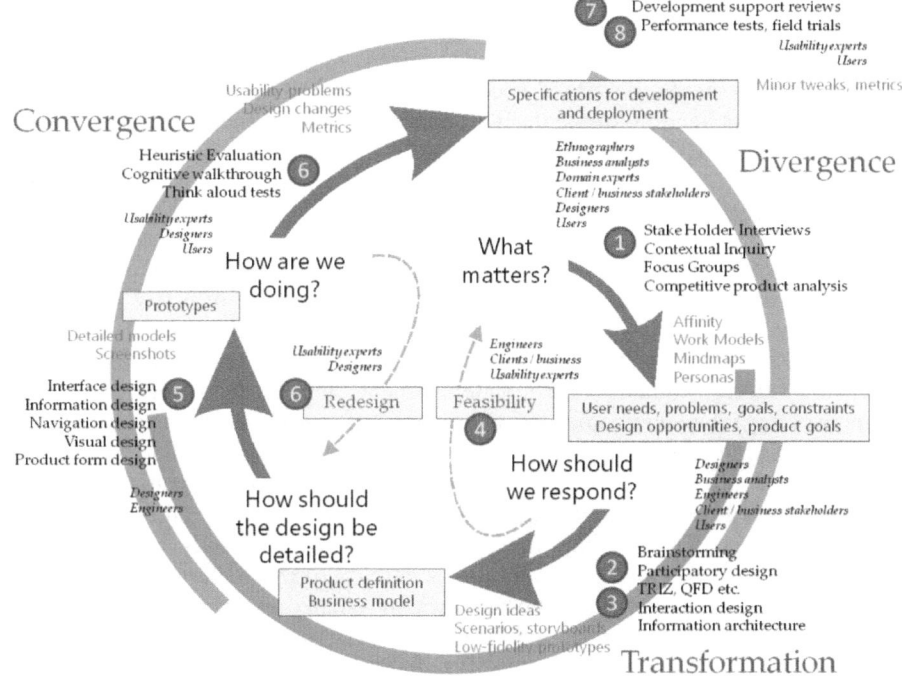

Fig. 1. Proposed framework for HCI design process

HCI activities, and associate them with typical methods, and deliverables. We organise the activities in phases, which we describe in terms of four questions derived from [12]: *What matters? How should we respond? How should the design be detailed? How are we doing?*

Figure 1 captures the phases, activities, methods, skills, and deliverables in a visual form. Table 1 summarises the same in a tabular view. Below, we describe this framework in detail. The framework is a flexible way of understanding and communicating the work of HCI designers in different contexts. Our objective is not to prescribe a one-size-fits-all HCI design process, but rather to articulate the typical HCI activities within which several methods and deliverables can be assimilated. Not all activities or methods may be essential in each instance of the process.

3.1   What Matters?

It is not only about what is "required" by someone. "What matters?" is a broader question and asks the design team to look at the problem at hand as holistically as possible. This question is answered through divergent thinking, looking beyond what had been specified in the design brief. The HCI activity associated with this phase is user studies, user modelling, and market analysis (activity 1 in Table 1). To understand the key concerns of the users, the stakeholders, the domain, and the context deeply, the team uses methods such as stakeholder interviews, contextual user interviews, focus groups, field observations, log analyses etc. The team may also study related issues such as the environmental, social, or cultural aspects. Most teams would do a benchmark analysis of competitive products. This is a very multi-disciplinary phase where ethnographers, business analysts, domain experts, client / business stakeholders, designers, and potential users are involved. At the end of this phase, the team gets a good understanding of users' needs, problems, goals, and constraints. They also have a good understanding of the design opportunities. The phase ends with identifying product goals, including usability goals.

3.2   How Should We Respond?

This is a holistic question as well. Now the design team is not just describing the situation but also transforming the problem space so that one or a few solutions become evident. The team begins with ideation (activity 2 in Table 1). With their creativity, but also using a range of ideation techniques such as brainstorming, synectics, participatory design, quality function deployment, and TRIZ (theory of inventor's problem solving) the team comes up with a range of design ideas that solve the problems and realise the opportunities.

The ideas could be wild and divergent to begin with, but eventually the team reaches a coherent understanding and articulation of the context and creates a meaningful, holistic response – a high-level product definition (activity 3 in Table 1). In interaction design, the product definition is often expressed through personas and scenarios. Sometimes, low-fidelity prototypes are created to support the scenarios. If design involves a new hardware, the form factor is modelled. If it involves software, wireframes of the screens are created. Buxton calls these techniques as 'sketching user experiences' [17].

In this phase, a multi-disciplinary team is involved, including designers, business analysts, engineers, and client / business stakeholders. If the method of participatory design is used, users are also involved. The product goals guide the team in this phase, but the product goals are also reviewed.

The first loop in the framework is the *feasibility* loop that occurs just after the product definition. Here business and technical feasibility of the proposed product definition are assessed. If competing product definitions are still in contention, a choice is made. If none of the proposed product definitions is found to be feasible, the team goes back and think of more alternatives. At this stage, the design team may do a formative evaluation of the product definition (activity 4 in Table 1), possibly by lightweight methods such as a heuristic evaluation or a cognitive walkthrough. The product definition would be refined to fix any problems found. At the end of this activity, product goals are finalised and technically and financially feasible product definition is agreed.

3.3 How Should the Design Be Detailed?

Once a feasible product definition is agreed upon, the detailed user interface is designed (activity 5 in Table 1). This activity completes the transformation and initiates the convergence. Designers explore the details of the user interfaces such as labels, icons, and behaviour of widgets. The text is written. Information is visualised. Visual elements such as typography, colours, fonts, and layouts are designed. Product form is finalised. Design decisions that seem particularly risky are prototyped first so that feedback on these can be sought early. This activity is primarily the designers' responsibility, though truly innovative designs may require collaboration between design, technology, and business. The output of this phase is one or more prototypes capturing and representing the design decisions.

3.4 How Are We Doing?

In this phase, the team seeks to converge to a usable solution quickly. The purpose of creating a prototype is to evaluate it. As it may happen, the initial design decisions do not fit all the users' needs. When a prototype is ready, a formative usability evaluation is done against the usability goals to identify potential problems with the design (activity 6 in Table 1). Card sorts and think-aloud tests are the most preferred method of evaluation at this stage, but other methods may also be used. Usability evaluators do the evaluations, though designers may also participate to get a first-hand feedback. The evaluation generates a list of problems and design ideas to fix them.

The second loop in the framework is that of *redesign*. As Gould and Lewis, interactive systems are particularly prone to having problems in the early designs [6]. After a round of evaluation, problems are fed back and products are redesigned until an acceptable solution is found. The fidelity of the prototypes keeps increasing through the iterations as more details are added. This cycle of design, prototype, evaluate, redesign needs to be tight, quick and consume as few resources as possible.

Changes to the design inevitably happen during software development. Some changes are inadvertent slip-ups that need to be corrected (e.g. an accidental change of typeface, colour, or layout). Other changes have to be made because the original design was not feasible. Yet other set of changes happen because there is a change in

Table 1. A multi-disciplinary framework for the HCI design process. Asterisk (*) denotes necessary deliverables.

Phases	Disciplines	HCI Activities	Methods	Deliverables
What matters?	Ethnographers, business analysts, domain experts, client / business stakeholders, designers, users	1. User studies, user modelling, market analysis	Stakeholder interviews Contextual inquiry Focus groups Competitive product analysis	Analysis of individual interviews User models such as affinity, work models, mind-maps, personas User needs, problems, goals and constraints* Opportunities for design interventions Product goals (including usability goals)*
How should we respond?	Designers, business analysts, engineers, client / business stakeholders, ethnographers, users	2. Ideation	Brainstorming Participatory design TRIZ QFD	Design ideas
		3. Product definition	Interaction design Information architecture	High-level use scenarios, storyboards Low fidelity prototypes, wireframes of software, foam models of hardware Business model Strategy, scope and structure of Garrett's model
Feasibility	Engineers, client / business stake-holders, usability experts	4. Formative usability evalua-tion 1 and re-finement	Heuristic evaluation	Refined and approved product definition and product goals* Technology feasibility approval* Business feasibility approval*
How should the design be detailed?	Designers, engi-neers	5. Design detail-ing	Interface design Information design Navigation design Visual design Product form design	Medium to high fidelity UI prototypes through iterations Structure, skeleton and surface of Garrett's model
How are we doing?	Usability experts, designers, users	6. Formative usability evalua-tion 2 and...	Heuristic evaluation Cognitive walkthrough Think aloud test Card sorting	Usability problems Metrics
		... refinement	Same as in design detail-ing	Refined, detailed UI prototypes* UI specification*
Dev. support	Designers, usability experts	7. Development support	Reviews during develop-ment	Minor tweaks
	Usability experts, users	8. Summative usability evalua-tion 3	Usability performance test Field trials	Usability approval* Metrics

requirements or change in technology platform. In all cases, ongoing collaboration between the design and engineering teams is important during software development – we call this development support (activity 7 in Table 1).

When an early version of the production code becomes available, it is a good idea to do a *summative usability evaluation* against the usability goals (activity 8 in Table 1). Often summative evaluation is done in a lab-based quantitative performance test. In some cases, it may be done by deploying the product in the field. Preferably, a summative evaluation is done by an external evaluator. The main outcome of a summative evaluation is (hopefully) a usability approval. A set of metrics could also emerge. Though summative evaluation is not supposed to affect the design, if serious usability problems are found, these ought to be fixed before release.

4   Recommended Weights for HCI Activities

The HCI activities in our framework must be integrated with the software engineering process model in use, so that they are applied in the practice of software development. Further, each activity may not be equally important in all situations. The importance of an activity would depend on the nature of the product, the context, and the experience of the team. In this section, we recommend the importance to be assigned to each HCI activity in our framework appropriate for typical contexts. However, note that the importance may vary in specific cases (some examples of which we point out). We express the importance of an activity by assigning it a weight on the scale of 0-5, where 0 indicates that the activity is not relevant, 1 indicates the activity is somewhat relevant, 2 indicates the activity is of typical importance, 3 indicates the activity is more important than usual, 4 indicates that the activity is very important, and 5 indicates that the activity is extremely important. Expressing the importance of these activities in this manner helps in direct evaluation of process metrics, as we describe in [18] and [19].

We will demonstrate the use of this framework with the waterfall model of software engineering. Despite criticisms, the waterfall model is still popular in the industry. In a survey of 200 practitioners, Neill and Leplante reported that the waterfall model was the most dominant and 35% of the practitioners claim using it [20]. In our experience, the waterfall model is used even more extensively in the Indian software industry.

To integrate our framework with the phases of the waterfall model, we suggest that the Communication phase of the waterfall model should include activities 1-4 of our framework, the Modelling phase should include activities 5-6 and the Construction phase should include activities 7-8 [21]. Table 2 lists our weight recommendations for each HCI activity when integrated with the waterfall model in this manner. Below, we describe our rationale for these weights.

In the beginning of a project, it is very important to understand the context of the user and the market scenario. Hence, the activities related to **user studies** and competitive product analysis is recommended a weight of 3 to 4. The weight can increase if the team is especially unfamiliar with the domain and the context, and can decrease if the team is very familiar with the domain and the context.

Table 2. Initial weights recommendations for HCI activities in the waterfall model

HCI Activity	Recommended weights
1. User studies, user modelling, competitive product analysis	3 – 4
2. Ideation with a multidisciplinary team	2
3. Product definition	1 – 3
4. Usability evaluation 1 of the product definition and refinement	1 – 3
5. User interface prototyping	4 – 5
6. Usability evaluation 2 of the user interface and refinement	4 – 5
7. Development support: ongoing reviews by usability team during development	3
8. Usability evaluation 3 of an early version	1 – 3

Ideation is an important activity. However, doing ideation formally as an independent activity may not be as important as generating ideas. Since user studies may also generate many ideas, the importance of explicit ideation is somewhat less. We therefore give it a weight of 2. However, extensive user studies may not be done if the product is not based on contextual data but on ideas, (for example, a toy, or an interactive installation). In such cases, the weight of ideation will go up.

Product definition is given a weight of 1 to 3 because we feel this activity can vary in importance. In situations where the product is very innovative or particularly unpredictable, the weight of this activity can go up. On the other hand, if the product is very predictable and what needs to be done is clearly understood by all, the weight can go down.

Detailed UI prototyping is the crux of the HCI design process as the main deliverables of HCI professionals come forth from it. This activity is therefore recommended a weight of 4 to 5.

In our framework, we identify three occasions where usability evaluation can be done – just after the product definition, after detailing out the user interface, and after an initial version of the working product becomes available. Of these, the first two are formative (aimed at improving the design), while the last one is summative (aimed at ensuring that all goals have been met). The formative evaluations are important as they directly affect the design. Between the two formative evaluations, we expect **usability evaluation 2 of the user interface** to be more important in many contexts as it will evaluate the design with many of its details in place. This evaluation is therefore recommended a weight of 4 to 5. We assume that if this formative evaluation was done well, the importance of doing the other two usability evaluations will be less.

Usability evaluation 1 of the product definition will usually have to be done on a very low fidelity prototype under very tight deadlines. Hence, we recommend a low weight for this step. In practice, the situations may vary somewhat. There may be opportunities (e.g. high-fidelity prototype was available early) and reasons (e.g. to demonstrate ideas to investors) to give more importance to the first formative evaluation. In this case, the weight of this usability evaluation can be increased and correspondingly, the weight for the next usability evaluation can be decreased.

Usability evaluation 3 of an early release is a summative evaluation and is expected to have little impact on design. Hence, it was also assigned a weight of 1.

However, in projects where user is expected to do critical tasks, this step will gain weight of up to 3.

Finally, we reckon that a lot depends on the continued contact between the HCI professionals and the development teams after the activity of detailed UI prototyping has been completed. Unanticipated UI changes may arise late in the project. In many companies, the HCI professionals are a shared resource and they keep moving from one project to the next before the earlier project is over. To emphasise the importance of **development support** and reviews of design changes during software development, we assign this step a weight of 3.

5 Validating Recommended Weights

5.1 Method

We derived the relative contributions of HCI activities in our framework to usability (and validated the weights proposed in section 4) with the help of simple linear regressions of each activity and a stepwise multiple linear regression of all activities on the usability of products in real-life industrial projects.

As a measure of the usability, we selected Usability Goals Achievement Metric (UGAM), a product metric that measures the extent to which the design achieves the usability goals. To calculate UGAM, high-level user experience goals are broken down into detailed, measurable goal parameters. For example, parameters for the high-level goal of *learnability* could be: options / data / information should be easy to find, user should take little time to learn, user should be able to learn on his own, the product should be consistent with its earlier version, etc. Each goal parameter is assigned a weight between 0-5. During a usability evaluation, each goal parameter is assigned a score between 0-100. UGAM is the sum of the weighted average of the scores,

$$UGAM = \frac{\sum W_p \times S_p}{\sum W_p}$$

where W_p is the weight of the goal parameter p and S_p is its score. UGAM is described in more detail in [18] and [19]. Goals and goal parameters are described in more detail in [22].

HCI professionals working in the Indian IT industry were invited to participate in the study. Participants were taught the method of calculating UGAM. They were also walked through the HCI activities in our process framework. First, participants were asked to calculate UGAM scores of the products delivered by their projects. Participants were then asked to assign a weight to each HCI activity based on their judgement of the importance of that activity in the context of their project. While they were shown the recommended weights described above, they were also given the freedom to assign a different score if they wished.

Finally, participants were asked to assign a score to each HCI activity from 0 to 100, where 100 represents the best case situation i.e. the activity was done in the best possible manner, with the highest fidelity, in the most appropriate phase of software development and with the best possible deliverables; 75 represents that the activity was somewhat toned down, but was still well-timed and well-executed; 50 represents an undecided state where the activity was done with some shortcuts or perhaps was not timed well; 25 represents that the activity was done with many shortcomings; and 0 represents the worst case situation where the activity was not done at all.

To help participants assign a score to each activity, we came up with detailed guidelines for evaluating each activity. For example, following are the guidelines for the activity 1 – user studies, user modelling, and competitive product analysis:

1. *Both organizational data gathering and user studies are done before requirements are finalized.*
2. *User studies are done in the context of the users by the method of contextual inquiry.*
3. *User studies are done with at least 20 users in each profile.*
4. *User studies are done by people with experience in user studies in a similar domain of at least 2 projects.*
5. *The findings including user problems, goals, opportunities, and constraints are analyzed, documented, and presented in an established user modelling methodology such as personas, work models, affinity diagram, etc.*
6. *Competitive / similar products and earlier versions of the products are evaluated for potential usability problems, at least by using discount usability evaluation methods such as heuristic evaluation, and are benchmarked.*
7. *User experience goals are explicitly agreed upon before finalizing requirements.*

100 = All the above are true, the activity was performed exceptionally well, 75 = At least five of the above are true, including point 7, or all the above are true, but point 3 had fewer than 20 users per profile, the activity was performed reasonably well, 50 = At least three of the above are true, including point 7, the activity was done with some shortcuts and / or perhaps was not timed well, 25 = Only two of the above are true, the activity was done poorly with many shortcomings, 0 = None of the above are true, the activity was not done.

Detailed guidelines for all activities are available online [23].

5.2 Weights Assigned by Participants

A total of 36 participants submitted 50 projects (some participants submitted more than one project). The HCI related experience of participants was between 1-7 years. The participants came from a wide variety of companies including large contracted software development companies, smaller contracted software development companies, multi-national companies with large product development centres in India, one large, internationally popular internet company, and five smaller product development companies. Only the projects following the waterfall model were used for the analyses presented in this paper.

Table 3 lists the averages of weights actually assigned by participants for HCI activities and their standard deviations. Participants do not seem to have deviated substantially from our recommendations.

Table 3. Initial recommendations for weights of the HCI activities and the average and the standard deviation of weights actually assigned by participants to those HCI activities (N = 50).

HCI Activity		Recommended weights	Assigned weights average	Assigned weights SD
1.	User studies, user modelling...	3 – 4	3.7	0.8
2.	Ideation with a multidisciplinary team	2	2.5	0.7
3.	Product definition	1 – 3	3.1	0.7
4.	Usability evaluation 1 of product definition...	1 – 3	2.0	1.1
5.	User interface prototyping	4 – 5	4.5	0.6
6.	Usability evaluation 2 of the user interface...	4 – 5	3.8	0.8
7.	Development support...	3	3.2	0.8
8.	Usability evaluation 3 of an early version...	1 – 3	1.9	1.0

5.3 Weights Derived from Regression Analysis

The score of each HCI activity is a measure of the fidelity of that HCI activity. UGAM is a measure of usability goal achievement in the project. The UGAM score is arrived at independently of the scores of HCI activities. If we can find the relative effect of the scores of HCI activities on the UGAM scores, this could be a way of evaluating the impact of HCI activities on the usability.

Separate simple linear regressions were performed assuming the scores of each of the eight HCI activities to be the predictor variables and UGAM to be the criterion variable (Table 4). In case of each HCI activity, a significant model emerged and the activity score had a positive significant Pearson's correlation with UGAM ($0.56 > R > 0.33$, $0.32 > R^2 > 0.11$, $0.30 >$ adjusted $R^2 > 0.09$, $22.399 > F > 5.796$, $p <= 0.02$, two-tailed). All coefficients were positive. All lower bounds of the 95% confidence intervals of the coefficients were also positive.

We can conclude that all HCI activities recommended in Table 2 affect UGAM positively. The scores of the HCI activities seem to be affecting the UGAM scores to varying degrees – some HCI activities have a larger effect on UGAM than others. The strongest correlations, largest adjusted R^2 values, and largest coefficients were observed for the HCI activities of user interface prototyping, usability evaluation of the user interface and refinement, development support, and user studies, user modelling, competitive product analysis. This justifies our 3+ weight recommendations for these activities (Table 2) and also the 3+ average weight assigned by participants (Table 3).

The adjusted R^2 value in a simple linear regression represents the extent to which a predictor variable affects the criterion variable. We could possibly assign weights to the HCI activities derived in proportion to the adjusted R^2 values we show below in column 4 of Table 6.

Using the stepwise method, a multiple regression was performed assuming the scores of the eight recommended HCI activities as predictor variables and UGAM as the criterion variable. The most significant model returned these values: $R = 0.784$, $R^2 = 0.614$, adjusted $R^2 = 0.580$, $F = 8.533$, $p < 0.005$. The four HCI activities identified above also emerged as significant predictors in this model (Table 5). The scores on these four HCI activities predicted 58% of variation in UGAM (adjusted $R^2 = 0.580$).

Table 4. Summary of simple linear regressions on UGAM as criterion variable and the scores of individual HCI activities as predictor variables on merged project scores (N = 50). The top four correlating activities have been highlighted.

	Model								95% conf. interval for B	
	R	R^2	Adj. R^2	F	Sig.	B	t	Sig.	Lower Bound	Upper Bound
User studies	0.445	0.207	0.190	12.517	0.001	0.221	3.538	0.001	0.095	0.346
Ideation	0.384	0.148	0.130	8.326	0.006	0.190	2.886	0.006	0.057	0.322
Prod Def	0.406	0.165	0.148	9.481	0.003	0.227	3.079	0.003	0.079	0.375
UE 1	0.351	0.123	0.105	6.748	0.012	0.162	2.598	0.012	0.037	0.287
UI Proto	0.564	0.318	0.304	22.399	0.000	0.299	4.733	0.000	0.172	0.426
UE 2	0.534	0.285	0.270	19.126	0.000	0.249	4.373	0.000	0.134	0.363
Dev Support	0.532	0.283	0.268	18.967	0.000	0.216	4.355	0.000	0.116	0.315
UE 3	0.328	0.108	0.089	5.796	0.020	0.134	2.407	0.020	0.022	0.246

These four HCI activities had a positive, significant coefficient ($p <= 0.023$) and the lower bound of the 95% confidence interval for all coefficients was positive. The variance inflation factors (VIFs) of all predictor variables are well below 4, indicating that there is no multi-collinearity among the predictor variables. This implies that the assumption that the HCI activity scores are independent variables was acceptable for the purpose of the stepwise multiple regression.

Table 5. The most significant model in the SPSS output of stepwise multiple linear regression on UGAM as criterion variable and the ratings of HCI activities as predictor variables (n = 50)

R	R^2	Adj. R^2	Std. Error of the Estimate	Change Statistics				
				R Square Change	F Change	df1	df2	Sig. F Change
0.784	0.614	0.580	7.702	0.073	8.533	1	45	0.005

	Unstandardised Coefficients		Standardised coefficients	t	Sig.	95% Confidence Interval for B		Collinearity Statistics
	B	Std. Error				L. Bound	U. Bound	VIF
(Constant)	33.794	4.024		8.398	0.000	25.690	41.889	
Usability Eval 2	0.154	0.048	0.332	3.208	0.002	0.057	0.250	1.247
Dev Support	0.123	0.040	0.306	3.064	0.004	0.042	0.204	1.165
User studies	0.138	0.047	0.286	2.921	0.006	0.043	0.233	1.116
UI Prototyping	0.133	0.057	0.253	2.346	0.023	0.019	0.247	1.354

Brace et al. suggest that the standardised coefficients of the predictor variables in a multiple regression can be used to compare the relative contribution of each predictor variable to the criterion variable and assess the strength of the relationship [24]. We could possibly assign weights to the HCI activities derived in proportion to these standardised coefficients as shown in column 5 of Table 6.

Table 6. A comparison of our recommended weights, average weights assigned by participants, weights derived by scaling up adjusted R^2 values from simple linear regressions (SLRs) and from scaling up the standardised coefficients of the stepwise multiple regression (MR)

HCI Activity		Recommended weights	Assigned weights	Derived weights scaled from	
				SLRs	MR
1.	User studies, user modelling...	3 – 4	3.7	3.1	4.3
2.	Ideation with a multidisciplinary team	2	2.5	2.1	-
3.	Product definition	1 – 3	3.1	2.4	-
4.	Usability evaluation 1...	1 – 3	2.0	1.7	-
5.	User interface prototyping	4 – 5	4.5	5.0	3.8
6.	Usability evaluation 2 of the UI...	4 – 5	3.8	4.4	5.0
7.	Development support...	3	3.2	4.4	4.6
8.	Usability evaluation 3...	1 – 3	1.9	1.5	-

6 Conclusions

Drawing from literature, we proposed a framework comprising of 8 HCI activities. By using simple linear regressions, we could demonstrate that each of these activities had a significant positive correlation with the usability metric UGAM. In a stepwise multiple regression, four of these HCI activities accounted for 58% of the variation UGAM. We can conclude that while all activities in the framework affect usability, the identified four HCI activities are relatively more important. The statistical analyses were in consonance with our original recommendations and with the weights assigned by practitioners, as summarised in Table 6 above. Perhaps the most underestimated HCI activity during recommendation and assignment was the support that HCI teams need to give during the software development, though it was not a complete surprise.

A possible critique of our method could be that we showed the recommended weights to the participants before they assigned theirs. While this could have been an approach, it must be noted that that neither the recommended weights, nor the weights assigned by participants play a role in the regression analyses, which are based on the UGAM scores and activity scores alone. The weights derived from the regression analyses validate both the recommended and the assigned weights.

Another possible critique could be about our assumption that the scores of HCI activities are independent variables. Although the activity scores are naturally related (teams likely to score well on some HCI activities are likely to score well on others), it was essential to use them as predictor variables as it is the only way to establish their effect on usability. We minimised the bias by prescribing guidelines for evaluating each activity. The statistics did not show any multi-collinearity among the HCI activity scores.

Knowing which HCI activities are important would be useful in many contexts, particularly when resources are scarce and tradeoffs need to be made. Designers can use the rigorous, higher fidelity methods on activities that are more important, and make do with discount methods on less important activities. This knowledge would be useful in integrating HCI activities in software engineering processes – HCI professionals can insist on including the important activities, while conceding the relatively less important ones. The weighted average of the scores of activities could be used as a process metric as we describe in [18] and [19].

We used our framework of HCI activities, the waterfall model, UGAM as the product metric, and projects from the Indian IT industry to find the relative contribution of various HCI activities. Our results may be generalised within these choices. Other researchers could use other frameworks, other process models, other product metrics, and / or other contexts in a similar way to identify the activities that matter in those contexts.

Acknowledgements

We thank Sanjay Tripathi, Pramod Khambete, Ved Prakash Nirbhay, Deepak Korpal, Atul Manohar, Aniruddha Puranik, Prof. UA Athavankar, Prof. Umesh Bellur, Prof. S Sudarshan, and all participants in the studies for their suggestions, assistance, and contributions.

References

1. Archer, B.: Systematic Method for Designers. Council of Industrial Design (1965)
2. Jones, C.: Design Methods, Seeds of Human Futures. Wiley- Interscience, Chichester (1970)
3. Lawson, B.: The Design Process Demystified. Butterworth Architecture, Butterworths (1980)
4. Cross, N.: Engineering Design Methods, 3rd edn. John Wiley & Sons, Chichester (2000)
5. Laseau, P.: Graphic Thinking for Architects and Designers. Van Nostrand Reinhold Company, New York (1980)
6. Gould, J., Lewis, C.: Designing for Usability: Key Principles and What Designers Think. Communications of the ACM 28(3) (1985)
7. Nielsen, J.: Usability Engineering. Morgan Kaufmann, San Francisco (1993)
8. Kreitzberg, C.: Managing for Usability. In : Multimedia: A Management Perspective. Wadsworth, Belmont (1996)
9. Dix, A., Finlay, J., Abowd, G., Beale, R.: Human-Computer Interaction, 2nd edn. Prentice Hall, Englewood Cliffs (1998)
10. Preece, J., Rogers, Y., Sharp, H.: Interaction Design, Beyond Human-Computer Interaction, 1st edn. John Wiley & Sons, Chichester (2002)
11. Sharp, H., Rogers, Y., Preece, J.: Interaction Design, Beyond Human-Computer Interaction, 2nd edn. Wiley India, Chichester (2007)
12. Beyer, H., Holtzblatt, K.: Contextual Design. Morgan Kaufmann, San Francisco (1998)
13. Cooper, A., Reimann, R.: About Face 2.0. Wiley, Chichester (2003)
14. Mayhew, D.: Usability Engineering Lifecycle. Morgan Kaufmann, San Francisco (1999)
15. Garrett, J.: The Elements of User Experience. New Riders, Indianapolis (2003)
16. Gulliksen, J., Göransson, B., Bovie, I., Blomkvist, S., Persson, J., Persson, J., Cajander, A.: Key Principles for User-centred System Design. Behaviour and Information Technology 22(6) (2003)
17. Buxton, B.: Sketching User Experiences. Morgan Kaufmann, San Francisco (2007)

18. Joshi, A., Tripathi, S.: User Experience Metric and Index of Integration: Measuring Impact of HCI Activities on User Experience. In: International Workshop on the Interplay between Usability Evaluation and Software Development, Pisa (2008)
19. Joshi, A., Sarda, N., Tripathi, S.: Measuring Effectiveness of HCI Integration in Software Development Processes. Journal of Software System (in press, 2010) (Corrected Proof), doi: 10.1016/j.jss.2010.03.078
20. Neill, C., Laplante, P.: Requirements Engineering: The State of the Practice. IEEE Software 20(6) (2003)
21. Joshi, A., Sarda, N.: HCI and SE: Towards a 'Truly' Unified Waterfall Process. In: Aykin, N. (ed.) HCII 2007. LNCS, vol. 4559, pp. 108–112. Springer, Heidelberg (2007)
22. Joshi, A.: Usability Goals Setting Tool. In: 4th Workshop on Software and Usability Engineering Cross-Pollination: Usability Evaluation of Advanced Interfaces, Uppsala (2009)
23. Joshi, A.: Index of Integration, http://www.idc.iitb.ac.in/~anirudha/ioi.htm (accessed 2009)
24. Brace, N., Kemp, R., Snelgar, R.: SPSS for Psychologists, 2nd edn. Palgrave Macmillan, China (2003)

AFFINE for Enforcing Earlier Consideration of NFRs and Human Factors When Building Socio-Technical Systems Following Agile Methodologies

Mohamed Bourimi[1,2], Thomas Barth[2], Joerg M. Haake[1],
Bernd Ueberschär[3], and Dogan Kesdogan[2]

[1] FernUniversität in Hagen, Cooperative Systems, 58084 Hagen, Germany
bourimi@gmail.com
[2] University of Siegen, Chair for IT Security, 57076 Siegen, Germany
[3] Leibniz Institute of Marine Sciences at the University of Kiel, 24105 Kiel, Germany

Abstract. Nowadays, various user-centered and participatory design methodologies with different degree of agility are followed when building sophisticated socio-technical systems. Even when applying these methods, non-functional requirements (NFRs) are often considered too late in the development process and tension that may arise between users' and developers' needs remains mostly neglected. Furthermore, there is a conceptual lack of guidance and support for efficiently fulfilling NFRs in terms of software architecture in general. This paper aims at introducing the AFFINE framework *simultaneously* addressing these needs with (1) conceptually considering NFRs early in the development process, (2) explicitly balancing end-users' with developers' needs, and (3) a reference architecture providing support for NFRs. Constitutive requirements for AFFINE were gathered based on experiences from various projects on designing and implementing groupware systems.

1 Introduction

Nowadays, a shift is taking place from single-user-centered usage to support multi-user needs and hence covering many collaboration measures and social aspects. The needed technical support for these users' activities in many important areas of our professional and leisure life activities is provided through collaborative applications also known as groupware as well as social software. According to Shneiderman and Plaisant *"an extrapolation of current trends leads to the suggestion that most computer-based tasks will become collaborative because just as most work environments have social aspects"* [1]. Thus, software systems and applications supporting collaboration are considered as socio-technical systems in the Computer-Supported Cooperative Work (CSCW) as well as Human-Computer Interaction (HCI) research fields [2]. Because socio-technical systems are characterized by complex scenarios which are mostly reflected e.g. in the user interface, HCI and CSCW also focus nowadays on human aspects of the development of computer technology in collaborative settings. While the goals of interaction are mostly covered by functional requirements (FRs), users' preferences (e.g. usability) and concerns (such as privacy and security) are related to non-functional requirements (NFRs). According to [3], FRs define what the

R. Bernhaupt et al. (Eds.): HCSE 2010, LNCS 6409, pp. 182–189, 2010.
© IFIP International Federation for Information Processing 2010

system does and therefore its functionality whereas NFRs define how a system has to be. Many CSCW and HCI key literature studied NFRs such as usability in socio-technical and the trade-offs, which could arise between them, e.g. privacy and awareness trade-offs in those systems. However, various literature state that current approaches do not adequately consider generally NFRs from the beginning in the development processes such stated in [3]. Thus, recently many development approaches especially in the area of socio-technical systems follow user-centered and participatory design in combination with agile methodologies in order to efficiently react on end-users' emerging needs and (change) requirements [4,5,6]. In our opinion, even when a given NFR is considered from the beginning (i.e. usability in user-centered or participatory design), it is mostly contemplated separately from other NFRs and factors. When considering that socio-technical systems mostly represent a special category of distributed systems that are known to be difficult to design and maintain, tensions could arise between project stakeholders (i.e. end-users and developers) especially in agile settings. Furthermore, current approaches often not explicitly address the gap of mapping NFRs into the underlying system architecture. In this paper, we present the AFFINE (Agile Framework For Integrating Non-functional requirements Engineering) *simultaneously* addressing these needs.

We first present identified needs in Section 2. Next, we describe our approach consisting of the AFFINE framework in Section 3 and our conclusions in Section 4.

2 Problem and Requirements Analysis

Software development processes can be seen as complex collaborative social processes. In order to reduce the potential complexity of these processes and assure the delivery as well as the quality of the products, many models (e.g. the well-known waterfall, prototyping, and spiral model) tried to structure the software development processes and define their behavior e.g. by introducing roles and defining software development life cycles. Latter include common phases like the requirements analysis, design, development, testing, and support phases. In contrast to the classical defined process models, agile process models and methodologies intend a better reaction on unexpected problems often by consideration of human factors. They are empirical processes that cannot be consistently repeated and therefore require constant monitoring and adaptation [7]. However, Balzert states in [8] that according to a coarse classification of the activities independently of a given development processes, one could generally differentiate between two main phases, namely, the *solution specification phase* and the *solution construction phase*. While most of the activities of the specification phase can be classified as requirements engineering activities, the activities of the construction phase target mapping a given solution specification to a concrete technical solution. Different software engineering practices recognized the critical importance of NFRs for the specification and construction of software systems in general. A classical work addressing NFRs is [3] state that software engineering practices concentrate on FRs, rather than NFRs. Furthermore, the authors cite that NFRs are generally stated informally during the requirements analysis, are often contradictory, difficult to enforce, and to validate during software development process. Based on further literature, they state that not taking NFRs properly into account is acknowledged to be the most expensive and difficult to correct once the software has been implemented and thus, there is a need to deal comprehensively with such requirements during the system development process. The concrete needs we address in this paper were identified based on one of the long-running project CURE (Collaborative Universal Remote Education) we were able to follow. This project has a very representative character since its needs correspond to identified needs in other literature. The CURE platform was developed at the FernUniversität in Hagen (FuH) to support different collaborative learning and collaborative work scenarios [9]. The development process followed in CURE is an agile process called the Oregon Software Development Process (OSDP) described in [10]. Applying OSDP considered end-users' feedback of the participating departments at the FuH. Representatives of students and instructors from various disciplines such as mathematics, electrical engineering, computer sciences and psychology were participating in the usage and evaluation of the prototypes resulting from each OSDP-iteration. Even though OSDP considers conceptually NFRs in form of a NFR backlog, their consideration was not earlier enough to overcome drawbacks in the construction phase. In the case of CURE, responding to end-users wishes related to NFRs (e.g. usability of the web interface, performance of the synchronous communication means and awareness provision in the shared workspaces) was interrupted in order to meet the delivery, integration deadlines and budget. CURE was extended in various sub-projects (e.g. [11,12,13]). Most of these works were primarily concerned with improving NFRs which were classified as insufficiently covered by the developed system or tried to address new needs emerged through the usage of the system. Ambler states in [14] that NFRs and constrains are difficult to consider in projects following agile methodologies. A conceptual consideration of NFRs in the followed methodology avoids delegating their fulfillment to the intuition of involved people that could result in intentional or accidental negligence. Thus, we identify the need of *conceptually enforcing the consideration of all relevant NFRs and possible trade-offs early in the development process (N1)*.

Involving end-users in an agile process could be very expensive. Especially when an agile methodology is followed in the end-users as well as developers are often experiencing continuous communication tensions. Developers are often asked to change, e.g., user interfaces or functionality, which seemed to be agreed upon earlier. Furthermore, on the one hand end-users and developers have different terminology for the same things or the same terminology for different things. On the other hand, members of the same development team might have different backgrounds and terminologies. This is also crucial in the case that different partners and/or distributed teams are cooperating in the same project. Communication problems are well known in the software engineering field and do not concern only agile methods. The same methodology may not be imposed to different stakeholder in the project, since involved parties may already have elaborated methodologies and processes as well as have different interests and goals (i.e. using their own software pieces or products etc.). Indeed, recent studies show that the most frequent failure source are communication problems with more than 70% [15] and that 33% of the projects are negatively affected or cancelled because of changing the requirements [16]. Based on our experiences we argue that this is especially expensive when following an agile development process. Even though agility assure the close involvement of end-users, latter are mostly not experienced in communicating requirements to the developers [8]. Thus we identify the second need of *explicitly balancing end-users' with developers' needs when following agile development method(ologie)s (N2)*.

The design and evaluation of socio-technical systems is still a challenge because of the exploratory nature of these applications [1]. Indeed, people involvement varies and the usage can range from occasional to frequent according to a given setting and circumstances. The same socio-technical system can lead to different evaluation results in different social environments [2]. The evaluation of socio-technical systems needs methodologies and approaches that allows for rapid and cost-effective development and usage of prototypes. Shneiderman and Plaisant mention that *"while software engineering methodologies are effective in facilitating the software development process, they have not always provided processes for studying the users, understanding their needs, and creating a usable interface"* [1]. Depending on the project specific situation, development costs need often to be reduced. Software should not be built from scratch each time in the development process. In [17], Grudin addresses challenges for groupware developers and suggests that adding new functionality to an accepted application is more adequate than developing a new application. This is a typical case when building many socio-technical systems or while their evolution. At a first glance, adding new functionality and enhanced interaction possibilities to existing systems seems attractive. However, adding new functionality often requires adding and modifying a lot of source code. This often complicates the API and requires a redesign of the domain model. Furthermore, Paech et al. argues in their position paper [18] that FRs and NFRs as well as architecture should not be separated. The emerging changes are especially crucial when considering costs in terms of (re-)design, implementation and retrofitting costs. Thus, added functionality to socio-technical systems is reflected in growing complexity of their classes and/or components. Thus, the extension or retrofitting and the integration of new components in these systems represent realistic scenarios, which have to be considered in terms of development costs. However, it is important that by freezing changes, the design of the system stays extendable for future extensions and retrofitting. Thus, we formulate the third need as follows: *The development method must be supported at the architectural and construction level to assure meeting N1 and N2 at minimal cost. A Kind of reference architecture providing support for NFRs is needed (N3)*. While **N1** is more concerned with the specification phase of a given socio-technical system and **N3** with its construction phase, **N2** still overlapping both phases when following an agile methodology. S*imultaneous* consideration of **N1-N3** is therefore required.

3 Our Approach: AFFINE

Introducing an agile method at the level of the development process is the key to satisfy **N1** and **N2** at the organizational level in our opinion. In order to reduce the complexity of the involvement of our method in various phases of the followed development process in a given project, we propose as an integral component Scrum [28]. Scrum can be seen as a process for empirical control of software development, which helps in handling changing requirements more efficiently by considering human factors in the development process of both; customers (in our case end-users) and project stakeholders in general. Based on our experiences in various projects, the main strengthens of Scrum consists of (1) the simplicity in terms of roles defined (Scrum master, product owner, and development team), development steps to be followed (e.g. development periods called sprints), documentation to be produced (e.g. sprint backlog), and meetings to be held (e.g. daily Scrum), (2) balancing the needs of the customers and developers through consensus enforcement for a given deliverable and continuous communication (e.g. in the daily Scrum meetings), (3) creating awareness on ongoing project tasks (also in daily Scrum e.g.), and (4) allowing for better as well as faster handling of detected, non-expected problems during the development process, which generally results (by right application) in better acceptance of the delivered product with low costs.

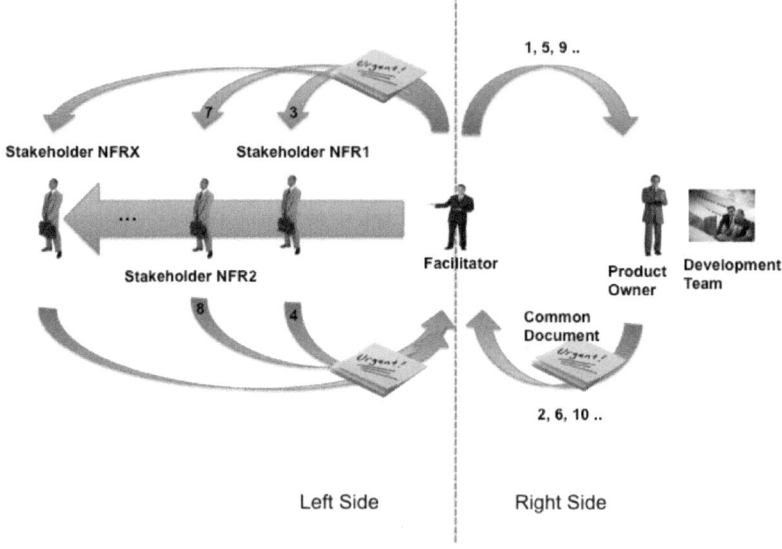

Fig. 1. The Scrum based AFFINE method

The right side of Figure 1 represents broadly a typical Scrum development procedure. A facilitator (in our case the Scrum master) as well as the product owner and development team interact with each other in order to drive the product development. This interaction is represented as loop involving them all together. Since the facilitator moderates the interaction, we represent such loop as an arrow starting and ending in the facilitator role. In Scrum, a sprint backlog document might be updated in such loop. Numerating this loop in our representation does not imply that the interaction is carried out in a giving sequence inside it. The left side of the same Figure shows our extension of a typical Scrum process to enforce the earlier consideration of NFRs. There, we introduce the role of a NFR stakeholder (mostly experts), who is concerned with the fulfillment and consideration of a respective NFR. The same facilitator has to moderate the circulation of the common document to the first stakeholder (according to prior prioritization), who has to update the document (e.g. adding warnings, requirements or changing them etc.). The structure of the common document and its content have to be defined from the project involved parties. However, circulating only one document, which contains all needed information for the development of given product, should avoid potential inconsistencies and information lost. After updating the document (at least by annotating that it was reviewed and maybe admitted without changes from the respective stakeholder), the document returns to the facilitator(s) and loops again over the left side. By admission without changes, the facilitator might shorten this iteration and directly forward the document to the next stakeholder. If any change happens in late circulations at the level of a stakeholder, the document returns to the facilitator, has to be circulated in the right side, and finally has to begin the circulation at the first stakeholder at the left side. We suggest the following informal steps for N1 and N2:

1. Involvement of all stakeholders of the project and introducing the role of the facilitator (one or more according to the project setting).
2. Goals or use cases (UC) identification of the intended processes (by defining the set of FRs). The facilitator has e.g. to guarantee the same terminology is used and has to detect miss-satisfaction signs in the different phases.
3. Alignment of all NFRs that have to be considered prioritizing them according to the project goals or UCs.
4. Responsible and experts for each goal or UC as well as NFR have to be chosen.
5. Circulating a single document (to avoid syncing various documents) containing the set of goals or UCs and their specification and modeling (by considering aligned FRs and NFRs at the same time). For this, UML or similar notations could be helpful in order to estimate efforts. The circulation has to be performed by the facilitator according to the priority of the NFRs. If a breakdown is identified in the circulation loop, the document has to be send back to the responsible of the first affected NFR (ordinarily with higher priority). If many NFRs are simultaneously affected, a meeting of the responsible and experts has to be organized. When conflicts arise, the facilitator intervenes in order to reach consensus. Since the facilitator is normally only a supporting role, his main goal consists in delivering the result while preserving satisfaction of end-users and project stakeholders. However, the final decision has to be made by the responsible(s) or at least by the coordination entity of the project.
6. The circulation ends when reaching the goals i.e. by implementing the UCs and testing them (also through the end-users).

Those steps have to be executed for each project iteration. If the project is organized according big work packages, following a divide and conquer methodology could be helpful. In order to optimize the requirements gathering, user-centered design and modeling steps (for instance by using established methods like prototyping) and UML or ER diagrams (as mentioned before) could be useful.

Finally, we want to mention, that the facilitator does not represents a critical point in this procedure. Any person familiarized with development activities should be able to act within this process as a facilitator. Further, if Scrum is integrated as an agile method, the Scrum certification exam ensures needed qualification of a facilitator. Related to **N3**, SOA is currently assessed as the next step forward in the design, development, operation, and organization of large-scale distributed systems (see e.g. [22]).

Characteristics like loose coupling, discovery of artifacts during design/run time, and the ability to reuse services to enable efficient adaptation of a system to changing requirements (e.g. changes in users behavior, processes) are not supposed to be provided by an architectural approach for the first time. Learning from preceding approaches, characteristics like the commitment to open standards and the separation of architectural concepts from their technical implementation led to a widespread acceptance of service-oriented principles in commercial as well as scientific communities. Since in our context NFRs are in the focus of attention, the inherent possibility of tailoring an SOA at design time according to the actual needs by carefully selecting the specifications to implement is an adequate means to realize these requirements [22]. Beyond this, NFRs like usability and performance in socio-technical systems can only be assessed during runtime and in close cooperation with the end-user. As already discussed in this paper, an early consideration of NFRs during the lifecycle of an SOA leads to reduced development cost. Integrating different stakeholders into the development of an SOA is one approach to handle this; a Service Life Cycle Model focusing on SOAs stakeholders as a prerequisite for governing an SOA throughout its lifecycle is presented in [23]. Since NFRs are crosscutting concerns, the positive synergy between aspect-oriented programming (AOP) techniques and SOA for satisfying NFRs implementation was beneficial in our case. The architecture of the CURE-based sub-projects described in the related publications supports different kind of clients (i.e. Eclipse RPC thick client for the collaborative design editor [11], normal and AJAX browser clients for the retrofitted CURE [12], and mobile as well as ubiquitous clients for the ubiquitous CURE [13]) with the same SOA/AOP layer. Thereby, different kinds of architecture families also are supported (based the on client-server model, replicating or P2P). Surely, this is due because the context of these sub-projects could be satisfied with such single layer. Nevertheless, if different contexts have to be supported, various instances of the SOA/AOP layer could be deployed. So we mean that our AOP/SOA-based generic architecture meets **N3** with a high genericity.

4 Conclusion

In this paper, we proposed the AFFINE framework that aims at *simultaneously* addressing three needs when developing socio-technical systems by following agile methodologies. The three needs were identified from the long-running project CURE as well as based on relevant HCI and CSCW literature gathered experiences. The main idea of AFFINE is to use an agile method including Scrum as an integral part. The agile method is user-centered and considers human factors, which could affect the success and acceptance of the developed socio-technical systems. The method enforces conceptually the earlier consideration of NFRs while the suggested supporting architecture provides a generic reference architecture for developing socio-technical systems in agile development settings. Furthermore, AFFINE is independent from a specific software development process and applicable for different phases of the followed process in a given project. The concrete suggestion to use SOA and AOP at the technological level showed their advantages in first evaluations. The proposed framework is now successfully being applied in the ongoing work of many projects led by us as first empirical evaluations show. Future work aims at collecting more experiences and refining AFFINE.

References

1. Shneiderman, B., Plaisant, C.: Designing the User Interface: Strategies for Effective Human-Computer Interaction, 4th edn. Pearson Addison Wesley, London (2005)
2. Gross, T., Koch, M.: Computer-Supported Cooperative Workspace. Oldenburg, Bombay (2007)
3. Chung, L., Nixon, B.A.: Dealing with non-functional requirements: three experimental studies of a process-oriented approach. In: ICSE 1995. ACM, New York (1995)
4. Jokela, T.: Assessment of user-centred design processes - lessons learnt and conclusions. In: Oivo, M., Komi-Sirviö, S. (eds.) PROFES 2002. LNCS, vol. 2559, pp. 232–246. Springer, Heidelberg (2002)
5. Schümmer, T., Lukosch, S., Slagter, R.: Empowering end-users: A pattern-centered groupware development process. In: Fukś, H., Lukosch, S., Salgado, A.C. (eds.) CRIWG 2005. LNCS, vol. 3706, pp. 73–88. Springer, Heidelberg (2005)
6. Lieberman, H., Paterno, F., Wulf, V. (eds.): End User Development. Springer, Heidelberg (2006)
7. Highsmith, J.: Agile software development ecosystems. Addison-Wesley, Reading (2002)
8. Balzert, H.: Lehrbuch der Softwaretechnik, Basiskonzepte und Requirements Engineering,, 3rd edn. Spektrum (2008)
9. Haake, J.M., Schümmer, T., Haake, A., Bourimi, M., Landgraf, B.: Supporting flexible collaborative distance learning in the cure platform, vol. 1. IEEE Computer Society, Los Alamitos (2004)
10. Schümmer, T., Slagter, R.: The oregon software development process (2004)
11. Bourimi, M.: Collaborative design and tailoring of Web based learning environments in CURE. In: Dimitriadis, Y.A., Zigurs, I., Gómez-Sánchez, E. (eds.) CRIWG 2006. LNCS, vol. 4154, pp. 421–436. Springer, Heidelberg (2006)
12. Bourimi, M., Lukosch, S., Kühnel, F.: Leveraging visual tailoring and synchronous awareness in Web-based collaborative systems. In: Haake, J.M., Ochoa, S.F., Cechich, A. (eds.) CRIWG 2007. LNCS, vol. 4715, pp. 40–55. Springer, Heidelberg (2007)
13. Bourimi, M., Kühnel, F., Haake, J., Abou-Tair, D., Kesdogan, D.: Tailoring collaboration according privacy needs in real-identity collaborative systems. In: CRIWG (2009)
14. Ambler, S.W.: Beyond functional requirements on agile projects. Dr. Dobb's Journal 33(10) (2008)
15. Huth, S.: Marktstudie probleme und fehler im requirements-engineering,
   http://www.sigs-datacom.de/wissen/artikel-fachzeitschriftel/
   artikelansicht.html?tx_mwjournals_pi1%5BshowUid%5D=2479
   (accessed 2010)
16. Emam, K.E., Koru, A.G.: A replicated survey of it software project failures. IEEE Softw. 25(5) (2008)
17. Grudin, J.: Groupware and social dynamics: eight challenges for developers. Communications of the ACM 37(1) (1994)
18. Paech, B., Dutoit, A.H., Kerkow, D., Knethen, A.V.: Functional requirements, non-functional requirements, and architecture should not be separated. Technical report, Proceedings of the International Workshop on Requirements Engineering (2002)
19. Schwaber, K.: Scrum overview, http://codebetter.com/blogs/
   darrell.norton/pages/50339.aspx (accessed August 2010)
20. Erl, T.: Service-Oriented Architecture (SOA): Concepts, Technology, and Design. Prentice Hall PTR, Englewood Cliffs (2006)
21. Gu, Q., Lago, P.: A stakeholder-driven service life cycle model for SOA. In: IW- SOSWE 2007: 2nd International Workshop on Service Oriented Software Engineering. ACM, New York (2007)

Understanding Formal Description of Pitch-Based Input

Ondřej Poláček and Zdeněk Míkovec

Faculty of Electrical Engineering, Czech Technical University in Prague,
Karlovo nam. 13, 12135 Prague 2, Czech Republic
{polacond,xmikovec}@fel.cvut.cz

Abstract. The pitch-based input (humming, whistling, singing) in acoustic modality has already been studied in several projects. There is also a formal description of the pitch-based input which can be used by designers to define user control of an application. However, as we discuss in this paper, the formal description can contain semantic errors. The aim of this paper is to validate the formal description with designers. We present a tool that is capable of visualizing vocal commands and detecting semantic errors automatically. We have conducted a user study that brings preliminary results on comprehension of the formal description by designers and ability to identify and remove syntactic errors.

Keywords: Non-verbal Vocal Interaction; Vocal Gesture; Formal Description; User Study.

1   Introduction

The *Non-Verbal Vocal Interaction* (NVVI) can be described as a method of interaction, in which sounds, other than speech, are produced. There are several approaches described in the literature which include using pitch of a tone, length of a tone, volume, or vowels in order to control the user interfaces. The NVVI is an interaction method that has already received a significant focus within the research community. It has been used as an input modality for people with motor disabilities [7][3] as well as voice training tool [2]. It is a method that shares some similarities with *Automatic Speech Recognition* (ASR). However, when comparing both interaction styles, several differences are revealed. Several reports, including mouse emulation [1] or controlling real-time games [7], suggest that NVVI is better fitted to continuous control rather than ASR. NVVI is cross-cultural and language independent [8]. Unlike ASR, NVVI generally employs simple signal processing methods [3]. Due to NVVIs limited expressive capabilities, ASR is better at triggering commands, macros or shortcuts. NVVI should be considered as a complement to ASR rather than replacement.

To design an application controlled by speech a set of word patterns or grammar must be defined. This grammar will then allow the ASR to recognize a range of expected words used in utterances. Likewise, a designer can also use a similar formal method for pitch-based NVVI.

R. Bernhaupt et al. (Eds.): HCSE 2010, LNCS 6409, pp. 190–197, 2010.

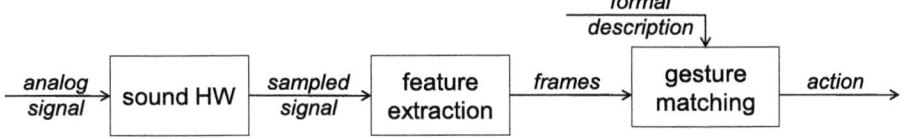

Fig. 1. NVVI signal processing pipeline

The signal processing pipeline for most pitch-based NVVI systems is depicted in Figure 1. Pitch is extracted from the sampled signal in a short discrete periods of time called frames. The typical duration of one frame is approximately 20 ms. The formal description of the NVVI and a stream of frames are then matched together, followed by generation of an appropriate action.

2   Formal Description

When designing a set of voice gestures, the designer must describe an ideal pitch profile for each gesture. These ideal pitch profiles are then referred to as *gesture templates* and they are usually represented in graphic form as shown in Figure 2. However, the users are unable to produce an ideal pitch profile. The interpretation of gesture templates by the user is referred to as *gesture instances*. An example of the relationship between a gesture template and its instances is depicted in Figure 2. Note that slightly different instances share the same semantics defined by the gesture template which is in this case an increasing tone. Once gesture templates are designed in a graphic form, they can be described by a *Voice Gesture Template* (VGT) expressions. Design of VGT expression is described in detail in [5]. These expressions are similar to regular expressions. They have two terminal symbols p and s that correspond to pitch and silence. They also use an operator * for repetition and operator | for the choice. However, there are several symbols with different meanings, for example brackets [ ] which are used for more sophisticated conditions and brackets <> which are used for output definitions to trigger an action. The use of VGT expressions is illustrated in Figure 3. The gesture template depicted in Figure 3 describes instances which start under midi note 60 and increase in pitch to more than 4 midi notes. Midi notes [4] are numerical representations of traditional notes in western music notation, for example, midi note number 60

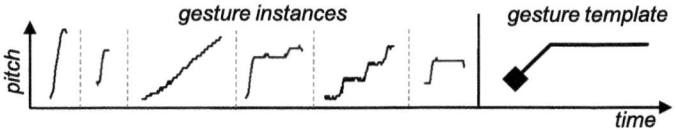

Fig. 2. Relationship between a gesture template and its instances

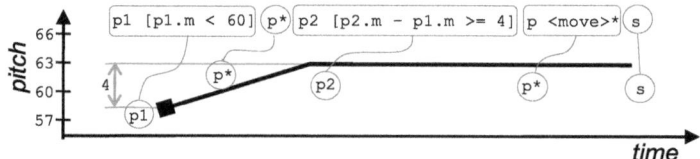

Fig. 3. VGT expression and its graphical representation of gesture template

corresponds to c'. The Figure 3 also illustrates the relation of VGT expression and the graphic representation of the gesture template. This process can be divided into four parts:

1. In the first part, the frame p1 is matched to the expression when its pitch is under midi note 60. This is ensured by the condition [p1.m < 60] where the attribute .m is a midi note value of the frame p1;
2. Then all pitch frames p* are matched until the difference between the pitch of a current frame and the frame p1 is higher than or equal to 4 midi notes (frame p2). This is ensured by the condition [p2.m - p1.m >= 4];
3. After satisfying the condition in the 2nd step, all pitch frames p <move>* are matched and the output symbol move is triggered with each frame;
4. The processing of the template is completed, when a silent frame s is matched.

3   Semantic Errors

Semantic information, that describes pitch profiles of gesture templates, is encoded by a VGT expression. However, the description of gesture templates may be affected by semantic errors which cannot be detected while parsing the expression. A semantic error can also appear in a VGT expression when a new gesture template is added to the expression. The expression must be checked by tedious experimenting that involves user input to see if all templates are recognized correctly. Our research has identified two frequent types of semantic errors which cause improper behavior in gesture recognition – *ambiguous* and *unreachable* templates.

Two gesture templates are ambiguous if there is at least one gesture instance that satisfies both templates. The reason this error frequently occurs is due to an imprecise template description. In a real application there is typically a large number of instances fulfilling the condition of ambiguity. This semantic error is typically demonstrated by the generation of two or more output symbols in one frame.

The gesture template is unreachable when there is no instance matching the template. This can, for example, be caused by a condition that is always false, the template does not take into account human capabilities, or there is another gesture template that prevents the unreachable template from matching instances.

3.1   Semantic Error Detection

Detection of semantic errors, which are described above, requires analysis of gesture instances that can be generated by a VGT expression. We have implemented
a tool which is capable of displaying possible gesture instances and automatically
identifying semantic errors. It also allows deeper understanding of matching an
instance to an expression by tracking its pitch profile. After generating all possible instances that match the expression, the tool checks if each instance belongs
to just one template (ambiguity condition) and if each template has at least one
instance (unreachability condition).

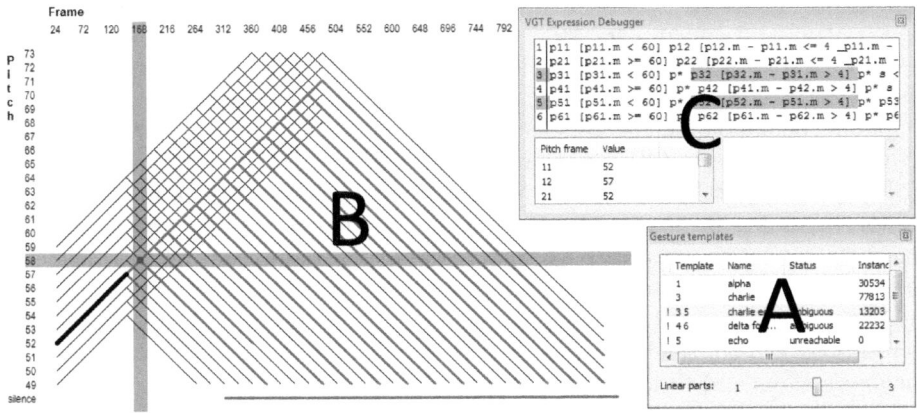

Fig. 4. Tool for vocal gestures visualization and semantic error detection

The user interface of our tool is depicted in Figure 4. Part A of the Figure
shows a dialog which contains a list of templates and number of instances. The
dialog shows semantic errors within the VGT expression by displaying both
ambiguous and unreachable templates (see the *Status* column). The user can
display instances by selecting an appropriate row. When selecting a row with
ambiguous templates, instances cause the ambiguity are displayed in part B.

Gesture instances are shown in the part B of Figure 4. The horizontal axis
represents frames converted into timestamps in milliseconds and the vertical
axis represents pitch using midi note numbers [4] starting with silence at the
bottom. The black lines represent the generated gestures. When there are a lot
of instances and their typical pitch profile is not visible, the user can display
these instances and track them from the beginning to the end. When tracking
an instance, the corresponding position of a VGT expression is highlighted in
the VGT Expression Debugger (dialog in part C). Horizontal and vertical bars
represent the current position, the bold line represents the part of an instance
that has been already tracked and the blue lines show the further extending of
a current instance.

The VGT expression is shown in dialog C. The current position of tracked instance is highlighted directly in the VGT expression by a yellow background, allowing the user to inspect how the instance is matched to its template. This is a very useful feature when inspecting instances that correspond to two or more ambiguous gestures, as the user can now clearly see the cause of the ambiguity. Current pitch values of numbered pitch frames are shown below the expression.

4 User Study

The aim of the user study was to find out whether the designers could understand VGT expressions, and to demonstrate the usefulness of the tool described in the previous section. Eight designers were recruited to participate in the study. Each participant (mean age=29.6, SD=2.8) had some previous experience with NVVI – four of them knew the interaction method, three had used it at least once and one had previously designed an NVVI application. Seven of the participants considered themselves as interaction designers and the remaining one as a usability expert. All participant were familiar with regular expressions.

The participants were given approximately 20 minutes of training, which involved discussing the syntax of two VGT expression examples as well as semantic errors. The participants were asked to complete three tasks. In each task they were told to recognize the gesture templates in given VGT expression by describing them orally and sketching a graphic representation of each template. They were also asked to identify any semantic errors that may have been present in the expressions and to propose a solution for each. However, they were not told to write a new corrected expression due to limited time of each session. One session lasted approximately one hour. Participants were divided into two groups of four – Group A and B. *Group A* was allowed to use the tool described above, whereas *Group B* was not allowed to use any aid.

Task #1

In the first task participants were told to analyze the following VGT expression:

```
p1 p* (p2 [p2.m - p1.m > 4] p* s <alpha> |
       p3 [p2.m - p2.m > 8] p* s <bravo>)
```

The expression above describes the two templates as depicted in Figure 5a. The *alpha* template defines instances where pitch increases by 4 or more midi notes. The *bravo*'s instances have to increase by 8 midi notes. However, the *bravo* template is unreachable, as the condition in the *alpha* template is always matched earlier.

Group A (Use of tool): Each participant correctly understood the templates and discovered that the gesture *bravo* was unreachable. Two participants proposed a partially correct solution.

Group B: One participant misunderstood the *bravo* template and consequently could not see an error. The other participants miscategorized the error as ambiguous. Two participants proposed a partially correct solution.

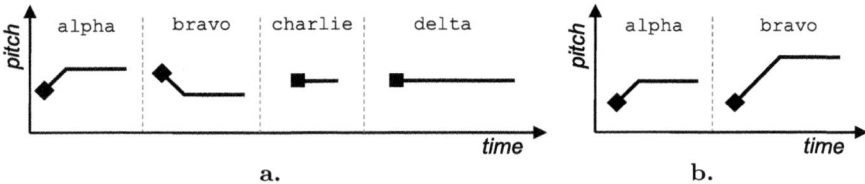

Fig. 5. a. Gesture templates in the task #1 **b.** Gesture templates in the task #2

Task #2

The second task contained gestures used in the *Tetris* game controlled by humming [7]. The participants were again told to analyze the VGT expression:

```
p1 p*
    (p2 [p2.m - p1.m > 4] p <alpha>* s |
     p3 [p1.m - p3.m > 4] p <bravo>* s) |
p*200;600 s <charlie> |
p*500; s <delta>
```

The expression above describes the templates depicted in Figure 5b. *Alpha* instances have to increase in pitch by 4 or more midi notes, whereas the *bravo* instances have to decrease by the same amount. *Charlie* instances are short tones of 200 to 600 ms and *delta* instances are all those that are longer than 500 ms. Two ambiguities are present in the expression. The first one is a time overlap in *charlie* and *delta* templates. The solution is to modify one of the limits. The second error is a pitch overlap between *alpha, bravo* and *charlie, delta* templates, due to the latter two not defining a pitch limit. The solution is to limit the pitch in *charlie, delta* templates to within ±4 midi notes.

Group A (Use of tool): Each participant understood the presented templates. One participant incorrectly identified the gestures initially, but corrected their interpretation after using the tool. All four were also able to locate all errors and propose a correct solution for each error.

Group B: Unlike the three others, one participant was not able to describe *alpha* and *bravo* templates correctly. All four participants were able to find ambiguity between *charlie* and *delta*. The second error was found by three participants, who proposed a correct solutions for each of the errors.

Task #3

The most complex VGT expression was analyzed in the last task. The expression defines six of the eight templates used in keyboard controlled by humming [6].

```
p11 [p11.m< 60] p12 [p12.m-p11.m<=4 & p11.m-p12.m<=4]* s<alpha> |
p21 [p21.m>=60] p22 [p22.m-p21.m<=4 & p21.m-p22.m<=4]* s<bravo> |
p31 [p31.m< 60] p* p32 [p32.m-p31.m>4] p* s<charlie> |
p41 [p41.m>=60] p* p42 [p41.m-p42.m>4] p* s<delta> |
p51 [p51.m< 60] p* p52 [p52.m-p51.m>4] p* p53 [p53.m<=p51.m] p* s<echo> |
p61 [p61.m>=60] p* p62 [p61.m-p62.m>4] p* p63 [p63.m>=p61.m] p* s<foxtrot>
```

The six instances correspond to the following - 1. *alpha* to a straight low tone, 2. *bravo* to a straight high tone, 3. *charlie* to increasing tone by more than 4 midi notes, 4. *delta* to decreasing tone by more than 4 midi notes, 5. *echo* to a tone that increases by more than 4 midi notes and then decreases to at least its initial pitch and finally 6. *foxtrot* which is essentially *echo* vertically inverted. Ambiguities between *charlie* and *echo* and between *delta* and *foxtrot* are present due to the end pitch of *charlie* and *delta* templates not being limited.

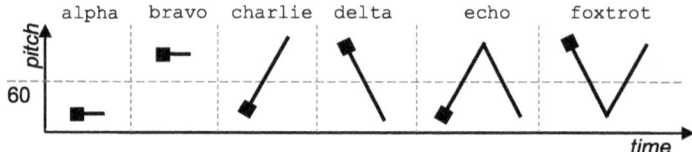

Fig. 6. Gesture templates in the task #3

Group A (Use of tool): One participant misunderstood *alpha* and *bravo* templates. Two participants incorrectly identified the templates initially, but corrected their interpretations after using the tool. Two participants thought there was an error present between *alpha* and *bravo*, but identified their mistake after using the tool. All participants located the error and three of them were able to propose correct removal solution.

Group B: Two participants incorrectly identified *alpha* and *bravo* templates as unreachable and were thus unable to sketch them. The other two participant incorrectly identified the templates as ambiguous. However, the other templates were understood by all participants, who were also able to identify the ambiguities and propose correct solutions.

5   Discussion

Using VGT expressions accelerates the process of building an NVVI application, as the matching algorithm no longer needs to be hard coded. The question, that is raised though, is whether designers are able to understand these VGT expressions. In most cases, participants from both groups correctly identified templates directly from VGT expression, which supported our assumption that VGT expressions can be understood by most designers. From total of 48 gestures that were examined in one group, there was two errors in the group A (use of tool) and seven error in the group B. What was slightly surprising was that participants from group A primarily relied on their own judgement rather than on the provided tool. However, they did use the tool from time to time to visually confirm their opinion or when they were unsure of the answer. In these situations the tool helped them to correctly understand the given templates and consequently to succeed in fulfilling the tasks. Thanks to the tool, participants from the group A also had no difficulty in detecting semantic errors. Although the participants from the group B were not as successful as group A, they were still able to locate a significant number of error occurrences. It seems that the use of the tool results in better understanding of VGT expressions and minimizes the overlooking of semantic errors. However, a further quantitative study is needed in order to support this hypothesis.

6 Conclusion

This paper discusses the formal description of pitch-based vocal input, used during the design process of NVVI applications. We have created a tool for automatic error detection and visualization of the formal description. Our research was focused on the comprehension of the formal description by designers and their ability to detect possible semantic errors with and without using the tool. Their ability to comprehend the formal description and to detect semantic errors was validated in a user study by eight interaction designers. Designers who used the tool were more successful in understanding the formal description. Further research concerning these results will be conducted in the future, including a comparative quantitative study to prove the efficiency of the gesture visualization tool.

Acknowledgments. This research has been partially supported by the MSMT research program MSM 6840770014 and the VitalMind project (IST-215387).

References

1. Harada, S., Landay, J.A., Malkin, J., Li, X., Bilmes, J.A.: The vocal joystick: evaluation of voice-based cursor control techniques. In: Proceedings of ASSETS 2006, pp. 197–204. ACM Press, New York (2006)
2. Hämäläinen, P., Mäki-Patola, T., Pulkki, V., Airas, M.: Musical computer games played by singing. In: 7th International Conference on Digital Audio Effects, pp. 367–371 (2004)
3. Igarashi, T., Hughes, J.: Voice as sound: using non-verbal voice input for interactive control. In: Proceedings of UIST 2001, pp. 155–156. ACM Press, New York (2001)
4. MIDI Manufacturers Association: Complete MIDI 1.0 Detailed Specification v96.1, 2nd edn. (2001), http://www.midi.org/techspecs/midispec.php
5. Poláček, O., Míkovec, Z., Sporka, A.J., Slavík, P.: New way of vocal interface design: Formal description of non-verbal vocal gestures. In: Proceedings of the CWUAAT 2010, pp. 137–144. Cambridge Press, UK (2010)
6. Sporka, A.J., Kurniawan, M., Slavík, P.: Non-speech Operated Emulation of Keyboard. In: Designing Accessible Technology, pp. 145–154. Springer, Heidelberg (2006)
7. Sporka, A.J., Kurniawan, S.H., Mahmud, M., Slavík, P.: Non-speech Input vs Speech Recognition: Real-time Control of Computer Games. In: Proceedings of ASSETS 2006, pp. 213–220. ACM Press, New York (2006)
8. Sporka, A.J., Žikovský, P., Slavík, P.: Explicative Document Reading Controlled by Non-speech Audio Gestures. In: Sojka, P., Kopeček, I., Pala, K. (eds.) TSD 2006. LNCS (LNAI), vol. 4188, pp. 695–702. Springer, Heidelberg (2006)

Application Composition Driven by UI Composition

Christian Brel, Philippe Renevier-Gonin, Audrey Occello, Anne-Marie Déry-Pinna,
Catherine Faron-Zucker, and Michel Riveill

I3S Laboratory (UMR 6070 - Université Nice - Sophia Antipolis et CNRS)
930 routes des colles – BP 145
{brel,renevier,occello,pinna,faron,riveill}@polytech.unice.fr

Abstract. Ahead of the multiplication of specialized applications, needs for application composition increase. Each application can be described by a pair of a visible part –the User Interface (UI) –and a hidden part –the tasks and the Functional Core (FC). Few works address the problem of application composition by handling both visible and hidden parts at the same time. Our proposition described in this paper is to start from the visible parts of applications, their UIs, to build a new application while using information coming from UIs as well as from tasks. We base upon the semantic description of UIs to help the developer merge parts of former applications. We argue that this approach driven by the composition of UIs helps the user during the composition process and ensures the preservation of a usable UI for the resulting application.

Keywords: User Interface Composition, Application Composition.

1 Introduction

There are more and more software tools: on the web, on Smartphones, on laptops, etc. Having so many widgets is interesting; however, to reach a friendly use, there is a need to compose them. For example, a Smartphone can provide its user with a diet list and an application that gives restaurants close to her and their menus. She would probably enjoy a second application filtering or emphasing dishes from her diet list.

To construct new applications by reusing other application sub-parts is a key challenge of Software Engineering. This is a mean to speed up development cycles. An interactive systems is composed at least of a functional part, usually called Fonctional Core (FC),and a User Interface (UI). Moreover, in the HCI research field, there is a strong recommendation of using a Task Model (TM) during requirements analysis. The TM describes the needs and the procedures to achieve these needs. The TM is not often explicitly implemented, but it can express the relationship between FC and UI entities. We choose to use UI as primary artifacts of the composition process because UI are the parts of applications manipulated by both developers and ergonomic designers. We aim at enabling them to reuse existing UI for creating new applications while preserving user requirements of individual original systems and keeping some of the links between the FC part and the UI part in the resulting system.

In this paper, we propose to combine information at the three levels: FC, UI and TM. For this, we base the composition process on the selection, extraction and placement of

R. Bernhaupt et al. (Eds.): HCSE 2010, LNCS 6409, pp. 198–205, 2010.

the existing application's UI as elementary composition actions to impact underlying task trees and FC part.The remainder of this paper is organized in 5 sections, respectively, the description of other UI composition works, the presentation of our model used in our composition, the overview of our composition process, the description of our implementation of the global process and finally the conclusion.

2 Related Work

This section presents related work on UI composition grouped by their entry point in the composition process according to the application cutting: the Functional Core (FC), the Task Model (TM) and the User Interface (UI). Each entry point addresses a specific problem of composition: presentation and layout consideration at the UI level, behavior of the application at the FC level, user needs at the TM level. We classify works related to UI compositions according to their approach: an "X" in the Table 1 means that corresponding work explicitly takes into account this part.

Table 1. Classification of composition approaches

	FC	UI	Tasks
Developing adaptable user interfaces [9]		X	
Amusing [8], ComposiXML [3]		X	
C3W [11]		X	
Task Models Merging [4]			X
Servface [7]	X		X
Compose [2]	X		X
Scenarios [12]		X	X
SOAUI [9], ALIAS [6], Transparent Interface[13]	X	X	

We group related works in four categories:

- Works only considering UI composition, either for defining specific toolkit for adaptive UI [9], either based on abstract definition of UI [8,3] or either adopting end-user programming [11],
- Works only considering TM composition (composition of two task trees [4]),
- Works deriving Tasks in FC composition and later in UI composition, because of generation UI from service annotation [7] or thanks to specific adaptable couple FC-UI [2] or deriving Tasks in UI [12]
- And Works considering both FC and UI composition. The main goal in [13] is to maintain a stable UI for using a composition of volatile service. The SOAUI approach [9] derives web service composition into UI composition, by searching the best-fitting UI in a repository for each service and then UI composition. The aim of [6] is to deduce the UI composition from the FC composition.

We notice a lack in underlying composition processes. Either the design of original applications' UI with man-crafted properties such as ergonomic or usability is lost, or both FC and UI parts are no longer connected together in the resulting application, or there is no UI reuse. In the context of fast development processes, reusing UI without keeping ergonomic and usability criteria is useless. Loosing links between the UI and the FC parts engenders human interventions to connect the two parts which is error prone and fastidious for large applications.

So we propose in our approach to mix information from all the levels to improve the application composition. The collaboration between the three levels are expressed in a unifying model, we call Enhanced Task Tree (ETT), presented in the next section.

3   Enhanced Task Tree

In our approach, the process is guided by the composition of former UI and by their reuse to build the new application. Our work is based on a model that lets consider information from Functional Core (FC) and UI and from Task Model (TM).

3.1   Connecting Conception and Implementation of the Interactive System

We assume the decomposition in two parts of an application: the FC and the UI. Links between both parts are difficult to analyze in the code, so we use an external description with references to some running objects. We use the task model (TM) as a pivot. The TM is established at design time from requirements and user models. We enhance it with information from the running objects. For each initial application and for each task, we add semantic annotations. In the following, we call "UI block" one piece or a group of pieces of UI. Fig. 1 shows an overview of the relationships between the different entities: tasks, UI Blocks and FC part. As a result, to implement our model, we need to retrieve from all the composed applications both their tasks description and the links between parts of their UI and parts of their FC. This knowledge is represented in a so-called Enhanced Task Tree.

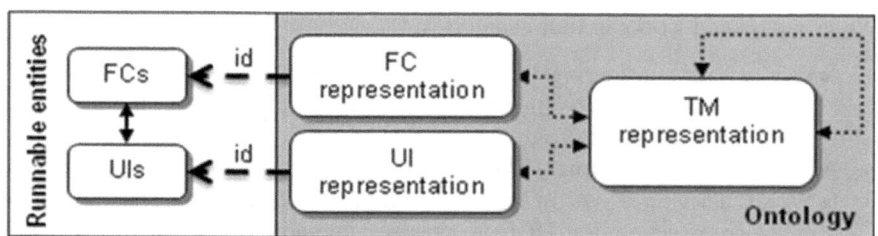

Fig. 1. Links between tasks, UI tree and FC

3.2   Enhanced Task Tree Definition

We define three sets for each application:

- Let UI the set of UI blocks.
- Let T the set of tasks.
- Let FC the set of functionalities.

The sets FC, UI and T of an application are defined by analyzing this application with the aim of extracting knowledge to create an enhanced task tree (ETT). Such a task tree includes the description of UI (blocks and layout) and links with the Functional Core (FC). This analysis is performed by developers.

Based on the ontology presented in the right part of the Fig. 1, we represent an ETT by a knowledge graph linking the multiple conception levels: it captures the links between the tasks in T and the UI blocks in UI, and between the tasks in T and the functionalities in FC. A task may be linked to at least one FC or UI entities. A UI (and respectively a FC) is at least linked to one task.

With ETTs, we are able to extract the right part of the reused UI in order to place them in the new UI without losing the links with the FC. ETTs enable composition at different levels that we can express through functions. In the remainder of section 3, we present the composition functions we specified for each of the three levels.

3.3 Selection/Extraction of Tasks at UI level

To represent the links between information, we define three functions:

Let δ a function associating to a UI block the corresponding tasks and its inverse δ^{-1} associating to each task its corresponding UI blocks:

$$\delta : UI \longrightarrow T^+; u \mapsto \{t_1,...,t_n\} \qquad \delta^{-1} : T \longrightarrow UI^+; t \mapsto \{u_1,...,u_m\}$$

In order to go further than the simple UI hierarchical relationship of container-component, we can identify each UI blocks $\{u_k\}$ connected with a given UI block "u",

i.e. $\left\{u_k, \forall k, \exists j, t_j \in \delta(u) \quad and \quad u_k \in \delta^{-1}(t_j)\right\}$. That connection is the

expression that all UI blocks $\{u_k\}$ are required to perform the tasks associated with the given UI block "u". So it makes sense to extend the selection from the single UI block "u" up to the set of UI blocks $\{u_k\}$, according to the acknowledgment of the developer.

3.4 Selection/Extraction of Tasks at Task level

Let ρ a function associating to each task all the tasks related to it:

$$\rho : T \longrightarrow T^+; t \longrightarrow \{t_1,...,t_n\} | \forall i \in \{1,...,n\}, r(t,t_i) \text{ where } r \text{ is a relation}$$

representing the temporal operations between tasks and the hierarchy between tasks from the CTT model [5].

Sometime, extracting only one task, like a dialog box to select a file, may have no sense, because the result of the task is not used. So if the developer has selected a task "t" through the UI blocks selection by selecting the set of Ui blocks defined by $\left\{u_k, \forall k, u_k \in \delta^{-1}(t)\right\}$, the developer has to extend that "t" up to $\rho(t)$. By this way, the developer can select some (or all) tasks directly related to "t". So, the function $\rho \circ \delta$ retrieves the tasks attached to a given UI block. The function χ representing the set of UI elements selected by extension of an initial selection:

$$\chi : UI^+ \longrightarrow UI^+$$

$$\chi(\{ui_1,...,ui_n\}) = \{ui_1,...,ui_p\} \mid p >= n \land \forall ui_{k \in \{n+1,...,p\}}, \exists j \in \{1,...,n\}, \exists t \in \rho(\delta(ui_j)) \mid ui_k \in \delta^{-1}(t)$$

3.5   Selection/Extraction of Tasks at FC level

Let γ a function associating to a task all its corresponding FC elements:

$$\gamma : T \longrightarrow FC^+; t \longrightarrow \{fc_1,..., fc_n\} \mid \forall i \in \{1,...,n\}, c(t, fc_i)$$ where c is a relation representing the links between a functionality and the task it implements.

Like ρ, γ enables extension of selection, but at a functional level, i.e. at the data processing level. The retrieval of the functionalities attached to a given UI block relies on the functions $\gamma \circ \delta$ and $\gamma \circ \rho \circ \delta$.

4   Composition Process

The goal of the process is to produce a new application resulting from the composition of UI of former applications. The new UI is composed of several parts reused from former UI and possibly of some new consolidating parts like graphical glue used to fill remaining voids.

Through a special UI, the user (i.e. a developer) loads each application containing functionalities (and corresponding UI blocks) to be inserted in the new application. The loading step corresponds to the construction of the multiple level descriptions introduced above. From each application's UI, he selects UI blocks to be reused. Thus, he can compose his new application. He obtains in only one application the different functionalities he wants to keep from the reused applications.

The construction of the new UI is done in three steps iterated during the building of the complete new UI:

1.   First, the developer makes a *selection* of pieces of UI to be reused in the new UI. Here we check whether the selected UI block is valid or not. To be valid, a UI block must enable the end user to completely perform one or more functionalities. He may either select an entire screen to add in the new UI, or select a UI block to be reused in the new UI, or select several UI blocks. In that case, the relative positions of the selected blocks in the initial UI are kept and they are placed in a new undividable UI block.
2.   If the selected UI block is not valid, we propose the *extraction* of complementary pieces of UI to "validate" the selection. During this extraction step, questions are asked to the developer to help the validation of the UI block. This step constitutes the extension of the selection.
3.   Once the selected UI block is valid, the third step consists in the *placement* of it in the new UI through various possible layouts. The selected UI is an entire screen, he has the possibility to place selected screen in the new screen flow. If it is a UI block, he can place it in the screen according predefined layouts that are proposed to the developer to define the placement in a screen or in a group of UI blocks.

5 Implementation: UI for Composing UI

We developed a proof of concept to perform a first validation of the different steps of the process we propose. It is made of (i) a UI to graphically compose several applications and (ii) several well-built applications. By "well-built application" we mean that it is developed with a clear separation between the UI and the Functional part. Moreover, both parts of the application are *"public"*: for the UI part, we can explore all UI Components starting from the main window (and its content pane); for the FC part, we get all the called methods, i.e. the Functional part is accessible through a *"façade"*. By "well-built application" we also mean that it is provided with an external description, its Enhanced Task Tree (ETT). The whole development is made in Java.

5.1 Enhanced Task Tree

ETTs are represented in RDF[1], the W3C standard for the Semantic Web; the ontology is represented in RDFS[2], the W3C standard for light-weight ontologies. To implement our composition mechanism, we use the Corese [1] semantic web engine to process and query the RDF representations of the different parts of the application. We implement the functions δ, ρ and γ by SPARQL[3] queries over the RDF(S) representation of the ETT.

Our model of tasks is based on CTT [5] and our UI model is based on MARIA [7] (we added some UI elements like graphical glue for the description of UI component tree). In our RDF models, there are references to Java Objects both for UI and FC. Thus, we define a unique ID for each UI component, based on the main class of the application and the place of the UI component in the component tree. For the Functional part, we define a unique ID based on its *"façade"* class and method name.

5.2 Selection and Extraction

We developed a UI for manipulating the different applications the user (i.e. a developer) wants to compose. This tool lets the developer compose his new application, place the different elements and save or load a composition already done. The developer performs the selection step by interacting with the former UI and by controlling those interactions with our tool for manipulating. Indeed, our tool enables to activate or deactivate the interaction in the former UIs (by adding / removing initial graphical event listeners) and the selection process (by adding / removing our own graphical event listeners)

The extraction step is interleaved with the selection step: each time a (group of) UI component(s) is selected, its extraction is determined as a set of questions asked to the developer. Because we have an access of the task tree corresponding to actions performed through the interface, we are able to warn the developer of the need of extracting other components linked to the selected component. The developer can deactivate the questioning.

---

[1] http://www.w3.org/RDF/
[2] http://www.w3.org/TR/rdfschema/
[3] http://www.w3.org/TR/rdf-sparql-query/

5.3 Placement

For this step, we propose to place components between each others, through relative positions like "above of", "on the right of", "on the left of", etc...

We express conditions with RDF properties and we transform these conditions in a Java layout. At the same time, the Corese engine deduces relative layouts thanks to a base of 14 inference rules we wrote. For example, from absolute positions of two different UI components, our rules enable Corese to deduce whether the first component is on the left, on the right, above or below the second component. This deduction is necessary to provide a relevant feedback to the developer during the placement step.

6 Conclusion

In this paper, we proposed an original process based on the manipulation of UI that improves the composition result in terms of UI design reuse while preserving the links between FC and UI parts.

Our process is made of three steps: selection, extraction and placement of former UI blocks. Each of these steps uses the enhanced task trees associated to the applications to compose and to build a new task tree keeping some links between the parts of applications. The originalities of the proposed process are: (i) in its starting point (the UI) but with a cover of also Task Model and Functional Core; (ii) in our commitment to reuse former UI (including their design properties). Moreover, its strengths are: (iii) in the possibility to build the resulting enhanced task tree in function of the user actions on the former UI and (iv) in the extraction of the right part of the UI and its placement in the new UI without losing the links with the FC.

Our approach must to be improved before performing test with developers. Indeed, we are working on merging UI blocks, at different levels (FC, TM or UI), according to the compatibility of manipulated entities and by importing adapters given by the developer.

Acknowledgments

Our work is funded by the DGE M-Pub 08 2 93 0702 project.

References

1. Corby, O., Dieng-Kuntz, R., Faron-Zucker, C.: Querying the semantic web with the corese search engine. In: 16th European Conference on Artificial Intelligence (ECAI 2004). IOS Press, Valencia (2004)
2. Gabillon, Y., Calvary, G., Fiorino, H.: Composing interactive systems by planning. In: UbiMob 2008, Saint Malo, France, mai 28 - 30, pp. 37–40 (2008)
3. Lepreux, S., Hariri, A., Rouillard, J., Tabary, D., Tarby, J.-C., Kolski, C.: Towards multi-modal user interfaces composition based on USIXML and MBD principles. In: Jacko, J.A. (ed.) HCI 2007. LNCS, vol. 4552, pp. 134–143. Springer, Heidelberg (2007)

4. Lewandowski, A., Lepreux, S., Bourguin, G.: Tasks models merging for high-level component composition. In: Jacko, J.A. (ed.) HCI 2007. LNCS, vol. 4550, pp. 1129–1138. Springer, Heidelberg (2007)
5. Mori, G., Paternò, F., Santoro, C.: Ctte: Support for developing and analyzing task models for interactive system design. IEEE Transactions on Software Engineering, 797–813 (August 2002)
6. Occello, A., Joffroy, C., Pinna-Déry, A.-M., Renevier, P., Riveill, M.: Experiments in Model Driven Composition of User Interfaces. In: Eliassen, F., Kapitza, R. (eds.) DAIS 2010. LNCS, vol. 6115, pp. 98–111. Springer, Heidelberg (2010)
7. Paternò, F., Santoro, C., Spano, L.D.: Maria: A universal, declarative, multiple abstraction level language for service-oriented applications in ubiquitous environments. In: Computer-Human Interaction (TOCHI), vol. 16 (November 2009)
8. Pinna-Déry, A.-M., Fierstone, J.: Component model and programming: a first step to manage Human Computer Interaction Adaptation. In: Chittaro, L. (ed.) Mobile HCI 2003. LNCS, vol. 2795, pp. 456–460. Springer, Heidelberg (2003)
9. Tsai, W.-T., Huang, Q., Elston, J., Chen, Y.: Service-oriented user interface modeling and composition. In: ICEBE 2008, Washington, DC, USA, pp. 21–28. IEEE Computer Society, Los Alamitos (2008)
10. Grundy, J.C., Hosking, J.G.: Developing Adaptable User Interfaces for Component-based Systems. Interacting with Computers 14(2), 175–194 (2002)
11. Fujima, J., Lunzer, A., Hornbæk, K., Tanaka, Y.: Clip, Connect, Clone: Combining Application Elements to Build Custom Interfaces for Information Access. In: Proceedings of UIST 2004, Santa Fe, NM, pp. 175–184 (2004)
12. Elkoutbi, M., Khriss, I., Keller, R.K.: Generating User Interface Prototypes from Scenarios. In: Fourth IEEE International Symposium on Requirements Engineering, RE 1999, Limerick, Ireland, pp. 150–158 (June 1999)
13. Ginzburg, J., Rossi, G., Urbieta, M., Distante, D.: Transparent interface composition in Web Applications. In: Baresi, L., Fraternali, P., Houben, G.-J. (eds.) ICWE 2007. LNCS, vol. 4607, pp. 152–166. Springer, Heidelberg (2007)

Methods for Efficient Development of Task-Based Applications

Vaclav Slovacek

Dept. of Computer Graphics and Interaction, Faculty of Electrical Engineering,
Czech Technical University in Prague, Karlovo nám. 13, 121 35, Praha 2, Czech Republic
slovavac@fel.cvut.cz

Abstract. This paper introduces methods for developing task-based applications by tightly integrating workflows with application logic written in an imperative programming language and automatically completing workflows especially with tasks that mediate interaction with users. Developers are then provided with completed workflow they may be used for further development. Automatic completion of workflows should enable to significantly shorten the development process and eliminate repetitive and error-prone development tasks. Information extracted from workflow structure and low level application logic may then be used to automatically generate low to high fidelity prototype user interfaces for different devices and contexts.

Keywords: Workflow, workflow processing, task modeling, generated user interface.

1 Introduction

The main goal of the research related to this paper is to introduce methodology that would enable efficient development of task-based applications using visual task modeling and present functionality of an ongoing task framework implementation.

Developing applications by first designing a task model and then automatically generate user interface provides developers with option to model application on higher levels of abstraction as task models abstract from device display resolutions, input methods, available user interface components, etc.

Modeling an application using workflows provides formal description of all processes in the application that is understandable by non-programmers. It enables to design and analyze the application on different levels of abstraction (using nested workflows) and enables eventually to detect design issues in the processes design [1].

Despite all the advantages listed above, current methods also suffer from significant drawbacks that prevent many developers from adopting task modeling as a method for developing applications. Developers have to learn formal semantics and although workflow schemas are easy to read they are much harder to design properly, especially when different tasks may run in parallel, cancel each other, etc.

Workflows may be used to automatically generate user interfaces (for example web forms that asks user for required input) and we believe that by making designing

R. Bernhaupt et al. (Eds.): HCSE 2010, LNCS 6409, pp. 206–213, 2010.

workflows simpler the workflows may be then used at least for rapidly designing low fidelity prototypes that may be modified by user interface designers, used for usability testing and finally converted to final user interfaces accelerating development cycle.

2 State of the Art

Common tool for task modeling are ConcurTaskTrees [2] that are used for hierarchical task analysis [3]. ConcurTaskTrees describe a high level task by hierarchically splitting it into subtasks. Abstract tasks that represent users intentions are split into elementary tasks. These tasks are either machine tasks (performed by a device a user is interacting with), user tasks (performed by a user) and interaction tasks (user interacting with the device). Complex branched processes are easier to express using workflow languages such as YAWL [4] and BPEL [5] that enable do define branching, iterations, etc. There are also several implementations of a workflow engines and visual editors available for both YAWL and BPEL.

There are several projects focused on automatic user interface generation. Project SUPPLE[6] currently enables to automatically generate user interfaces. It is possible to provide SUPPLE with data that are required to be entered by a user (specifying the type of data, name, allowed and expected values) and SUPPLE provides a user interface optimized for a specific user [7] enabling the user to enter the required data.

3 Framework

We focused on making the process of designing task-based applications as usable for developers as possible. We took advantage of currently existing technologies and built on knowledge of developer enabling them to quickly start developing more maintainable applications while providing methods for rapidly deliver low to high fidelity user interface prototypes that are integrated with application logic.

3.1 Workflow

We have chosen YAWL as a base language for our research because it covers all necessary patterns for describing any application logic unlike BPEL [4]. Also every BPEL process can be converted to an appropriate YAWL workflow [8]. We use a simplified YAWL notation closely described in [9] that reduces number of visual elements to describe a workflow.

We also do not use XPath and XQuery that are used in YAWL for branching conditions and data updates. Instead we delegate branching logic to an imperative programming language such as Java and provide an API for controlling execution of the workflow (e.g., choosing tasks should be executed). Using an imperative programming language for elementary application logic should be natural for most developers.

3.2 Task Types

Workflow is a descriptive form of defining tasks. Although workflows are efficient for describing high level processes, it generally fails to simply describe low-level application logic [10] that is much more efficiently described using imperative programming languages such as Java, ECMAScript, etc. By low-level application logic we understand operations that have no inner structure that should be exposed.

The problem with using an imperative language for implementing elementary tasks is that it is very hard to limit their functionality so it does not perform operations that should be rather defined in a workflow. Decision what is still considered elementary task depends on developers and thus a set of rules and recommendations for proper coding style should be introduced. Otherwise advantages of having a descriptive task-model may be lost as most of the application logic might be implemented in elementary tasks that have no inner structure and behave as black boxes.

We split tasks into implicit, triggered and user task types. These types differ by when they are executed. Implicit tasks are executed by the workflow engine automatically when they are reached in an executed workflow. Triggered tasks must be initialized from a user interface and are easily recognizable as they require an input data. Server stops processing workflow until it receives a triggering event with the required data from a user interface.

User tasks are similar to triggered tasks, but are directly accessible by user, so there must be a button or another interaction element visible that enables users to initialize the task. Developer is responsible for declaring user tasks to distinguish them from triggered tasks (e.g., using @*UserTask* annotation). This information is important for automatically generating user interfaces.

3.3 Execution Conditions

Execution conditions are conditions that must be satisfied for a task to be available for user. The conditions in our framework are identified by a unique id (e.g., fully qualified name of class that is used to evaluate if the condition is satisfied).

As the framework abstracts from how execution conditions are represented. It is possible to extend the support of execution conditions to Java Bean Validation [11], semantically described conditions, etc.

3.4 Execution Condition Satisfiers

Execution condition satisfier is a task that is automatically inserted before another task to satisfy its execution conditions. The condition satisfier itself may require different execution conditions to be satisfied and thus it might be necessary to add another condition satisfier preceding it (e.g., condition satisfier producing a user object instance, may require user name and password).

The framework abstracts from how a condition satisfier task satisfies an execution condition so different implementations may be used - e.g., implementation providing manually designed user interface to a user, implementation providing automatically generated user interfaces, implementation providing static data, etc.

4 Modifying Workflow

To simplify and accelerate workflow-based application development we propose a method for modifying workflow that completes the workflow automatically based on execution conditions extracted from source code of elementary tasks.

An application is a set of tasks the user may perform (the tasks the application was designed to perform). These tasks are usually implemented in elementary tasks and the rest of the workflow ensures they are performed in the desired order, under certain conditions (e.g., time, location), after required data get available, etc.

4.1 Satisfying Execution Conditions

The figure 1 shows four different representations of the same workflow. The workflow as defined by developer (a) contains just one task that requires a condition uniquely identified by the letter A (shown in the circle on the left side of the task) to be satisfied.

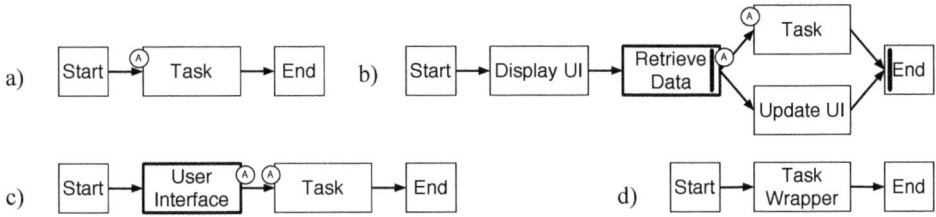

Fig. 1. The same task represented in 4 different ways - a) as defined by a developer, b) automatically completed, c) simplified semantic representation that is more readable by a developer, but not is semantically equivalent with (b), d) wrapping task with complex inner structure in form of nested workflow

The framework modifies the workflow (b) by adding a task (Display UI) that renders a user interface visible to user and then the execution stalls before executing task Retrieve Data waiting for user input (tasks requiring input from a user interface are marked by a thicker border). After a user provides the required data the original task is executed in parallel with another added tasks that notifies user about progress of the original task which may be important for user experience [12] (e.g., displaying a progress bar, showing notification when the task is finished, etc., depending on implementation).

Although the automatically completed workflow exactly represents the application behavior it is quite complex and adding such constructs to every task with unsatisfied execution conditions would lead to overly complex structure that might be difficult to work with.

Because of this the framework might represent the task by merging all the added tasks into a single task (User Interface) that precedes the original task as shown in (c), this however leads to losing the parallel branch that lets user informed about progress of the task.

The only acceptable pattern seems to be creating a wrapping task that encapsulates a nested workflow similar to the one shown in (b). As all execution conditions are solved inside the nested workflow there is no unsatisfied execution condition on the higher level and the higher level workflow is kept simple compared to (b) and (c).

4.2 Completing Workflow

Satisfying an execution condition a single task is useful for dealing with very simple patterns. Eventually satisfying execution conditions for each task individually may lead to generating poor user interfaces.

The figure 2 shows an example workflow having two sequentially executed tasks (a). Using the method described in the previous section the framework would provide two separate user interfaces preceding each task. However there is no other branching or conditional logic that would cancel the sequential execution thus the execution conditions may be collected and a user interface preceding execution of the first task may be provided asking user for input required for both tasks as shown in (b).

A different pattern is shown in (c) when a common user interface is used to get input necessary for both task and then asks for additional input necessary only for one of the branches (d) while the other branch may be executed while waiting for a user to input necessary data.

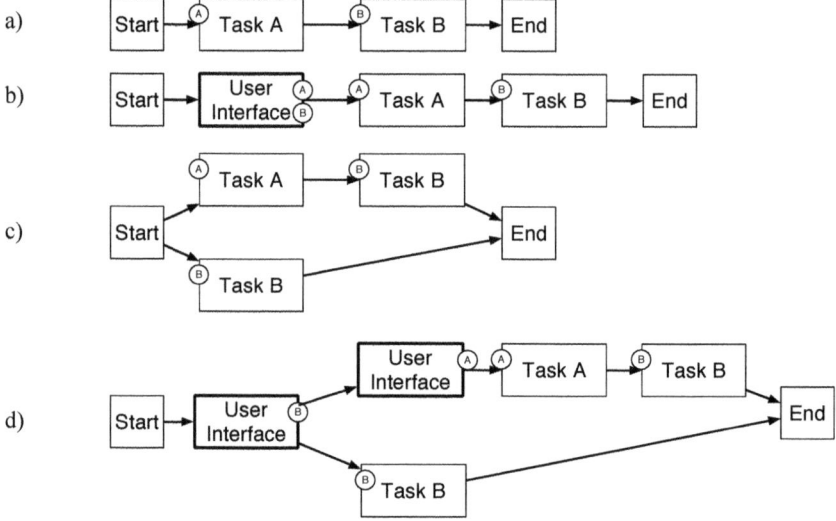

Fig. 2. Example workflows as defined by a developer (a), (c) and with automatically added condition satisfier tasks (b), (d)

5 Metadata Related to User Interfaces

Information necessary for rendering user interfaces is directly extracted from elementary task source code. A lot of information may be extracted from the source code using language reflection, which is supported by several programming languages[13], without a developer having to provide any additional information. The following Java code is an example of an elementary task as used in our framework:

```
@Title("title") @Description("description")
class Login implements UserInteraction {
   void execute(
      @NotNull DeviceContext requiredDeviceContext,
      @Title("title") @Description("description")
      @Input("username") String name,
      @Input("password") String password) {
         // application logic here
   }
}
```

The above code snippet contains enough information to be properly represented in a user interface. The framework extracts fields of the class and parameters of the *execute()* method. Based on their types and names defined in *@Input* annotation it injects appropriate values to class fields using inversion of control mechanism before calling the *execute()* method with appropriate parameters.

The class implements interface *UserInteraction* that extends interface *Interaction* common for every elementary task. As interfaces support inheritance they may be used to organize interactions into different groups. This may be used for better layout of automatically generated user interface (e.g., clustering of related user interface elements).

Additionally the code snippet above contains annotations (*@Title* and *@Description*) that provide closer description of both the interaction itself and the parameter expected to be provided by a user. These information may be used to properly represent the task in a user interface. We have introduced annotations that are a copy of Dublin Core [14] metadata tags used typically in XML to describe these properties of elementary tasks. The title may be for example used for a label related to a text field for input of the appropriate data and description for providing a tooltip closer describing the required input.

5.1 Task Importance

There are several ways how importance of tasks for a given application may be calculated. The framework enables to specify the importance of certain tasks manually (e.g., using *@Importance* annotation). This is a mechanism that tells which tasks are necessary in the application. This typically includes the tasks the application is designed for (e.g., volume control and channel switching in a TV application).

However specifying importance manually to all tasks is not very useful. Thus importance may also depend on user preferences (for example unexperienced user will not access color management settings of a TV), on an end-device used or any other environment properties.

Calculating transitive importance is used to propagate importance of individual tasks forward in the workflow. We simply do that by propagating the highest importance to previous tasks in a sequence. This ensures that the task is properly represented in the interface that is provided to user before it is even reached in a workflow. An example of the importance propagation is shown in figure 3 with workflow (b) showing transitive importance calculated from workflow (a) and workflow (d) showing transitive importance from workflow (c). In workflow (d) the importance is

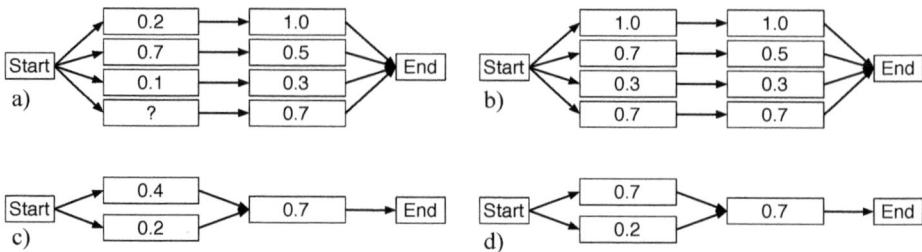

Fig. 3. Workflow with tasks with calculated importance (a) parallel tasks with individually calculated importance, (b) the workflow with transitive calculated importance, (c) sequential tasks with individually calculated importance, (d) the same workflow with transitive calculated importance

propagated only to a single branch that already has higher importance to prevent cluttering a user interface.

Calculated importance may then be used also for automatically generating user interfaces where more important tasks may be represented e.g., by larger buttons, more prominently placed controls, etc. Tasks with importance under a defined threshold may eventually not be visible in a very constrained environment (e.g., very small device screen).

We distinguish three different states of a workflow task. Task may be enabled (all execution conditions are satisfied) meaning that user may execute it. Task may disabled (at least one execution condition is not satisfied) causing all relevant user interface elements (e.g., button executing the task) to be disabled but still visible in the user interface thus keeping it consistent. Tasks that are in hidden state are not represented in the user interface and their controls simply disappear. As it would be difficult for a computer system to guess whether the tasks should be disabled or hidden developer has to declare that a task switches to disabled state (e.g., by adding *@AlwaysVisible* annotation).

6 Conclusion

We have introduced basic methods for automatically completing workflow models for developing applications that should simplify development of applications based on workflows.

We have strongly focused on process that would enable to automatically generate user interfaces directly from application logic implemented in an imperative programming language while managing the state transitions based on workflow description tightly integrated with an application low-level source code.

7 Future Research

We have not covered a situation that may occur when an execution condition is first satisfied by condition satisfier task, then concurrently made unsatisfied by another tasks and then a tasks requiring the execution condition to be satisfied is reached.

It would be possible to enclose blocks that depend on satisfying execution conditions into transactions. However as these transactions might involve user interaction there may arise problems with very long transactions blocking other processes in an application and problems with selecting proper items in a context to be locked. Transactions locking large part of a context for a long time may result in deadlock and/or may significantly slow down an application.

Research should also focus on usability of automatically generated user interfaces and analyze impact of methods described in this paper on development process.

References

1. Van Breugel, F., Koshkina, M.: Models and Verification of BPEL. Unpublished Draft (January 1, 2006)
2. Paternò, F., Mancini, C., Meniconi, S.: ConcurTaskTrees: A diagrammatic notation for specifying task models. Chapman & Hall Ltd., London (1997)
3. Stanton, N.: Hierarchical task analysis: Developments, applications, and extensions. Applied Ergonomics (January 1, 2006)
4. Van der Aalst, W., Ter Hofstede, A.: YAWL: yet another workflow language. Information Systems 30(4), 245–275 (2005)
5. Juric, M.B.: Business Process Execution Language for Web Services BPEL and BPEL4WS, 2nd edn. (2006)
6. Gajos, K., Weld, D.: SUPPLE: automatically generating user interfaces. In: Proceedings of the 9th International Conference... (January 1, 2004)
7. Gajos, K., Wobbrock, J., Weld, D.: Automatically generating user interfaces adapted to users' motor and vision....In: Symposium on User Interface (January 1, 2007)
8. Brogi, A., Popescu, R.: From BPEL processes to YAWL workflows. In: Bravetti, M., Núñez, M., Zavattaro, G. (eds.) WS-FM 2006. LNCS, vol. 4184, pp. 107–122. Springer, Heidelberg (2006)
9. Slovacek, V.: Towards Workflow-based Application Development Framework (2010)
10. Jelinek, J., Slavik, P.: GUI generation from annotated source code. In: Proceedings of the 3rd Annual Conference on... (January 1, 2004)
11. Bernard, E., Peterson, S.: JSR-303 Bean Validation. Bean Validation Expert Group (January 1, 2009)
12. Blackmon, M.: Cognitive walkthrough. In: Encyclopedia of Human-Computer Interaction
13. Gosling, J., Joy, B., Steele, G., Bracha, G.: Java (TM) Language Specification, The Java (Addison-Wesley). Addison-Wesley Professional, Reading (2005)
14. Weibel, S., Kunze, J., Lagoze, C., Wolf, M.: RFC2413: Dublin Core Metadata for Resource Discovery. RFC Editor United States (January 1, 1998)

Towards an Integrated Model for Functional and User Interface Requirements

Rabeb Mizouni[1], Daniel Sinnig[2], and Ferhat Khendek[3]

[1] College of Information Technology, UAE University, Al-Ain, UAE
mizouni@uaeu.ac.ae
[2] Faculty of CS and Elec. Engineering, University of Rostock, Germany
dasin@informatik.uni-rostock.de
[3] Dept. of Electrical & Computer Eng., Concordia University, Montreal, Canada
khendek@encs.concordia.ca

Abstract. Despite the widespread adoption of UML as a standard for modeling software systems, it does not provide adequate support for specifying User Interface (UI) requirements. It has become a common practice to separately use UML use cases for specifying functional requirements and task models for modeling UI requirements. The lack of integration of these two related models is likely to introduce redundancies and inconsistencies into the software development process. In this paper, we propose an integrated model, consisting of use case and task models, for capturing functional and UI requirements. Both artifacts are used in a complementary manner and are formally related through so-called *Anchors*. Anchors are use case steps that require further elaboration with UI-specific interactions. These interactions are explicitly captured in associated task models. The formal semantics of the integrated model is given with finite state automata.

Keywords: Functional Requirements, UML Use Cases, User Interface Requirements, Task Models, Integrated Requirements Model, Finite State Automata.

1 Introduction

UML has become the de-facto standard for software systems modeling. However, UML's support for User Interface (UI) development is deemed insufficient [1]. While UML diagrams are well suited for object-oriented analysis and design, the HCI community argues that a set of specialized models is needed to effectively specify users' characteristics and tasks, UI dialogue structures and layouts.

This divergence has been addressed by many researchers. Most attempts either define extensions for UML to capture HCI related information [2, 3] or, conversely, extend HCI models to cope with object-oriented features [4, 5]. An effective integration, however, is not simply a matter of expressiveness and the ability to convert or embed a model into another one. Instead, as Paternò [1] points out, specialized notations should be used in a complementary manner to efficiently support software engineers and UI designers in their work.

R. Bernhaupt et al. (Eds.): HCSE 2010, LNCS 6409, pp. 214–221, 2010.
© IFIP International Federation for Information Processing 2010

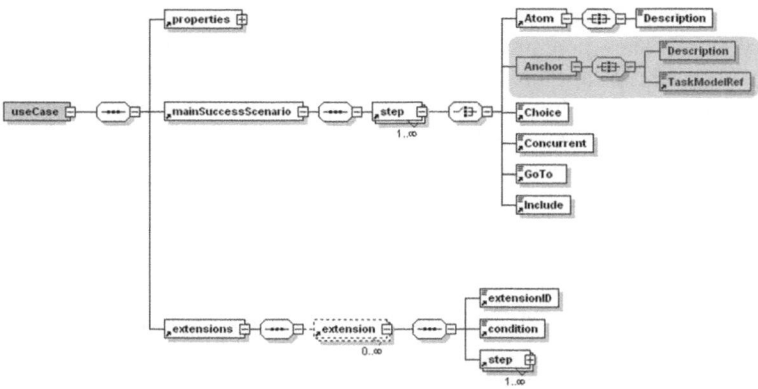

Fig. 1. Use Case Model Syntax with Anchor

In this paper, we define an integrated model for capturing functional and UI requirements. It is composed of two heterogeneous, yet interrelated parts: *UML use cases* and *HCI task models*. Use cases are the medium of choice for capturing functional requirements whereas task models are commonly used to specify the detailed user interactions with the system. Within our integrated model, use cases and task models are used according to their intended purposes establishing clear separation of concerns.

The research reported here builds upon our earlier work [6, 7] where we described a two-phase integrated development methodology for use cases and task models. In the *first* phase, an initial coarse grained use case model is developed, which, without delving into details, documents the primary interactions that actors will perform with the system in a step-by-step format. Additionally, for each use case, the software engineers identify a set of use case steps that require further elaboration with UI details. These steps are called *anchors*. In the *second* phase, each anchor is associated with a corresponding task model capturing UI-specific interactions. Concurrently, the coarse-grained use case model is further refined by taking into account alternative and failure cases that thus far have been considered only marginally.

In this paper we focus on the definition of an integrated model for functional and UI requirements to support such a methodology, including its syntax and semantics. The latter is defined by providing a formal mapping to the semantic domain of finite state automata.

2   Syntax of the Integrated Functional and UI Requirements Model

In this section we define the syntax of our integrated model for functional and UI requirements. As aforementioned, the model consists of two heterogeneous parts, a use case model and a set of task models, interlinked by a set of anchor points. Each individual use case corresponds to the structure portrayed in Fig. 1. The main success scenario as well as each extension consist of a sequence of use-case steps, which can be of six different kinds. *Atomic* steps are performed either by the system or a secondary actor. They contain a textual description, but do not consist of any sub-steps. *Anchors* are also atomic, but are performed by the primary actor and as such are related to the user interface. Anchor steps additionally contain a reference to a refining (UI-specific) task model. *Choice* steps provide the primary actor with the choice between several interactions. Each such interaction is (in turn) defined by a sequence of steps. *Concurrent* steps define a set of steps which may be performed in any order by the primary actor. *Goto* steps denote jumps to steps within the same use case. *Include* steps denote invocations of sub-use cases.

To illustrate our approach, let us consider a "Process Contact Request" use case. It depicts the interactions involved in processing contact requests, as it is typical in social networks such as LinkedIn and Facebook. The main success scenario describes the situation in which the primary actor directly accomplishes his goal of confirming a contact request. We also define two extensions to specify alternative scenarios, which occur when the primary actor fails to authenticate himself or refuses a contact request, respectively. The textual description of the use case is shown on the left hand side of Fig. 2.

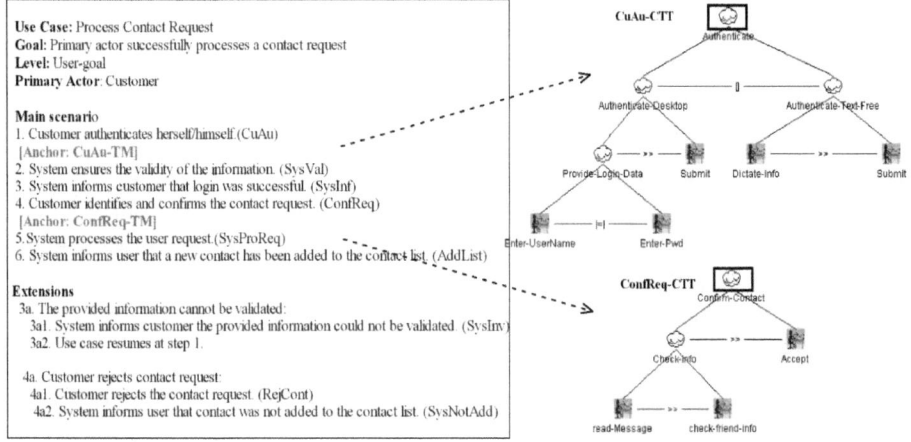

Fig. 2. Integrated Functional and UI Requirements Model of the "Process Contact Request" Use Case

The use case contains two UI-related steps 1 ("Authentication") and 4 ("Identification of Contact Request") which are defined as anchors and as such are related to refining task models. Both steps do not detail how the step-goals are achieved. These interactions are UI-specific and are captured in the corresponding task models. For example, the authentication step (CuAu) may require that the user enters his/her name and password in any order (Desktop UI), or that the user dictates his/her login information (Text-Free Voice UI). Both possibilities are expressed by the binary choice operator ([]) in the corresponding task model (CuAu-TM). In a similar manner, use case step 4 (ConfReq) is associated with a task model (ConfReq-TM), specifying UI interactions for confirming a contact request.

3 Semantics of the Integrated Functional and UI Requirements Model

This section defines a formal semantics for our integrated model. We start by defining the well-known semantic domain of finite state automata. We then portray how the use case and task model parts of the integrated model are mapped separately into the semantic domain. Finally, we define a merging procedure that integrates the various individual semantic representations into a common behavioral model.

3.1 Semantic Domain

The semantics for our integrated model is given by a mapping to a finite state automaton.

Definition 1 (Finite state automaton). An automaton is defined as a 5-tuple (S, s^0, S^f, L, E) where S is the set of states, s^0 is the initial state, S^f is the set of final states, L is the set of labels, and $E \subseteq S \times L \times S$ is the set of transitions.

Definition 2 (Trace). A trace of an automaton A is a sequence of transitions $e = q_0.q_1.q_2.\ldots.q_{n-1}$ where $q_0 = (s_0, l_0, s_1) \in E$ such that $s_0 = s^0$, $\forall i, 1 \leq i < n-1$ $q_i = (s_i, l_i, s_{i+1}) \in E$, and, $q_{n-1} = (s_{n-1}, l_{n-1}, s_n) \in E$ where $s_n \in S^f$.

Informally, a trace is a word of the language accepted by the finite state automaton when it starts from its initial state and ends in one of its final states for the trace. In what follows, we use operational semantics for our definitions. Equations of the following form $\dfrac{a\,;b}{c}(Cond)$ denote that a AND b IMPLY c. $Cond$ is the condition for the applicability of the rule.

3.2 Semantics for Use Cases and CTT Task Models

This section outlines the separate mappings of the use case and task model into the semantic domain. For the sake of conciseness, only a high-level overview will be given while the full details can be found in [8].

The semantic mapping from a use case model into an automaton is defined in a bottom-up manner, starting with the mapping of individual use case steps. Each of the six kinds of use case steps enumerated in Fig.1 has its own specific mapping to an FSM. *Atomic* steps and *Anchor* steps map to elementary FSMs consisting of only an initial state and a set of final states, connected by a transition that represents the use case step. A *Choice* step maps to a composite FSM consisting of the initial states of each choice's FSM. A *Concurrent* step is the product machine of its constituent FSMs. *Goto* steps map to an FSM with a single state defined to be equivalent to the initial state of the FSM representing the target of the jump. The complement FSM of an *Include* step consists of two states: one identified with the initial state of the FSM of the main success scenario of the invoked sub-use case, and the other identified with all final states of the sub-use case's FSM.

Now that individual use case steps can be formally represented by automata, we can link arbitrary sequences of steps using *sequential composition*, by unifying the final states of the first operand with the initial state of the second one. In the next step, we map the main success scenario and each extension of the use case to a set of automata, each being the result of the sequential composition of the automata representing the individual use case steps. Finally, the entire use case is mapped into an automaton, by merging the automata representing the main success scenario and all its extensions.

Similar to the semantic mapping of use cases, the mapping of CTT task models to automata is performed in a bottom-up manner. Each atomic task is mapped into an atomic automaton. Composite tasks are represented by more complex automata, which result from the composition of the automata representing sub-tasks. We have defined the following composition operations: *sequential composition* (●), *choice composition* (#), *parallel composition* (||), and *iterative composition* (*). The full details of the mappings are given in [8].

3.3 Automaton of the Integrated Model

In this section, we elaborate how the individual use case and task model automata are merged into a single automaton, representing the behavioral semantics of our integrated requirements model.

Intuitively, the behavior of the integrated requirements model can be summarized as follows: At first, the integrated model adopts the behavior of the use case model up until an *Anchor* step is encountered. At this point, the integrated model adopts the behavior of the associated CTT model depicting how the primary actor may accomplish the step-goal using a particular UI. Thereafter, the integrated model again resumes with the behavior of the use case model. This alternating continues until the scenario comes to an end.

The behavioral merge of finite state automata has been addressed in many research projects [6, 9-11]. Since in our integrated model use cases and task models are utilized in a complementary −non-overlapping− manner we choose one of the existing *explicit* automata composition techniques [6, 10, 11] to merge the respective use case and task model automata. Similar to our work presented in [6], the merge of use case and task model automata is based on imperative expressions. Each expression specifies (1) the use case and the CTT automata to be merged, (2) the anchor where the merge is performed, and (3) a *Refine* operator that specifies how the actual merge is performed. The evaluation of the expression yields a new automaton where the use case transition representing the anchor step has been replaced by the corresponding CTT automaton. We define *Refine* operator semantics next.

Let $A=(S,s^0,S^f,L,E)$ be an automaton and let $tr(A)=\{e \mid e \text{ is a trace of } A\}$ be its set of traces. We define the set $tr(A, ep)$ to be the set of traces of A passing through the anchor ep as: $tr(A,ep)=\{e \in tr(A), e= q_0.q_1.q_2....q_{n-1}, \forall 0 \leq i \leq n-1 \; q_i \in E \mid \exists \; q_i = ep\}$. It represents the set of traces where ep appears as a transition in the trace. Additionally, we define $Pref(A,ep)$ (respectively postfixes $Post(A,ep)$) as the set of prefixes (respectively postfixes) of the traces of the automaton A passing through ep. More formally, let $e=q_0.q_1.q_2....q_{n-1}$ be a trace of automaton A. $u= q_0.q_1....q_{i-1} \in Pref(A, ep)$ if $(q_i = ep)$ (respectively, $r=q_{i+1}....q_{n-1} \in Post(A, ep)$ if $(q_i = ep)\}$. Consequently, a trace $e \in tr(A,ep)$ can be written as: $e=u.ep.r$ where $u \in Pref(A,ep)$ and $r \in Post(A,ep)$.

Definition 4 (Refine Operator): Let $A=(S_1,s^0_1,S^f_1,L_1,E_1)$ and $B=(S_2,s^0_2,S^f_2,L_2,E_2)$ two automata, and $C=(S_3,s^0_3,S^f_3,L_3,E_3)$ be the resulting automaton by applying the *Refine* operator at the anchor $t=(s,a,s')$. Furthermore, let $tr(A)$ and $tr(B)$ be the traces of automata A and B, respectively. Then, the set of traces $tr(C)$ of the resulting automaton C is constructed using the following rules:

$$\frac{(e \in tr(A)\,/\,tr(A,t))}{e \in tr(C)} \quad (1)$$

$$\frac{(e \in tr(A,t));(\exists u,r \mid e = u.t.r \; where \; u \in \Pr ef(A,t), r \in Post(A,t)); e_b \in tr(B))}{u.e_b.r \in tr(C)} \quad (2)$$

Equation (1) shows that all traces of A not passing through the anchor point are traces of the automaton C. Equation (2) shows that for all traces of A passing through t, the transition t is replaced by the traces of B.

The construction the final merged automaton is an iterative process, where the resulting automaton from a composition is used as an input to a subsequent composition until a fixpoint is reached (i.e., all anchors have been replaced by respective task model automata). At the end of the composition, the derived automaton is the semantic representation of the integrated requirements model. Fig.3 portrays the various automata involved in our "Process Contact Request" example. The automaton representing the use case is given in Fig. 3 (a). The task model automata representing the refinements of the "authentication step" and the "confirm contact" step are given in Fig. 3 (b) and Fig. 3 (c). Finally, Fig. 3 (d) illustrates the resulting automaton representing the integrated model.

4 Related Work

Since UML was developed with little attention to UI related issues, several proposals have been put forward to close this gap. Most of them fall into one of the following categories: (1) Extensions to UML for the purpose of capturing HCI-related information [2, 3], (2) extensions to HCI models for capturing object-oriented features [4, 5] and (3) development methods promoting the integration of HCI and OO models [12].

Paternò [1] proposes a method for integrating use case diagrams and task models. Use cases denote core functionalities offered by the system which are refined by a set of task models. However, the scenario descriptions entailed in each use case are not taken into account. Another approach that falls under the first category is presented by Noberga *et al.* [2]. Motivated by the fact that the current UML standard provides insufficient support for modeling interactive systems, a mapping from CTT task models to UML activity diagrams is proposed. The mapping is complemented by an extension of UML with high-level syntactic constructs related to task modeling.

Da Silva and Paton [5] propose UML*i* as a modeling language for interactive systems. UML*i* extends UML with UI diagrams for describing abstract interaction objects. According to their eight-step methodology, use cases are employed to define high-level functionalities which are further refined by a set of user tasks captured in extended UML activity diagrams. A set of logical links, placed between the various

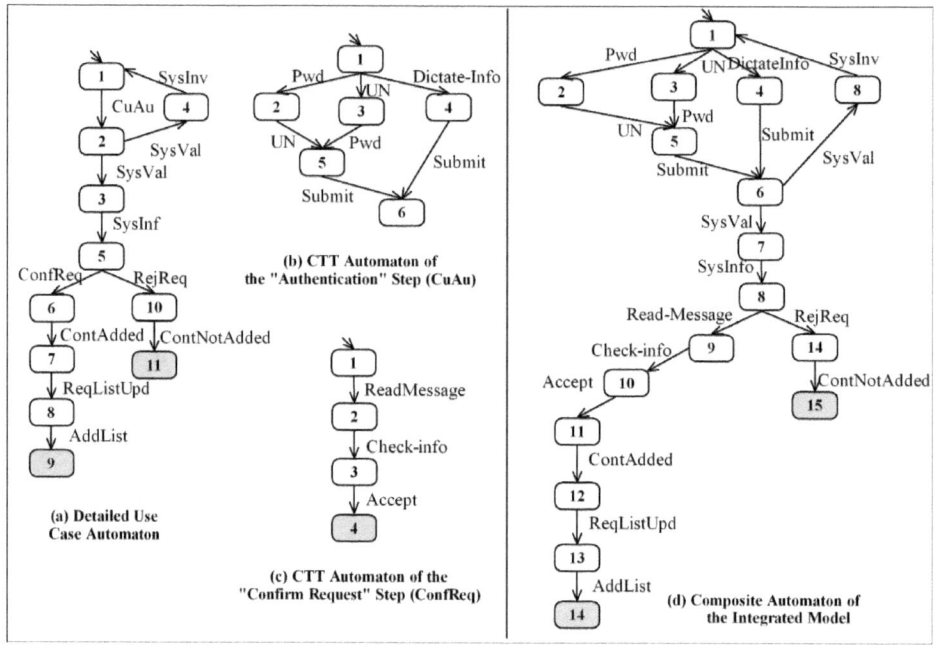

Fig. 3. Composition Example

use cases and the activity diagrams, establishes traceability between UI details and the corresponding functional requirements.

Rosson [13] proposes a scenario-based approach to object-oriented analysis and design. In order to integrate usability concerns with functional modeling, a system is modeled by a set of *instance scenarios*. In a bottom-up approach the various scenarios are processed and serve as a basis for the creation of the object model. Nunes and Conha [4] point out that UML provides inadequate support for modeling architectural concerns of interactive systems and propose their Wisdom framework to fill this gap. While mainly based on existing UML models, Wisdom introduces a CTT-like notation to capture the dialogue between users and the application.

5 Conclusion

In order to overcome the insufficient support for UI modeling in UML, we have proposed an integrated model to capture functional and UI requirements. This integrated model is the outcome of a larger undertaking, first discussed in [7], that investigates methods for efficient collaboration between software engineers and UI designers while preserving clear separation of concerns. The integrated model is comprised of two well-established models – UML use cases and CTT task models – interrelated through a set of Anchors. We have defined a formal syntax and semantics for the integrated model. The latter is given in terms of a finite state automaton.

As future work, we plan to carry out comprehensive case studies and to apply our approach and notation to industrial-strength projects. We are currently developing tool support for authoring and validating the integrated model. We envision that our tool will support the reuse of task model specifications (either within the same project or among different projects). In many cases, the interactions specified by task models are independent from the application domain and consequently can be reused across projects. Other future avenues are related to the extension of the integrated model to encompass other UI-related artifacts such as user and dialogue models and the generation of integrated test cases.

References

1. Paternò, F., Santoro, C.: Support for Reasoning about Interactive Systems through Human-Computer Interaction Designers' Representations. Comput. J. 46(4), 340–357 (2003)
2. Nobrega, L., Nunes, N.J., Coelho, H.: Mapping ConcurTaskTrees into UML 2.0. In: Gilroy, S.W., Harrison, M.D. (eds.) DSV-IS 2005. LNCS, vol. 3941, pp. 237–248. Springer, Heidelberg (2006)
3. Bastide, R.e.: An Integration of Task and Use Case Metamodels. In: HCI International, San Diego, CA, USA, 19/07/09-24/07/09 (2009)
4. Nunes, N.J., o e Cunha, J.o.F.:Towards a UML profile for interaction design: the Wisdom approach (2000)
5. de Paula, M.i.G., da Silva, B.S., Barbosa, S.D.J.: Using an interaction model as a resource for communication in design. In: CHI 2005: CHI 2005 extended abstracts on Human Factors in Computing Systems, pp. 1713–1716 (2005)
6. Mizouni, R., et al.: Merging partial system behaviors: composition of use-case automata. IET Software 1(4), 143–160 (2007)
7. Daniel, S., Rabeb, M., Ferhat, K.: Bridging the gap: empowering use cases with task models. In: Proceedings of the 2nd ACM SIGCHI Symposium on Engineering Interactive Computing Systems, ACM, Berlin (2010)
8. Sinnig, D.: Use Case and Task Models: Formal Unification and Integrated Development Methodology, Department of Computer Science and Software Engineering, Concordia University, Montreal (2008)
9. Chechik, M., et al.: Partial Behavioral Models for Requirements and Early Design. In: MMOSS, 06351 (2006)
10. Leue, S., Mehrmann, L., Rezai, M.: Synthesizing ROOM Models from Message Sequence Chart Specifications. Technical Report 98-06, ECE Dept., University of Waterloo, Canada (October 1998)
11. Uchitel, S., Kramer, J., Magee, J.: Behavior Model Elaboration using Partial Labeled Transition Systems. In: ESEC/FSE 2003 (2003)
12. Lu, S., et al.: Generating UML Diagrams from Task Models (2003)
13. Rosson, M.B.: Integrating development of task and object models. ACM Commun. 42(1), 49–56 (1999)

Author Index

GPSR Compliance

*The European Union's (EU) General Product Safety Regulation (GPSR)
is a set of rules that requires consumer products to be safe and our
obligations to ensure this.*

*If you have any concerns about our products, you can contact us on
ProductSafety@springernature.com*

In case Publisher is established outside the EU, the EU authorized
representative is:

Springer Nature Customer Service Center GmbH
Europaplatz 3
69115 Heidelberg, Germany

Batch number: 09474016

Printed by Printforce, the Netherlands